PREFACE

1. Scope

This publication provides doctrine for the conduct of stability operations during joint operations within the broader context of US Government efforts. It provides guidance for operating across the range of military operations to support US Government agencies, foreign governments, and intergovernmental organizations, or to lead such missions, tasks, and activities until it is feasible to transfer lead responsibility.

2. Purpose

This publication has been prepared under the direction of the Chairman of the Joint Chiefs of Staff (CJCS). It sets forth joint doctrine to govern the activities and performance of the Armed Forces of the United States in joint operations and provides the doctrinal basis for interagency coordination and for US military involvement in multinational operations. It provides military guidance for the exercise of authority by combatant commanders and other joint force commanders (JFCs) and prescribes joint doctrine for operations, education, and training. It provides military guidance for use by the Armed Forces in preparing their appropriate plans. It is not the intent of this publication to restrict the authority of the JFC from organizing the force and executing the mission in a manner the JFC deems most appropriate to ensure unity of effort in the accomplishment of the overall objective.

3. Application

a. Joint doctrine established in this publication applies to the joint staff, commanders (CDRs) of combatant commands, subunified commands, joint task forces, subordinate components of these commands, and the Services.

b. The guidance in this publication is authoritative; as such, this doctrine will be followed except when, in the judgment of the CDR, exceptional circumstances dictate otherwise. If conflicts arise between the contents of this publication and the contents of Service publications, this publication will take precedence unless the CJCS, normally in coordination with the other members of the Joint Chiefs of Staff, has provided more current and specific guidance. CDRs of forces operating as part of a multinational (alliance or coalition) military command should follow multinational doctrine and procedures ratified by the United States. For doctrine and procedures not ratified by the United States, CDRs should evaluate and follow the multinational command's doctrine and procedures, where applicable and consistent with US law, regulations, and doctrine.

For the Chairman of the Joint Chiefs of Staff:

WILLIAM E. GORTNEY
VADM, USN
Director, Joint Staff

Intentionally Blank

TABLE OF CONTENTS

APPENDIX

GLOSSARY

FIGURE

Intentionally Blank

EXECUTIVE SUMMARY
COMMANDER'S OVERVIEW

- **Describes the nature of stability operations.**

- **Presents the principles of stability operations.**

- **Stresses the need for unified action in stability operations.**

- **Discusses stability operations design and planning.**

- **Explains the stability operations functions of security, humanitarian assistance, economic stabilization and infrastructure, rule of law, and governance and participation.**

Stability Operations

Stability operations are various military missions, tasks, and activities conducted outside the US in coordination with other instruments of national power to maintain or reestablish a safe and secure environment, provide essential governmental services, emergency infrastructure reconstruction, and humanitarian relief.

The Department of Defense (DOD) has learned through the difficult experiences of both Iraq and Afghanistan that success is not only defined in military terms; it also involves rebuilding infrastructure, supporting economic development, establishing the rule of law, building accountable governance, establishing essential services, and building a capable host nation (HN) military responsible to civilian authority.

The Department of State (DOS) is charged with responsibility for leading a whole-of-government approach to stabilization that includes the array of US Government (USG) departments and agencies, including DOD and component Services and agencies. Within this broad approach, **the primary military contribution to stabilization is to protect and defend the population, facilitating the personal security of the people and, thus, creating a platform for political, economic, and human security.**

The missions, tasks, and activities that make up stability operations fall into three broad categories: initial response activities,

Initial response activities aim to provide a safe, secure environment and attend to the immediate humanitarian needs of a population.

Transformational activities are generally a broad range of security, reconstruction, and capacity building efforts.

---

transformational activities, and sustainment activities.	Activities that foster sustainability encompass long-term efforts that capitalize on capacity building and reconstruction activities to establish conditions that enable sustainable development.
	During major operations and campaigns, stability operations are particularly emphasized following the achievement of major combat objectives. However, major operation and campaign plans must feature an appropriate balance between offensive, defensive, and stability operations in all phases.
	During crisis response and limited contingency operations, the balance of stability and combat operations varies widely with the circumstances. Many crisis response and limited contingency operations, such as foreign humanitarian assistance (FHA), may not require combat. Others, such as strikes and raids, may not require stability operations. Still others, such as counterinsurgency (COIN), will require a delicate balance of offense, defense, and stability operations throughout the operation.
Peace operations.	Peace operations encompass multiagency and multinational crisis response and limited contingency operations involving all instruments of national power with military missions to contain conflict, redress the peace, and shape the environment to support reconciliation and rebuilding and facilitate the transition to legitimate governance.
Counterinsurgency.	COIN is comprehensive civilian and military efforts taken to defeat an insurgency and to address any core grievances. COIN requires joint forces to both fight and build sequentially or simultaneously, depending on the circumstances. Stability operations are fundamental to COIN—stability operations are the "build" in the COIN process of "clear, hold, build."
Foreign humanitarian assistance.	FHA consists of DOD activities, normally in support of the United States Agency for International Development (USAID) or DOS, conducted outside the US, its territories and possessions to relieve or reduce human suffering, disease, hunger, or privation.
Nation assistance (NA). *Military support to stabilization efforts during*	During military engagement, security cooperation, and deterrence activities, stability operations play an important role in joint operations conducted in consonance with the geographic combatant commanders' theater campaign plan

peacetime generally takes the form of presence and NA operations.

objectives and support the objectives of individual country teams. US nation assistance (NA) is civil or military assistance (other than FHA) rendered to a nation by US forces within that nation's territory during peacetime, crises or emergencies, or war, based on agreements mutually concluded between the United States and that nation.

Stability operations executed during major operations or campaigns or during crisis response and limited contingency operations normally take place in fragile states or regions.

A fragile state is a country that suffers from institutional weaknesses serious enough to threaten the stability of its central government. The fragile states framework, used in interagency forums, can help the joint force commander (JFC) develop a foundational understanding of the operational environment. The term "fragile states" describes a broad range of failing, failed, and recovering states. The framework has three categories of states: failed, failing, and recovering, although the distinction or exact transition between categories is rarely clear.

All military action should be assessed by its contribution toward achieving stabilization objectives, thus creating a platform for political, economic, and human security.

At the heart of the political problem lies a contest between the way political power is organized and who wields that power. Leaders of peacemaking efforts will need to convince decisive elites that their interests are best served through an accommodation with the approved political settlement, rather than renewed conflict. Where this is not possible, the use of military force can influence and alter the political dynamics, which may remove the barriers to any accommodation. The JFC should support DOS initiatives to engage all legitimate claimants to power in the society into the political process. The main objective in most cases should be to allow the main contenders to continue their competition under new rules that favor peaceful over violent means, giving all an opportunity for power sharing.

Legitimacy is a condition based upon the perception by specific audiences of the legality, morality, or rightness of a set of actions, and of the propriety of the authority of the individuals or organizations in taking them.

If an operation is perceived as legitimate, the audience has a strong impulse to support the action. Establishing and strengthening the legitimacy of the HN government in the eyes of the HN population is the foundation of stabilization efforts; stability operations conducted by military forces must maintain this focus. Even after rudimentary civil authority is established, the JFC's effectiveness in coordinating a more unified response or activity may depend on the partnering organization's perception of the legitimacy of the military operations, as well as the perceptions of the local population.

Principles of stability operations.	Although the principles of joint operations apply to all aspects of any joint operation, emphasis on certain principles and their applicability during stability operations is appropriate.
Direct every military operation toward a clearly defined, decisive, and attainable objective.	**Objective.** The objective of a stabilization effort is to achieve and maintain a workable political settlement among the HN government, competing elites, and the wider population.
Seize, retain, and exploit the initiative.	**Offensive.** Failing to act quickly to gain and maintain the initiative in stabilization efforts may create a breeding ground for dissent and possible exploitation opportunities for enemies or adversaries.
Concentrate power at the decisive time and place.	**Mass.** Mass matters in stability operations, particularly when stability operations are conducted in a hostile environment (e.g., during a major operation or in COIN). Deploying a stability force that has the capability to satisfy the concurrent requirements to protect the population and neutralize hostile groups will be a major planning consideration.
Allocate minimum essential combat power to secondary efforts.	**Economy of Force.** Personnel should not presume that stability operations are "secondary" efforts, particularly during major operations and campaigns or even within the context of theater strategic planning efforts.
Seek unity of effort in every operation.	**Unity of Command.** Unity of command will help ensure that stability and combat operations are directed together toward their common objective. Stability operations must be closely coordinated with and through appropriate interagency authorities, as well as HN and other partner nation authorities as appropriate.
Apply appropriate combat capability prudently.	**Restraint.** Restraint requires the careful and disciplined balancing of protecting the people and infrastructure, conducting military operations, and achieving the overarching objectives of the operation. A single act can cause significant military and political consequences; therefore, when force is used, it must be lawful and measured.
Prepare for the measured, protracted application of military capability in support of strategic aims.	**Perseverance.** The stabilization of fragile states is, fundamentally, a protracted effort. The long-term focus of transformational stability activities and activities that foster sustainability requires a conviction among the local

population that external support for their government will be sufficient and enduring.

Committed forces must sustain the legitimacy of the operation and of the host government.

Legitimacy. The credibility of the HN government and its ability to generate consent is crucial. The population's attitude toward US or multinational forces may be a significant element in this but, ultimately, is of secondary importance.

Unified action.

One of the defining features of contemporary stabilization environments is the array of intervening participants present in the theater of operations. The range of external stakeholders could include various USG departments and agencies, allies—who themselves often have a multiagency presence—intergovernmental organizations (IGOs), nongovernmental organizations (NGOs), and private sector interests. Despite the differing organizational cultures, experiences, and timelines that inevitably will exist among stakeholders, it is imperative that there be a shared understanding of the national objectives and operational environment, cooperative planning and assessment, and coordinated, integrated when appropriate, actions and activities—unified action.

Civil-military operations involve the interaction of military forces with the civilian populace to facilitate military operations and consolidate operational objectives.

A civil-military operations staff element (cell, branch, or directorate) and appropriate employment of civil affairs (CA) forces provides connectivity and understanding that enables unity of effort within the headquarters and among stakeholders. Other enabling forces such as special operations forces (SOF), engineers, health service support, transportation, military police, and security forces provide the means to execute civil-military operations (CMO)-related tasks.

Stability Operations Design and Planning

It is the responsibility of combatant commanders and their subordinate joint force commanders (JFCs) to incorporate stability operations into the contingency and crisis action planning processes.

The design and development of operation plans that integrate offense, defense, and stability operations and integrate the Armed Forces contribution to stabilization efforts with the activities of interorganizational partners is the responsibility of JFCs and their staffs. JFCs must also ensure that subordinate commanders (CDRs) understand the overall design of the operation, including, in particular, how various military and civilian stability efforts interrelate and, when possible, integrate with each other and with combat missions, tasks, and activities, if any.

Particularly in stability operations, JFC, subordinate commanders, and staff at all echelons should interact with the leadership and elements of the lowest tactical units who encounter the local population and local security forces on a daily basis to help the JFC to develop insights about ongoing operational trends.

A holistic understanding of the operational environment enables the design of complementing offensive, defensive, and stability operations that, together in an appropriate and ever changing balance, achieve operational objectives. A holistic view of the operational environment encompasses physical areas and factors (of the air, land, maritime, and space domains) and the information environment (which includes cyberspace). In operations requiring a significant combat component, a holistic understanding of the environment that emphasizes civil factors alongside military factors helps ensure smooth transitions from operational phases that emphasize combat operations to those that emphasize stability operations. In operations with little or no combat, this holistic view is particularly valuable, as there may be no overt adversary military forces, but rather forces of nature, possibly covert adversary forces, and nonmilitary personnel, organizations, and other systems.

Strategic guidance.

In preparation for major stabilization efforts, the USG should undertake a conflict assessment in accordance with the Interagency Conflict Assessment Framework (ICAF) and in consultation with other USG agencies to include DOD. Lead agency determination and intergovernmental relationships will be recommended during this process. The various departmental roles and supported and supporting responsibilities need to be synchronized through the National Security Council in a reconstruction and stabilization plan.

Designing and planning stability operations.

The goal of design and planning is to develop a comprehensive approach that integrates the capabilities and contributions of many diverse participants toward a common purpose.

In developing this overarching design and plan, the JFC and staff employ the same principles of operational design and planning utilized in Joint Publication 5-0, *Joint Operation Planning.* Combat and stabilization are neither sequential nor binary alternatives; the JFC must integrate and synchronize stability operations with other operations (offense and defense) within each phase of any joint operation. The JFC's visualization of the operation will determine the emphasis to be placed on each type of mission or activity in each phase of the operation. As the design and plan for the operation evolve, the JFC maintains a constant focus on the objective of political settlement among competing elites in local societies and the need to protect and defend the population.

Arranging operations.

By arranging operations and activities into phases, the JFC can better visualize, integrate, and synchronize subordinate operations in time, space, and purpose.

Force planning.

The size and composition of the force will depend on the mission, the operational environment, and the JFC's concept of operations. However, since stability operations occur in the land domain, joint land forces (to include SOF) will normally provide the majority of the force required supported by joint air, maritime, and space forces.

Integrated design and planning.

Whenever possible, the wider international community, including the host nation (HN) and other multinational partners and nongovernmental organizations, should be incorporated into this integrated planning process.

Established policy and procedures are designed to support the military chain of command while engendering comprehensive, cooperative planning between military and civilian agencies of the USG to implement stabilization policy and direction. Interagency planning should be an iterative process that synchronizes diplomatic, development, and defense implementation planning and tasks with a view to developing unified action to achieve overall stabilization goals. JFCs should work closely with chiefs of mission and other civilian counterparts to establish appropriate structures and processes that will facilitate a shared understanding, integrated design and planning, and coordinated execution and assessment.

Special considerations.

In most scenarios, joint task forces will conduct stability operations. The planning and execution of these operations are fully integrated with the planning and execution of offensive and defensive operations, and should not be separated into a separate staff directorate. When the scope of the mission is almost completely focused on stability operations, with little or no combat mission, a JFC may establish a joint CMO task force to accomplish that mission.

Command and Control. Traditional military command and control does not apply to relationships with civilian departments and agencies. The JFC must be able to effectively coordinate and, when appropriate, integrate efforts between the joint force and interorganizational partners.

Intelligence. Intelligence production and information gathering in stability operations should be broadly focused and include collection and fusion of information concerning political, military, paramilitary, ethnic, religious, economic, medical, environmental, geospatial, and criminal indicators. The primary intelligence effort must focus on answering the CDR's priority intelligence requirements assisting in the accomplishment of the mission. While normally this will involve assessing potential threats to the mission (from forces external and internal to the affected population), the unique aspects of stability operations may result in significant or even primary emphasis being placed upon logistic, health, or political intelligence and intelligence support to information operations (IO) and CA.

Fires. Joint forces represent a potent combination of lethal and nonlethal capabilities. Although the presence of military forces may influence human behavior by demonstrating the potential for lethal action, security of the population, HN, or joint force cannot normally be assumed or achieved solely through the physical presence of military forces or the killing or capturing of adversaries. When required, military forces will have to neutralize and isolate irregular actors by winning the contests in both the physical domains and the information environment of the operational area.

Protection. Protection is a fundamental element in stability operations. The ability to provide physical security to the population and those conducting stabilization is often a primary reason for involvement by the Armed Forces of the United States in stabilization efforts. The protection function during stability operations emphasizes force protection, force health protection, and civil security.

Sustainment. Stability operations are often logistics and engineering intensive. Therefore, the overall logistic concept should be closely tied into the operational strategy and be mutually supporting. Planning also should consider the potential requirements to provide support to nonmilitary personnel (e.g., USG civilian agencies, NGOs, IGOs, indigenous populations and institutions, and the private sector).

Continuous assessment.

Continuous and timely assessments of the operational environment and the progress of operations are essential to measure progress toward mission accomplishment. Assessment occurs at all levels and across the entire range of military operations. Assessment in stability operations is as important as assessment in combat operations and can be more complex than traditional combat assessment. The results of stabilization activities will be very difficult to achieve, or indeed, to measure, and the CDR may therefore need to devote greater effort to this area if he is to gain a clear picture of progress.

Transitions.

The JFC must also be prepared to recommend a change in the strategic end state to political and military leadership if the original goals are no longer achievable.

Because the national strategic end state may be general or broad in nature, it may be difficult to determine whether and when military operations should be terminated. A requirement, therefore, exists, to determine the military end state and the termination criteria. The military end state is the set of required conditions that defines achievement of all military objectives. Establishing benchmarks tied to measurable conditions is normally more effective in determining when and where a transition from military to civil efforts and lead agent responsibilities should begin.

Training for stability operations.

Combatant commanders (CCDRs) should schedule interagency, IGO, and NGO coordination training as a part of routine training and exercise participation, and as training for a specific operation.

Stability Operations Functions

Stability operations functions.

The tasks within each function are crosscutting, generating effects across multiple sectors.

While the assignment of specific tasks and prioritization among them depends on the mission and conditions of the operational environment, the stability operations functions, as a framework, are a tool to help visualize the conduct of an operation, sequence necessary activities within an operation, and develop appropriate priorities for those activities and resource allocation. Individually, the functions encompass the distinct yet interrelated tasks that constitute stability activities in a functional sector. Collectively, they are the pillars upon which the USG frames the possible tasks required in a stabilization effort. The functions described here are security, humanitarian assistance, economic stabilization and infrastructure, rule of law, and governance and participation.

Strategic communication.

Joint force staffs must carefully ensure that messages are consistent with actions and vice versa.

Although not discussed specifically in any given functional area, strategic communication themes and messages, fully coordinated with other operational activities, enhance the legitimacy of HN forces and ultimately the stability of the HN. Public affairs and IO provide the "words," supported by the "deeds" of stability operations and CMO.

Stability Operations Functions—Security

The military provides the security on which stability can be built.

Security activities seek to protect and control civil populations, property, and territory. They may be performed as part of a military occupation during or after combat, to help defeat an insurgency, or in response to a humanitarian disaster. Security activities conclude successfully when civil violence is reduced to a level manageable by HN law enforcement authorities.

The security requirements vary greatly across the range of military operations, and the JFC should consider security actions based on the mission and his understanding of the operational environment.

In addition to providing security as required, a major joint force role in stabilization may be to provide support for security sector reform (SSR). Beyond simply providing security, SSR includes the broad set of policies, plans, programs, and activities that a government undertakes to improve the way it provides safety, security, and justice. Transformational activities and activities that foster sustainability in the security sector generally fall under the rubric of SSR.

To plan for and execute an intervention, CDRs and their staffs conduct an in-depth analysis to provide relevant background concerning existing dynamics that could trigger, exacerbate, or mitigate violent conflict. The key lies in the development of shared understanding among all agencies and countries involved about the sources of violent conflict or civil strife. This conflict diagnosis should deliver a product that describes the context, core grievances and resiliencies, drivers of conflict and mitigating factors, and opportunities for increasing or decreasing conflict.

Military contribution.

When the joint force is providing security, the Department of Defense will normally have the lead role in this area; otherwise, this area is generally led by the United States Agency for

Separating warring parties involves establishing distinct areas of control that keeps factions apart and allows the joint force to monitor their actions. The establishment of security fundamentally requires a monopoly on the use of force by a single entity. In stabilization efforts, the goal is normally to support a legitimate HN governmental authority that holds this monopoly, using it to protect the population, or to help that authority attain the monopoly. Toward this goal, joint forces take action to support efforts to end ongoing conflict, build HN security force capacity,

International Development's Bureau of Democracy, Conflict, and Humanitarian Assistance.

and disarm adversary forces. DOS's Bureau of Political-Military Affairs and various intelligence services could also play significant supporting roles.

Territorial Security. Side-by-side with the monopoly on the use of force, the HN government must also be in control of its borders, and must be able to reasonably monitor and control movement within its borders, particularly movement by adversaries. Territorial integrity is a necessary condition in which ordinary citizens and legitimate goods are able to move in relative freedom within the country and across its borders, while illicit commodities and individuals that present threats to security are denied free passage.

Public order is one of the functions of governance that affects early perceptions of the legitimacy of the state and thus will almost always be one of the first and most important public tasks.

Public Order and Safety. Although the Armed Forces of the United States are not designed or trained, by and large, to be a constabulary force, the joint force may be called upon to conduct certain constabulary functions on a temporary basis until HN or other security forces can assume those responsibilities. This requirement is largely driven by the size and presence of the joint force, particularly in the immediate aftermath of war or other devastating events.

Protection of Indigenous Infrastructure. Both the short - and long-term success of any stabilization effort often relies on the ability of external groups to protect and maintain critical infrastructure until the HN can resume that responsibility.

Protection of Personnel Involved in the Stabilization Effort. The joint force may be called upon to provide protection for civilian personnel from the United States or other nations that are assisting in the stabilization effort. Interagency or international memorandums of agreement will be required in this instance, laying out specific rules and responsibilities, as well as rules of engagement. Only on the rarest of occasions will military forces provide protection for NGO personnel, and only when directly requested; many NGOs feel that their reputation for neutrality, that is their independence from US or any other political and military influence, forms the basis of their security—joint forces must be careful not to impinge upon this reputation.

Threats and vulnerabilities.

Everyone present during stabilization efforts has the potential to influence the course of events in ways which may be positive or negative. The CDR will strive to understand the full range of participants and their motivations, aspirations, interests, and relationships. Generically, the participants can be divided into six categories based on their aims, methods, and relationships: adversaries, enemies, belligerents, neutrals, friendlies, and opportunists.

Security response.

Population Security. To provide protection to the population, JFCs employ a range of techniques. Not all will be popular.

Static protection of key sites (e.g., market places or refugee camps).

Persistent security in areas secured and held (e.g., intensive patrolling and check points).

Targeted action against adversaries (e.g., search or strike operations).

Population control measures (e.g., curfews and vehicle restrictions).

Countering Adversaries. Direct military action against adversaries may be a central component of a stabilization effort. In which case, setting the conditions for a negotiated political settlement will entail breaking the ideological, financial, or intimidatory links within and among different adversarial and belligerent groups, as well as between them and the broader population.

Tailored Approaches. A well-targeted, differentiated strategy for engaging the various participants can transform the strategic geometry of the conflict. Such a strategy may allow the CDR to co-opt once adversarial or belligerent groups into the emerging political settlement.

Security Force Organization. The JFC may organize joint forces into a number of different composite units for the purpose of establishing security in and among the population; these include framework forces, strike forces, surge forces, and specific focus task forces.

The HN government may require firm advice, as well as financial support, to sustain the capabilities required.

Security Force Assistance. The generation and subsequent training of indigenous security forces should be conducted in a coordinated manner with broader SSR initiatives such as the development of civilian oversight bodies, judiciary and detention institutions, as well as transitional justice mechanisms and disarmament, demobilization, and reintegration programs.

Transitions.

The JFC should consider moving from an international military security lead to an indigenous lead as soon as practicable. The ability to transfer this responsibility will be a function of two inputs: the threat and the capacity of indigenous security forces.

Stability Operations Functions—Humanitarian Assistance

The humanitarian assistance function includes programs conducted to meet basic human needs to ensure the social well-being of the population. Social well-being is characterized by access to and delivery of basic needs and services (water, food, shelter, sanitation, and health services), the provision of primary and secondary education, the return or voluntary resettlement of those displaced by violent conflict, and the restoration of a social fabric and community life.

Civilian development agencies generally break humanitarian assistance into three categories: emergency humanitarian and disaster assistance; shorter-term transition initiatives; and longer-term development assistance. These generally parallel the military approach of initial response activities, transformational activities, and activities that foster sustainability; however, in the civilian agencies, each category has distinct operational approaches, staff, and resources.

Armed Forces of the United States participation in humanitarian assistance generally falls into one of two categories. Humanitarian assistance that provides support to alleviate urgent needs in an HN caused by some type of disaster or catastrophe falls under the rubric of FHA. Humanitarian assistance conducted as part of programs designed to increase the long-term capacity of the HN to provide for the health and well-being of its populace typically falls under the rubric of NA.

Evaluation and assessment.

It is normally appropriate to base measures of effectiveness (MOEs) for humanitarian assistance on *The Sphere Project Humanitarian Charter and Minimum Standards in Disaster Response*. The Sphere Project, developed by IGOs and NGOs involved in humanitarian assistance, recommends key indicators for provision of water, sanitation, food, health, shelter, and non-food items in disasters, and establishes voluntary minimum standards for each sector.

Military contribution.

Dislocated Civilian (DC) Support Missions. These missions are specifically designed to support the assistance and protection for DCs. A "dislocated civilian" is a broad term primarily used by DOD that includes a displaced person, an evacuee, an internally displaced person, a migrant, a refugee, or a stateless person. These persons may be victims of conflict or natural or man-made disaster. Typically, the United Nations (UN) or other IGOs and NGOs will build and administer camps, if needed, and provide basic assistance and services to the population. However, when the US military is requested to provide support, DC support missions may include camp organization (basic construction and administration); provision of care (food, supplies, medical attention, and protection); and placement (movement or relocation to other countries, camps, and locations).

Trafficking in Persons (TIP). Simply stated, TIP is modern-day slavery, involving victims who are forced, defrauded, or coerced into labor or sexual exploitation. Ongoing TIP in an area undermines ongoing stabilization efforts, as well as US and HN legitimacy. Ongoing security activities, such as border protection and freedom of movement activities, should support the HN's battle against TIP.

Emergency Food Assistance and Food Security. IGOs such as the World Food Programme, NGOs such as Cooperative for Assistance and Relief Everywhere, and USG agencies such as USAID can be expected to provide for the food needs of the relevant population. In some cases, military involvement may consist of providing security for food aid warehouses and delivery convoys in uncertain and hostile environments.

Shelter. Although the basic need for shelter is similar in most emergencies, considerations such as the kind of housing needed, the design used, what materials are available, who constructs the housing, and how long it must last will differ significantly in each situation.

Humanitarian Demining Assistance. DOD humanitarian demining programs are coordinated by the designated CCDR humanitarian mine action program manager, funded by the Defense Security Cooperation Agency Overseas Humanitarian, Disaster, and Civic Aid funds, and coordinated with interagency partners by the office of the Assistant Secretary of Defense for Special Operations and Low-Intensity Conflict and Interdependent Capabilities.

Public Health. Joint force operations to rebuild and protect infrastructure, potable water, proper sewage disposal, and essential health services that contribute significantly to the health of the HN population must be closely planned and coordinated with the HN ministries and USG agencies responsible for health sector redevelopment assistance. The JFC may employ forces to conduct medical humanitarian and civil assistance to support local military and civilian health systems or provide direct public health care to include primary medical, dental, veterinary, and other needed care. During stability operations the military may need to provide public health services for humanitarian reasons as well as to build community trust in the HN government.

Education. Military activities to support education programs generally focus on physical infrastructure.

Transitions.

Because humanitarian assistance is largely a civilian endeavor, with the military in a supporting role, the termination of US or multinational military humanitarian assistance activities will not normally coincide with the termination of international efforts.

Stability Operations Functions—Economic Stabilization and Infrastructure

The economic stabilization and infrastructure function includes programs conducted to ensure an economy in which people can pursue opportunities for livelihoods within a predictable system of economic governance bound by law.

Economic stabilization consists of restoring employment opportunities, initiating market reform, mobilizing domestic and foreign investment, supervising monetary reform, and rebuilding public structures. Infrastructure restoration consists of the reconstitution of power, transportation, communications, health and sanitation, fire fighting, education, mortuary services, and environmental control.

Economic and infrastructure security and development are inherently civilian undertakings; however, the presence of US forces will almost always have an impact, even indirectly, on this area. There may be times when more direct military involvement in economic development will be necessary: for example, when conditions restrict civilian movement or when civilian agencies have not yet arrived in the area.

Evaluation and assessment.

Each country has a unique economic structure based on its resources, the needs of the people, laws, customs, traditions, and level of development. The assessment should describe the situation, end state, CDR's intent, and national strategic objectives to stabilize a post-conflict economy, reduce the economic drivers of conflict, and increase institutional capacity. The four steps in conducting an economic assessment are: **compile a country economic profile; develop a country economic implementation plan; identify and analyze the economic drivers of any ongoing conflict; and prepare an economic section for inclusion in an initial staff estimate.**

Military contribution.

Employment Generation. Providing employment is an immediate peacekeeping task, a post-conflict objective, and a means of establishing the foundation for future economic growth and political stability. Key determinants of the appropriate nature of the military role in employment generation include the general security environment, the condition of the economic-related infrastructure, the scope of the need for employment generation programs, and the access of civilian responders to the area.

Monetary Policy. Establishing a central bank system and basic monetary policy is foundational to a recovering economy. The military contribution to this establishment is peripheral and should be thought of strictly in terms of providing required security, supporting resources (e.g., USG office equipment, specific CA expertise).

Fiscal Policy and Governance. The military will contribute to HN fiscal actions by providing security for financial institutions and for cash distribution, including salary or contractual payments, as required.

Critical Infrastructure. The joint force may be called upon to support infrastructure development by providing security, funding and materiel, CA functional expertise, or construction.

Quick impact projects.

Quick impact projects (QIPs) are relatively short-term, small-scale, low-cost, and rapidly implemented stabilization or development initiatives that are designed to deliver an immediate and highly visible impact, generally at the local provincial or community level. In more permissive environments, it is only where there is a capability gap that cannot be filled by another actor, or where the military possesses particular specialist skills that QIPs are likely to be implemented by the joint force. Where provincial reconstruction teams (PRTs) or other interagency field-based teams (e.g., field advance civilian teams) exist, much of this activity will be funded, planned, and implemented by development agencies coordinated through the PRT or interagency team.

Other considerations.

Other considerations for economic stabilization and infrastructure include: ownership issues; cost recovery; getting services to those in need; contracting as a management tool; business, legal and regulatory environment; maintenance standards; security; and accountability, auditing, and financial oversight.

Transitions.

JFCs must anticipate the transition from military to civilian program management and plan actions supportive of the long-term strategy. Joint forces can provide immediate support for economic stabilization, but the programs are frequently not viewed as long-term solutions. To maximize project effectiveness, these projects should be sequenced with the work of international civilian agencies and with the private sector to ensure continuity of effort with employees, functions, and support. The military's role is to help restore normalcy and fill the gap until civilian-led, longer-term programs commence.

Stability Operations Functions—Rule of Law

The rule of law is fundamental to legitimate governance.

The rule of law function refers to programs conducted to ensure all individuals and institutions, public and private, and the state itself are held accountable to the law, which is supreme. Perceived inequalities in the administration of the law, and real or apparent injustices, are triggers for instability.

Security Sector Reform. SSR centers not only on the security forces of the HN, but also on broader rule of law initiatives. The overall objective of SSR is to provide an effective and legitimate public service that is transparent, accountable to civilian authority, and responsive to the needs of the public.

Staff Judge Advocate Review of Rule of Law Programs. Programs to influence the legal systems of the HN are not above the law. Apart from US policy considerations, stability operations in the rule of law must themselves be governed by the rule of law; actions must be reviewed to ensure that they comply with applicable provisions of US law, international law, and HN law, as well as any UN or other international mandate governing the intervention.

Evaluation and assessment.

The necessary first step is an effective assessment that is comprehensive enough to provide situational understanding of the status of rule of law and that describes the deficiencies in a country's justice and security systems and does so holistically.

One of the most important initial steps in conducting rule of law programs is determining what law applies in the HN. If the JFC lacks understanding of the HN legal system and how it functions, it will be difficult to make informed decisions about how US forces can or should operate in relation to that system.

Military contribution.

Establishing an Interim Criminal Justice System. When conditions require the restoration of governance, establishing an interim justice system is a prerequisite. Civilian agencies normally support the development of an interim criminal justice system; however, when operating in a failed state, especially during and immediately after conflict, the joint force may be required to supply military police, legal, CA, and other personnel to fulfill these roles.

Personal Property. One of the most vital services provided by the judiciary branch is the resolution of property disputes. Typically, the military's role in resolving disputes is limited unless the joint force implements these mechanisms in the absence of a functioning HN government.

War Crimes Tribunals and Truth Commissions. While a military governing authority may operate military commissions and provost courts, the international community oversees the conduct of war crimes courts, tribunals, and truth commissions.

Transitions.

The military's role in ensuring rule of law, other than providing security, is normally limited; however, when operating in a failed or failing state, especially during and immediately after conflict, the joint force may be required to play a direct role in capacity building of justice systems and security sectors. As soon as the security situation warrants, these programs should be transitioned to civilian agencies, either from the US or multinational partners, or those of the HN.

Stability Operations Functions—Governance and Participation

Stable governance provides a foundation on which rule of law and economic activity can thrive and become drivers of security and stability.

Governance and participation refers to programs conducted to help the people to share, access, or compete for power through nonviolent political processes and to enjoy the collective benefits and services of the state. Stable governance is characterized by a government that provides essential services and serves as a responsible steward of public resources; government officials who are held accountable through political and legal processes; and a population that can participate in governance through civil society organizations, an independent media, and political parties. Military substitution for absent international civilian leadership should be considered a temporary solution, and civilian expertise and advice integrated into the planning process through appropriate reachback or in-theater advisors.

Evaluation and assessment.

The Democracy and Governance Assessment is an assessment framework developed by USAID, designed to assist civilian and military leaders prioritize and administer HN governance areas needing assistance. Data collection and analysis may involve a combination of research and interviews or focus group sessions with key country stakeholders. Particularly when combined with the Interagency Conflict Assessment Framework assessment of any ongoing conflict, the Democracy and Governance Assessment helps identify and assess key issues, key people, and key institutions in HN governance.

Military contribution.

Support National Constitution Processes. When the HN has no government, as may be the case during immediate post-conflict reconstruction or interventions in failed states, developing a national constitution is typically an important first step to establishing a foundation for governance and the rule of law. The military can support this process both with CA functional expertise, as required, and the provision of security and logistic support for key constitutional processes such as debates and balloting.

Support Transitional Governance. The military may support transitional governments through CMO support to civil administration (SCA) as well as providing security to governmental leaders and institutions of all branches of the government. Efforts to support transitional governance are shared between DOS and DOD, with leadership depending on the circumstances.

Support Local Governance. Even before national governance institutions and processes are established, the joint force should support the establishment of effective governance at the local level. The military support to local governance may include restoring essential services as required, providing CMO SCA, or providing security to governmental leaders and institutions of all branches of the government.

Support Anticorruption Initiatives. Corruption undermines confidence in the state, impedes the flow of aid, concentrates wealth into the hands of a generally unelected, unaccountable, and illegitimate minority, and provides elites with illicit means of protecting their positions and interests.

Support Elections. While civilian agencies and organizations that maintain strict transparency guide the elections process, military forces provide the support that enables broad participation by the local populace. This certainly includes security, but may also include logistic support.

Local governance and building on local capacities.	Joint force governance efforts should build on the foundations of existing capacity—however insubstantial they are, be they formal or informal, be they national or local. By identifying existing capacities on which to build, governance capacity building is more likely to develop approaches that are both systemically desirable and culturally feasible.
Essential services.	Whether following a US intervention or during peacekeeping operations, COIN operation, or other intervention, or in response to a natural disaster, the restoration of essential services in a fragile area is a key action to achieve security. This basic function of local governance is often lost during conflict and other disasters; efforts to restore governance, particularly at the local level, should focus on essential services—generally referred to as SWEAT-MSO: sewage, water, electricity, academics (meaning schools), trash, medical, safety, and other considerations.
	As with all stability operations, the joint force follows the lead of other USG agencies, particularly USAID, in the restoration of essential services. In many circumstances, local or international development and humanitarian organizations may be operating in theater and able to fulfill this function. The military contribution will be focused on enabling them to expand their access to the population. However, only military forces may be able to operate in some areas.
Elections.	In a post-conflict environment, elections are often one of the first and most visible steps toward nonviolent political transition, signaling the transfer of authority from the international community to HN leaders.
Without the establishment of a secure environment, an election is prone to failure.	In this context, the ability of US or multinational forces to conduct an election support mission successfully, in particular through achieving a secure environment, can be critical to the establishment of a legitimate government and attainment of overall mission objectives. The JFC, or liaisons, should participate in principals, donors, implementing agencies coordination to help coordinate and integrate security and election implementation strategies.

Media.

The media can be an important accountability mechanism for the government, helping to maintain the rule of law. Additionally, media can be useful in identifying gaps in government services through advocacy.

Joint forces may establish media outlets to meet the need to convey information to the public immediately, to dispel rumors, and to counteract the effects of hate speech and inflammatory propaganda. These efforts are often designed to preempt or compete with media outlets controlled by adversaries. The joint force may need to fill the vacuum in the provision of critical information to the population about stabilization activities, especially when free and independent media are lacking.

Support to civil administration.

SCA is assistance to stabilize a foreign government. SCA consists of planning, coordinating, advising, or assisting with those activities that reinforce or restore civil administration.

SCA in friendly territory includes advising friendly authorities and performing specific functions within the limits of authority and liability established by international treaties and agreements. SCA in occupied territory encompasses the establishment of a transitional military authority, as directed by the Secretary of Defense, to exercise executive, legislative, and judicial authority over the populace of a territory that US forces have taken from an enemy by force of arms until an indigenous civil government can be established.

Other considerations.

The burdens of governance require culturally astute leaders and joint forces capable of adapting to nuances of religion, ethnicity, and a number of other considerations essential to success.

The military force should, consistent with security requirements, respect the religious celebrations and the legitimate activities of religious leaders.

Archives and records, current and historical, of all branches of the former government should be secured and preserved. Large quantities of mail and other documents are often found in post offices or at other points of central communications. The joint force should seize, secure, and protect such materials until the forces can process and deliver them.

In general, the joint force protects and preserves all historical and cultural sites, monuments, and works; religious shrines and objects of art; and any other national collections of artifacts or art.

Successful capacity building relies on dependable vetting processes to screen potential civil servants from the HN. These processes help CDRs select qualified, competent officials while reducing the threat of security risks.

Transitions.

Poorly timed and conceived transitions create opportunities for hostile groups to exploit. This is particularly the case if the HN government fails to adequately discharge a responsibility that was previously successfully discharged by intervening organizations. Such an outcome severely undermines population confidence in the government.

The transition of governance to HN authorities will not occur by default. Establishing sustainable governance must involve extensive international and interagency coordination from the very beginning to ensure a successful transition. Joint force support to governance should focus on restoring the capacity of the HN, as well as enabling the other USG agencies and IGOs. All MOE, end state, transition, and termination planning should reflect this goal.

CONCLUSION

This publication provides doctrine for the conduct of stability operations during joint operations within the broader context of USG efforts. It provides guidance for operating across the range of military operations to support USG agencies, foreign governments, and IGOs, or to lead such missions, tasks, and activities until it is feasible to transfer lead responsibility.

Intentionally Blank

CHAPTER I
STABILITY OPERATIONS

"We secure our friends not by accepting favors but by doing them."

Thucydides
History of the Peloponnesian War (431 BC)

1. Nature of Stability Operations

a. The Department of Defense (DOD) has learned through the difficult experiences of both Iraq and Afghanistan that success is not only defined in military terms; it also involves rebuilding infrastructure, supporting economic development, establishing the rule of law, building accountable governance, establishing essential services, building a capable host nation (HN) military responsible to civilian authority. In short, we must employ multiple instruments of national power to build a foreign nation's (FN's) internal capacity in a preventive mode to help them to defend themselves and maintain stability, or to enable the transition of responsibility back to the host country after defeat of an active insurgency. The US also expends resources to bring stability to areas and peoples affected by natural or man-made disasters.

b. Many agencies of the US Government (USG) as well as many intergovernmental organizations (IGOs) and nongovernmental organizations (NGOs) distinguish between disaster response/humanitarian assistance activities, development activities, and post-conflict reconstruction and stabilization activities, along with a variety of the individual organizations' ongoing programs and aid assistance. However, in all cases the purpose of these efforts is to help move a HN or FN from instability (and particularly the violent conflict that often accompanies increased instability) to increased stability (and reduced violent conflict). Significant destabilizing factors challenge sustainable peace and security around the world. Such challenges range from acts of nature (e.g., earthquakes and typhoons) to the direct and indirect consequences of the choices and actions of governments and other entities affecting the populations of the world. Drivers of conflict, including oppression, natural disaster, fanaticism, competition for resources, residual territorial claims, ethnic tension, and the desire for power are exacerbated by terrorism, transnational crime, and ethnic violence. Successful conflict transformation relies on the ability of intervening entities to identify and reduce the primary drivers of ongoing or future violent conflict and instability in a region or individual HN, while building regional and HN capacities to manage them. The comprehensive efforts by the US and its partners to stabilize states in crisis (including both natural disaster response and intervention in violent conflicts) and to build the capacity of fragile states are referred to in this publication as stabilization efforts. The US priorities for stabilization efforts are based on the degree of impact on US strategic interests and the ability to mitigate the impact through intervention. Each individual case is judged by political leaders against these broad determinants.

c. Stabilization efforts are primarily the responsibility of development and US Foreign Service personnel from across the USG. The Department of State (DOS) is charged with responsibility for leading a whole-of-government approach to stabilization that includes the array of USG departments and agencies, including DOD and component Services and agencies. DOS also coordinates US interagency participation in a comprehensive approach to stabilization efforts that includes not only the US, but also the HN, other nations, IGOs, cooperating NGOs, and other participants. Within this broad approach, **the primary military contribution to stabilization is to protect and defend the population, facilitating the personal security of the people and, thus, creating a platform for political, economic, and human security.** Beyond protecting the population, however, a combination of factors arising from national strategic objectives, requirements of the operational environment, and the capacity of the joint force may drive the Armed Forces of the United States to directly participate in other stabilization efforts during the conduct of stability operations. Stability operations are various military missions, tasks, and activities conducted outside the US in coordination with other instruments of national power to maintain or reestablish a safe and secure environment, provide essential governmental services, emergency infrastructure reconstruction, and humanitarian relief.

d. Joint forces may lead stabilization activities until other USG agencies, foreign governments and security forces, or IGOs assume the role. The conduct of stability operations is a core US military mission that the Armed Forces are prepared to conduct with proficiency equivalent to combat operations. Joint forces support stabilization activities led by other USG departments or agencies, foreign governments and security forces, IGOs, or when otherwise directed.

e. Force is rarely the defining element that delivers success; instead, it is best used as an enabler of diplomacy. Complex problems of fragile states require comprehensive solutions—a full range of measures to promote HN growth and to protect it from subversion, lawlessness, insurgency, and other threats to stability. Ultimately, such a strategy, developed by the HN for itself (sometimes referred to as an internal defense and development [IDAD] strategy), must focus on building viable political, economic, security, and social institutions that respond to the needs of society. Its fundamental goal is to prevent a downward spiral of instability by forestalling and defeating threats and by working to correct conditions that may prompt violence. Stability operations support comprehensive solutions represented by the IDAD strategy.

f. Figure I-1 introduces a simple, idealized model that illustrates the elements of a stable state: human security; economic and infrastructure development; governance and the rule of law. While these elements can be analyzed individually, it is potentially distorting to view them separately. The stability of the state depends upon how well these elements are performed and the manner in which they interact, and the commitment of key members of that society to maintain or promote a standard acceptable to the populace.

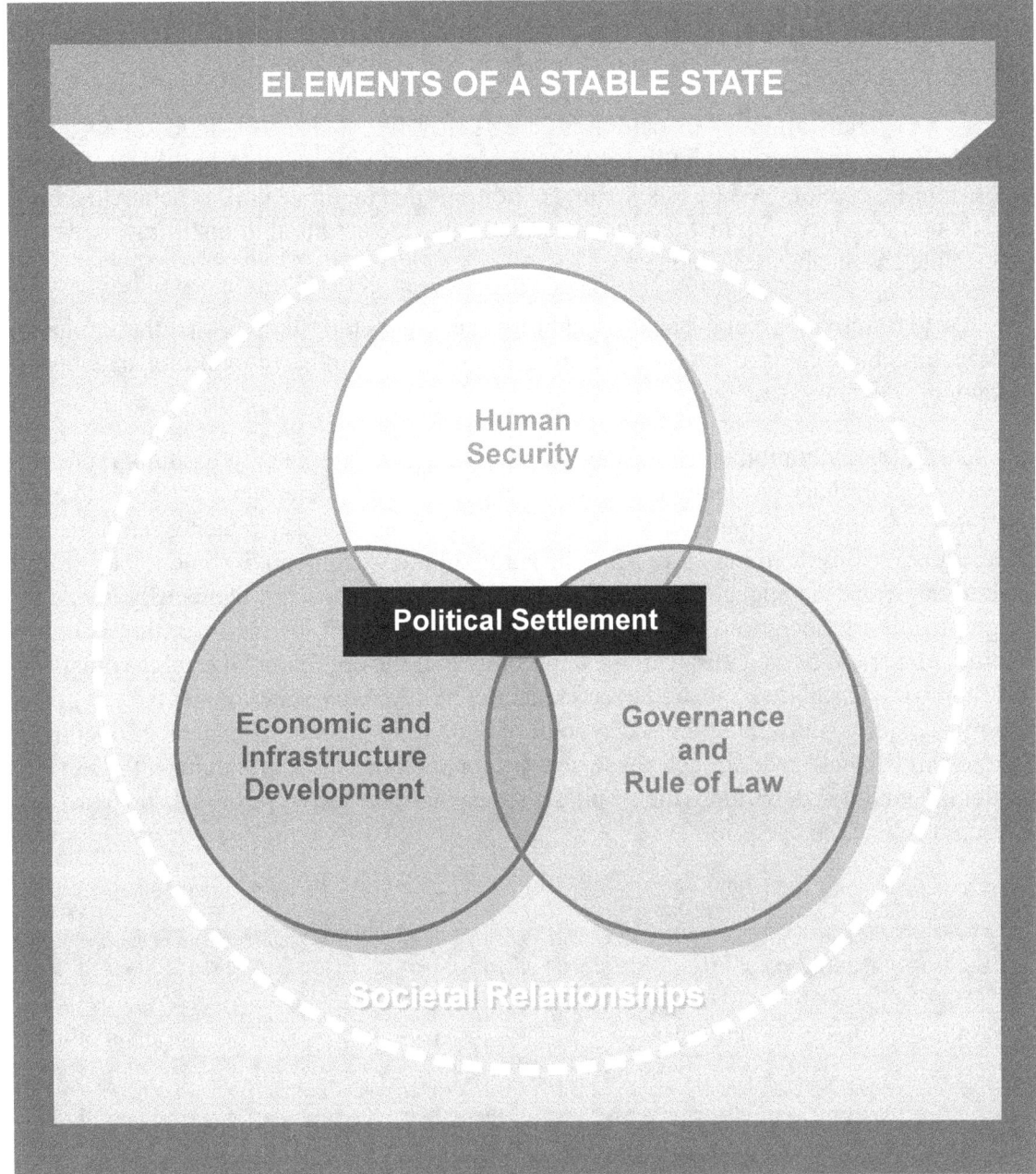

Figure I-1. Elements of a Stable State

2. Stability Operations Across the Range of Military Operations

a. The missions, tasks, and activities that make up stability operations fall into three broad categories: initial response activities, transformational activities, and sustainment activities.

(1) Initial response activities generally are tasks executed to stabilize the operational environment in an area in crisis, for instance during or immediately following conflict or a natural disaster. Initial response activities aim to provide a safe, secure environment and attend to the immediate humanitarian needs of a population. They support

efforts to reduce the level of violence or human suffering while creating conditions that enable other organizations to participate safely in ongoing efforts.

(2) Transformational activities are generally a broad range of security, reconstruction, and capacity building efforts. These activities aim to build HN capacity across multiple sectors. While establishing conditions that facilitate unified action to rebuild the HN and its supporting institutions, these activities are essential to instilling conditions that enable sustainable development.

(3) Activities that foster sustainability encompass long-term efforts that capitalize on capacity building and reconstruction activities to establish conditions that enable sustainable development.

b. Military operations vary in size, purpose, and combat intensity within a range that extends from military engagement, security cooperation, and deterrence activities to crisis response and limited contingency operations, and, if necessary, major operations and campaigns, as illustrated in Figure I-2. The nature of the security environment may require US military forces to engage in several types of joint operations simultaneously across the range of military operations. Whether the prevailing context for the operation is one of traditional warfare or irregular warfare (IW), or even if the operation takes place outside of war, combat and stabilization are never sequential or alternative operations; the joint force commander (JFC) must integrate and synchronize stability operations with other operations (offense and defense) within each phase of any joint operation. The commander (CDR) for a particular operation determines the emphasis to be placed on each type of mission or activity in each phase of the operation.

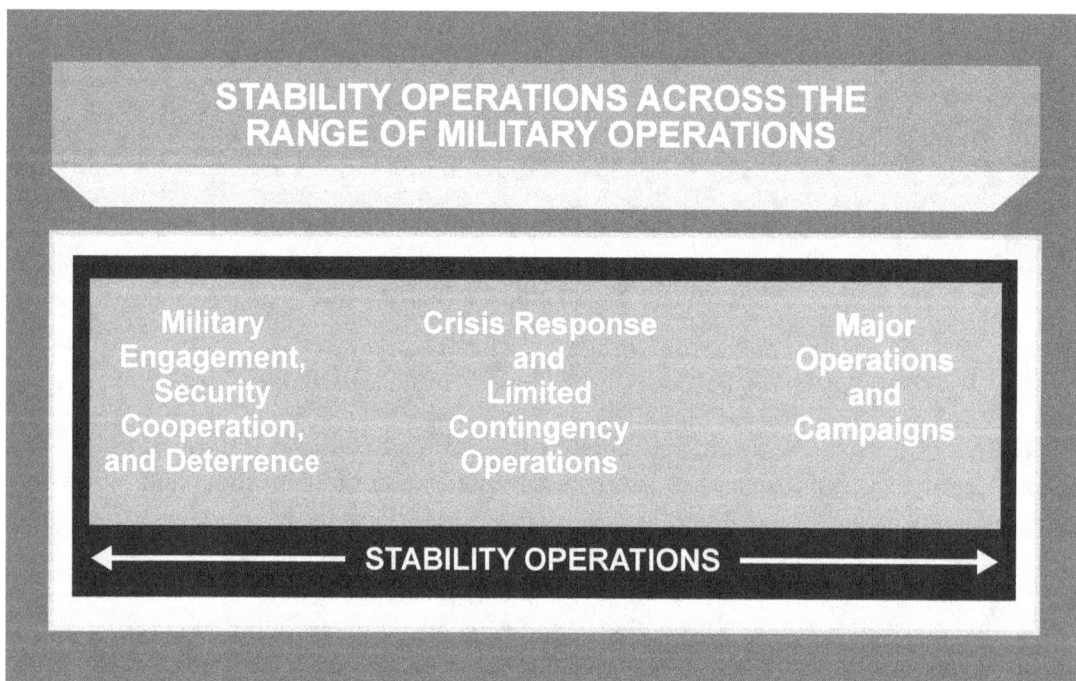

Figure I-2. Stability Operations Across the Range of Military Operations

For further details on the range of military operations, refer to Joint Publication (JP) 3-0, Joint Operations.

(1) During major operations and campaigns, stability operations are particularly emphasized following the achievement of major combat objectives. However, major operation and campaign plans must feature an appropriate balance between offensive, defensive, and stability operations in all phases. An exclusive focus on offensive and defensive operations in earlier phases may limit appropriate development of basic and supporting plans for follow-on phases and ultimately strategic success. Even while sustained combat operations are ongoing, there will be a need to establish or restore civil security and control and provide humanitarian relief as succeeding areas are occupied, bypassed, or returned to a transitional authority or HN control.

(a) During stabilization, initial response activities will dominate stability operations. The joint force should focus on establishing civil security to protect both the joint force and the civilian population, and meeting the humanitarian needs of civilians affected by war. Simultaneously, the JFC should maintain the momentum of the operation by working with partners to support the restoration of essential services and repair and protect critical infrastructure, if the security situation permits.

(b) The military's predominant presence and its ability to command and control (C2) forces and logistics under extreme conditions will often require the JFC to assume the lead in stabilization efforts during major operations and campaigns, even as USG lead transfers to an agency other than DOD. Additionally, the level of violence, particularly while sustained combat operations are ongoing, may delay the introduction of civilian personnel, leaving the lead agency without the capacity to execute civil administrative and other stability functions. During this critical period, only the joint force may have capability to execute civil administration, stabilization, and reconstruction efforts until well after combat objectives are accomplished. The disparity between authority and capability varies widely among theater strategic, operational, and tactical levels and is heavily dependent on the level of violence and threat of armed resistance.

(2) During crisis response and limited contingency operations, the balance of stability and combat operations varies widely with the circumstances. Many crisis response and limited contingency operations, such as foreign humanitarian assistance (FHA), may not require combat. Others, such as strikes and raids, may not require stability operations. Still others, such as counterinsurgency (COIN), will require a delicate balance of offense, defense, and stability operations throughout the operation.

(a) Peace operations (PO) encompass multiagency and multinational crisis response and limited contingency operations involving all instruments of national power with military missions to contain conflict, redress the peace, and shape the environment to support reconciliation and rebuilding and facilitate the transition to legitimate governance. PO include peacekeeping operations (PKO), peace enforcement operations (PEO), peacemaking (PM), peace building (PB), and conflict prevention efforts. PO normally include a large stability operations component, in the form of PB. PB provides the reconstruction and societal rehabilitation that offers hope to resolve conflict. PKO and PEO include predominantly combat actions that establish the conditions that enable PB to succeed. PB promotes reconciliation, strengthens and rebuilds civil infrastructures and institutions, builds confidence, and supports economic reconstruction to prevent a return to conflict. PB tasks are at times called "post-conflict reconstruction actions." Regardless of which term is applied to such an operation, stability operations play a key role. Some instability will exist concurrently with PB. PB usually begins during PKO or PEO and continues after they are concluded.

For further detail, refer to JP 3-07.3, Peace Operations.

(b) COIN is comprehensive civilian and military efforts taken to defeat an insurgency and to address any core grievances. COIN requires joint forces to both fight and build sequentially or simultaneously, depending on the circumstances. Stability operations are fundamental to COIN—stability operations are the "build" in the COIN process of "clear, hold, build."

For further detail on COIN, refer to JP 3-24, Counterinsurgency Operations.

EXAMPLE OF STABILITY OPERATIONS IN A MAJOR OPERATION

On 20 December 1989, the US committed forces in Panama to protect US citizens, secure the Panama Canal, support democracy for the people of Panama, and apprehend Manuel Noriega. As the Panamanian Defense Forces were neutralized, widespread looting and general lawlessness reduced Panama to a state of anarchy. The units of the task force had to quickly bring some sort of order to both the cities and the countryside. Everything from providing medical care and emergency food and water to supporting the training of local police was required. On 22 December, President George Bush sent in 2,000 additional troops to support the 22,500 already there in conducting stability operations. While the military had achieved its initial objectives, President Bush declared that the mission was not over until stability had been established. Over 200 civil affairs and 250 psychological operations personnel bolstered the newly installed government of President Guillermo Endara. As the situation became more stable and the democratic process began to take hold, Operation JUST CAUSE ended on 31 January 1990. The troops were pulled out and the military presence in Panama returned to its pre-invasion strength of about 13,500.

SOURCE: Joint Military Operations Historical Collection

(c) FHA consists of DOD activities, normally in support of the United States Agency for International Development (USAID) or DOS, conducted outside the US, its territories and possessions to relieve or reduce human suffering, disease, hunger, or privation. FHA is conducted to relieve or reduce the results of natural or man-made disasters or endemic conditions that might present a serious threat to life or that can result in great damage to or loss of property. FHA provided by US forces is limited in scope and duration. The foreign assistance provided is designed to supplement or complement the efforts of the

HN civil authorities or agencies that have the primary responsibility for providing that assistance.

For further detail on FHA, refer to JP 3-29, Foreign Humanitarian Assistance.

(d) Crises may occur suddenly or develop over a period of time. Although joint forces may operate in an HN to forestall crises, military intervention is often not directed until the crisis has deteriorated beyond the ability of civilian agencies to respond effectively, either due to a high level of violence or the requirement for capabilities and capacities unique to the military (e.g., heavy lift capabilities or robust C2 capacities). Prior to entry in an operational area, the JFC, in collaboration with other USG departments or agencies, should identify what the military may be required to contribute in the way of stability operations, recognizing that military provision is a last resort and that the main responsibility lies with international organizations and the HN government, IGOs, and the private sector. In a hostile environment, the military may be widely involved in such provision. Ideally, the military should transition this responsibility as quickly as possible.

(e) Initial response activities will dominate stability operations at the beginning of crisis response and limited contingency operations as the joint force confronts the crisis. Circumstances will normally require the JFC to gain the initiative quickly to stem and ultimately reverse the crisis. As the crisis turns, the joint force may transition focus to transformational activities and activities that foster sustainability in an attempt to avert future crises. The decision for the joint force to continue these efforts to alleviate underlying causes of the crisis is a political decision and will vary with the circumstances. During operations in which the military must continue to protect the population until stabilization efforts have transformed the crisis (e.g., COIN or PO), direct participation by the military in transformational and sustaining activities across all sectors is more likely. During operations in which the military is not required to conduct ongoing missions to protect the population (e.g., most FHA operations), military forces normally withdraw after immediate response activities are complete or transferred to civilian agencies. In either case, military expertise falls largely in areas focused on the security sector. Support for security sector reform (SSR) and defense reform may be key components of the military's transformational activities that foster sustainability.

(3) During military engagement, security cooperation, and deterrence activities, stability operations play an important role in joint operations conducted in consonance with the geographic combatant commanders' (GCCs') theater campaign plan objectives and support the objectives of individual country teams. Military support to stabilization efforts during peacetime generally takes the form of presence and nation assistance (NA) operations.

(a) Sustained joint force presence in a region helps promote a secure environment in which diplomatic, economic, and informational programs designed to reduce the drivers of conflict and instability can flourish. Presence can take the form of forward basing, forward deploying, or pre-positioning assets. Joint force presence often keeps unstable situations from escalating into larger conflicts.

**EXAMPLE OF STABILITY OPERATIONS IN A CRISIS RESPONSE/
LIMITED CONTINGENCY OPERATION**

On 28 December 2004, the US committed forces to Southeast Asia to respond to the 26 December 9.15-magnitude earthquake that struck off the west coast of Indonesia and the ensuing series of devastating tsunamis throughout the region. Only 10 days after the earthquake and tsunamis struck, Operation UNIFIED ASSISTANCE included over 25 ships, 45 fixed-wing aircraft, and 58 helicopters, working with US Government, host nation, and international partners. Although stability operations were the primary component of this foreign humanitarian assistance (FHA) mission, defensive activities were constant; in particular, ongoing insurgencies in Indonesia and Sri Lanka as well as large numbers of refugees and concerns about US intentions by the largely Muslim population made force protection a top priority. In UNIFIED ASSISTANCE, which lasted only about six weeks, the primary goal was to provide immediate response humanitarian assistance in the form of life-sustaining water, food, and medicines. The joint force generally avoided transformational stability activities, although the hospital ship USNS Mercy assisted in rebuilding Indonesia's emergency medical services. At the operational level, Operation UNIFIED ASSISTANCE succeeded in assisting with transportation and communications so as to enable the flow of aid. At the strategic level, this FHA operation assisted in improving diplomatic relations, increasing military-to-military cooperation, and fostering public good will.

SOURCE: *Waves of Hope: The US Navy's Response to the*
Tsunami in Northern Indonesia
Bruce A. Elleman
Naval War College Newport Papers No. 28

(b) US NA is civil or military assistance (other than FHA) rendered to a nation by US forces within that nation's territory during peacetime, crises or emergencies, or war, based on agreements mutually concluded between the United States and that nation. NA operations support the HN by promoting sustainable development and growth of responsive institutions. The goal is to promote long-term regional stability. NA programs include, but are not limited to, security assistance, foreign internal defense (FID), humanitarian and civic assistance (HCA), building partnership capacity, and military civic action (MCA). These operations will have a significant stability operations component.

For further details on NA, refer to JP 3-0, Joint Operations, *JP 3-22,* Foreign Internal Defense, *and JP 3-57,* Civil-Military Operations.

(c) Joint forces normally conduct NA and other military engagement, security cooperation, and deterrence activities in relatively stable states. As such, activities that foster sustainability will dominate, though transformational activities may also play an important role. Military participation in stabilization efforts outside of war or crisis response generally focuses on SSR, especially training counterpart military units in both combat and stability operations.

EXAMPLE OF STABILITY OPERATIONS DURING MILITARY ENGAGEMENT, SECURITY COOPERATION, AND DETERRENCE ACTIVITIES

Every year, US forces conduct stability operations in Central America, South America, and Caribbean nations during US Southern Command's military civic assistance program, NEW HORIZONS. During NEW HORIZONS, military forces from the US and a host nation (HN) work together to refine skills of the HN military's engineers, medical personnel, and support staff, mainly by conducting immediate response and transformational stability activities together in the neediest areas of the HN. Task Force NEW HORIZONS works with HN ministries and provincial governments to identify and complete the humanitarian missions.

SOURCE: US Southern Command

---

c. Military health support for stability operations is a core US military mission that the DOD military health system shall be prepared to conduct throughout all phases of conflict and across the range of military operations. Military health support for stability operations shall be given priority comparable to combat operations and be explicitly addressed and integrated across all military health system activities.

For further details, refer to JP 4-02, Health Service Support.

3. **Stability Operations in Fragile States**

a. Stability operations executed during major operations or campaigns or during crisis response and limited contingency operations normally take place in fragile states or regions. A fragile state is a country that suffers from institutional weaknesses serious enough to threaten the stability of its central government. Whether that fragility is caused by the removal of state institutions in military actions, ongoing systemic issues of economics or governance, a sudden onset disaster, or any other circumstances that may upset the balance of the elements of a stable state, the JFC must understand the context in which stability operations are executed. The fragile states framework, used in interagency forums, can help the JFC develop a foundational understanding of the operational environment. The framework describes different levels of fragility and the direction and speed of movement along the framework. States move within the fragile states framework based on the relationships among the elements of a stable state.

b. The term "fragile states" describes a broad range of failing, failed, and recovering states (see Figure I-3). The stability of these states depends on the commitment of key members of that society to maintain or promote a standard acceptable to the populace. When joint forces commence operations in an area, the state may be at any point along the fragile states framework; thus, the starting conditions may be from a failed state to a recovering state. From that point, the joint or multinational forces and civilian agencies will attempt to move the state toward normalization, even as the presence of destabilizing factors (e.g., insurgents, ongoing natural disasters) may contribute to outbreaks of violent conflict. Movement along the framework does not have to be linear; the conditions can decline and

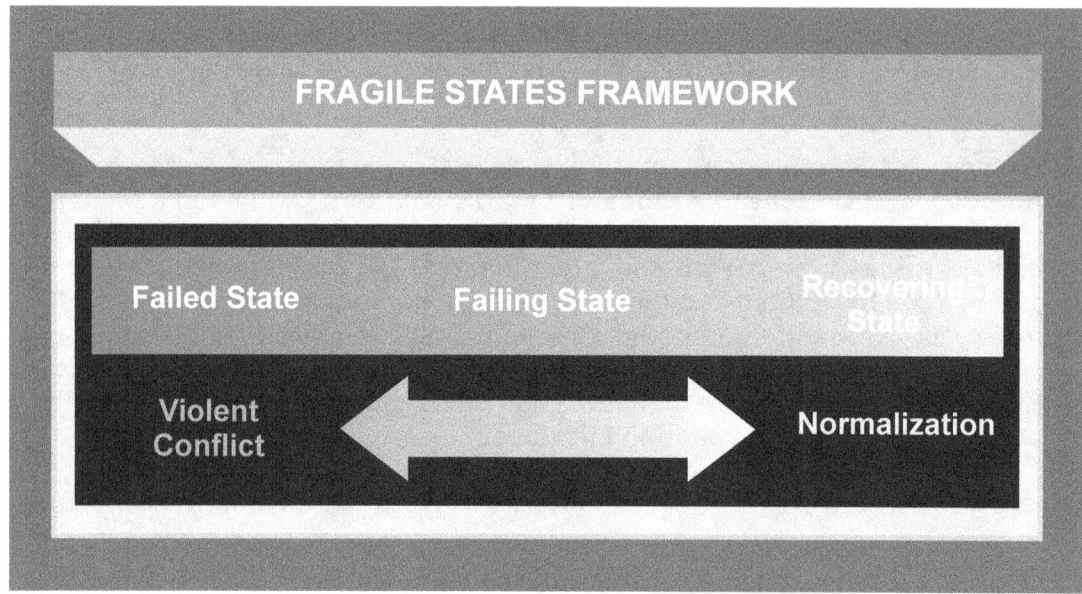

Figure I-3. Fragile States Framework

improve in separate iterations. Conditions on the Failed State/Violent Conflict end of the framework are more likely to require more military effort, particularly to provide civil security.

(1) The framework has three categories of states: failed, failing, and recovering, although the distinction or exact transition between categories is rarely clear.

(a) **Failed State.** A failed state may only have remnants of a government due to collapse or regime change or it may have a government that exerts weak governance in all or large portions of its territory. A failed state is unable to effectively protect and govern the population. A failed state may not have any government with which to work and, consequently, conducting stabilization efforts is difficult, especially with respect to establishing legitimacy of the government and governmental security forces. Under these extreme circumstances, the intervening authority may have a legal and moral responsibility to install a transitional authority. Even with a national government, a failed state may include large ungoverned areas (UGAs).

(b) **Failing State.** The failing state is still viable, but it has a reduced capability and capacity to protect and govern the population. Based on the situation and level of stability, a failing state may be transforming toward a recovering state or a failed state.

(c) **Recovering State.** The recovering state is moving toward normalcy but may have an imperfect level of viability. This state is able to protect and govern its population to some degree. A key consideration is whether the population considers the level of protection and governance acceptable and normal.

(2) The distinction among failed, failing, and recovering states is not always clear in practice, and it is more important to understand in which direction a state is moving along

the framework and how quickly than it is to categorize a state as failed or not. Therefore, the JFC, working in consultation with the country team, GCC, and combatant command staff, must distinguish between fragile states that are vulnerable to failure and those that are already in crisis.

(a) **Vulnerable States.** Vulnerable states are those states unable or unwilling to adequately assure the provision of security and basic services to significant portions of their populations and where the legitimacy of the government is in question. These states are not in crisis and may even be moving toward normalization, but their vulnerability to failure remains an important consideration for the HN government and any intervening forces.

(b) **Crisis States.** Crisis states are those states where the central government does not exert effective control over its own territory or is unable or unwilling to assure the provision of vital services to significant parts of its territory. Crisis states are already in failure or are quickly spiraling toward violent conflict.

For further details on the fragile states framework, refer to USAID's Fragile States Strategy (2005).

(3) States protect and defend their population from internal and external threats (i.e., provide civil security) to protect individuals from persecution, intimidation, reprisals, and other forms of systematic violence (i.e., personal security). In addition, states attempt to meet the basic physiological needs of the people. Human security, a requirement for building and sustaining stability, is met when the personal security needs and basic physiological needs (e.g., food, water, and shelter) of the population are met. Where the state lacks the capability or will to meet security needs, individuals tend to transfer loyalty to any group that promises to meet those needs, including adversarial groups such as insurgents and foreign fighters, as well as belligerents and opportunists. These groups can exploit human insecurity by providing money, basic social services, and even a crude form of justice. Securing the population, therefore, is fundamental to the development of HN government authority and ultimately the national security of the state.

(4) The political climate and economic and infrastructure development are characterized by the level of natural resources, degree of technological development, industrial base, communications network, and level of government revenue. These factors shape the ability of the state to provide stable governance and to ensure security in the long term, thereby reducing the drivers of conflict and instability and preventing the downward spiral from vulnerability to crisis and state failure.

(5) Governance and rule of law in a stable state is characterized by a sustainable political structure that permits the peaceful resolution of internal contests for power. The prospect of long-term stable governance only occurs when effective influence is exercised over a population and territory by methods viewed as broadly legitimate by the majority of the governed, though a brittle form of stability can exist using brutality and corruption. The rule of law is fundamental to legitimate governance; the ability to provide human security and to encourage economic stabilization is fundamental to effective governance over the long term.

(6) Human security, economic and infrastructure development, and governance and rule of law encompass the substantive functionalities and competencies of the state. However, the context is also determined by the societal relationships that underpin and are interwoven with these elements. In a stable state, the social, cultural, and ideological factors that bind society are broadly consistent with the manner in which state institutions discharge their responsibilities and gain consent from the population.

(7) The structures of a state are determined by a political settlement forged by a common understanding, usually among competing elites, that their interests or beliefs are served by a particular way of organizing political power. The political settlement is not necessarily a formal agreement, but is rather an understanding among those with power as to how political power is organized and exercised without resorting to violence; however informal, it is the foundation of a political process. Initially, a settlement may only involve elites, but must broaden out to include wider society and bring in excluded groups. It is the achievement of the political settlement, more than anything else, that is the most important marker of progress in stabilization.

(8) Degradation in any one of these areas may lead to erosion of the others. This in turn creates a web of poor governance, economic breakdown, and human insecurity that simultaneously stimulates and exacerbates conflict. This may cause, or be caused by, a collapse in the political settlement that regulates key societal and state relationships. Despite huge contextual variations—and every situation *is* different—this normally drives a downward spiral of state fragility. This can be characterized by decline or disintegration at the junction where human security, economic development, governance and the rule of law meet, leading to the unraveling of the political settlement.

c. People chronically deprived of human security can be both a cause and result of state fragility. A desperate population will turn to any provider when basic needs are insufficiently met. Opportunists and potential adversaries will seek to fill the vacuum where the HN is absent or ineffective. Failure to provide human security undermines the foundations of both the state and the region's stability as the people struggle for survival. Political progress is unlikely to take place in the midst of chronic human insecurity. Focusing on the population may not necessarily gain popular consent, but it is a key element in preventing potential and real adversaries from gaining undue influence. People need to believe that their situation is more likely to improve under the HN than its adversaries.

d. The fragile states framework and the elements of a stable state are tools to help understand the context in which stability operations are conducted. A stable state, as described in these tools, may be the overarching objective of stabilization efforts, but JFCs must be careful to avoid focusing too heavily on national institutions as a panacea for fragility and instability. Although capacity building at the national level plays a crucial role, societal strength and stability is ultimately rooted at the community level.

e. The scale of military involvement and commitment in stability operations can range from a single advisor to a sizeable joint force. Generally, early involvement and commitment to prevent a downward spiral in a fragile state will be considerably less onerous for intervening forces than the scale necessary to facilitate recovery of a failed state.

Intervention in a state that is failing, which nearly always involves a kaleidoscope of violent adversaries, is likely to be bloody, protracted, and costly. The resources required are substantial, and the costs, both in terms of casualties and treasure, will usually be painful and controversial.

4. Political Settlement

a. All military action should be assessed by its contribution toward achieving stabilization objectives, thus creating a platform for political, economic, and human security. At the heart of the political problem lies a contest between the way political power is organized and who wields that power. Leaders of PM efforts will need to convince decisive elites that their interests are best served through an accommodation with the approved political settlement, rather than renewed conflict. Where this is not possible, the use of military force can influence and alter the political dynamics, which may remove the barriers to any accommodation.

b. A collapsing political settlement is often the source, not just the symptom, of state fragility. If powerful elites believe that an existing or proposed political settlement is no longer in their interests they may actively seek to undermine it. This may include the use of large-scale violence to undermine the authority of the state. In such circumstances exacerbating and prolonging human insecurity, undermining development, and exacerbating weaknesses in governance and the rule of law may be a deliberate and central part of their strategy.

c. Stabilization efforts seek to reshape and stabilize a series of key relationships. The primary relationship is the triangular one between the HN government, competing (possibly violent) elites (of which there may be several), and the wider population. It is this set of relationships that holds the key to a sustainable political settlement.

d. A strategy of political settlement will entail the accommodation of competing elites, sometimes referred to as elite consolidation. Elites in this case are those individuals and groups with the power (including capacity for significant violence) to undermine existing political settlements and prevent the establishment of new ones. They can achieve this through their ability and aspiration to mobilize resources, decisive groups, or broad swaths of the population. Elites can generally be expected to accommodate themselves to political settlements on the basis of self-interest, but economics, ideologies, culture, and social relationships also matter. Therefore, political settlements of competing elites may not be stable in the long term. At least one side may continue to struggle for power and domination.

e. Negotiation and peace agreements may be a part of a political settlement, but they are not synonymous. A clear-cut victory of one group over another could lead to a political settlement if the losers believe that the chance of improving their position through further conflict is limited; personal security can be a strong motivation for accommodation. However, unequivocal victories in complex societal conflicts are rare. Usually, success is based on including elements of hostile groups in the political system.

f. In countries where legitimate institutions are weak and few, building a stable system of government is a long, difficult process.

g. The JFC should support DOS initiatives to engage all legitimate claimants to power in the society into the political process. The main objective in most cases should be to allow the main contenders to continue their competition under new rules that favor peaceful over violent means, giving all an opportunity for power sharing.

For further details on PM, refer to JP 3-07.3, Peace Operations.

5. Legitimacy

a. Legitimacy is a condition based upon the perception by specific audiences of the legality, morality, or rightness of a set of actions, and of the propriety of the authority of the individuals or organizations in taking them. This audience may be the US public, FN, the populations in the operational area, or the participating forces. If an operation is perceived as legitimate, the audience has a strong impulse to support the action. Establishing and strengthening the legitimacy of the HN government in the eyes of the HN population is the foundation of stabilization efforts; stability operations conducted by military forces must maintain this focus. Although secondary to the legitimacy of the HN, the JFC should strive to promote the legitimacy of the intervening force as well. This comes into play, for example, when the JFC needs to work in partnership or closer alignment with key NGOs or IGOs such as the European Union (EU). Even after rudimentary civil authority is established, the JFC's effectiveness in coordinating a more unified response or activity may depend on the partnering organization's perception of the legitimacy of the military operations, as well as the perceptions of the local population.

b. A political settlement is unsustainable if the HN government is unable or unwilling to build sufficient authority and legitimacy. All governments exercise control through a combination of consent and coercion. Legitimate governments function with the tacit consent of the governed and are generally stable, whereas regimes generally considered illegitimate rule entirely or mainly through coercion. The more a state relies on coercion, the greater the likelihood of collapse if that power is disrupted. The rule of law is fundamental to legitimate governance. Legitimate governance can be undermined by many issues, including criminal activity (e.g., corruption, illegal trafficking), incompetence, bias, disregard for the rule of law, abuse of established traditions, and disenfranchisement of key stakeholders. However, rule of law is likely to be institutionalized in varying forms dependent upon the social, cultural, and political mores of the particular society. The local population determines legitimacy; it cannot be imposed by an external entity.

c. Authority of the state or intervening forces or organizations is dependent upon the successful amalgamation and interplay of four factors:

(1) **Mandate:** The perceived legitimacy of the mandate that establishes the intervening authority and even the mandate that establishes the state authority of the HN, whether through the principles of universal suffrage, or a recognized and accepted caste/tribal model.

(2) **Manner:** The perceived legitimacy of the way in which those exercising the mandate conduct themselves, both individually and collectively.

(3) **Consent:** The extent to which factions, local populations, and others consent to, comply with, or resist the authority of those exercising the mandate. Consent, or its absence, may range from active resistance, through unwilling compliance, to freely given support.

(4) **Expectations:** The extent to which the expectations and aspirations of factions, local populations, and others are managed or are met by those exercising the mandate.

d. The JFC must distinguish between the justification for intervention as spelled out in policy for the operation and the ongoing legitimacy accorded to the joint force in view of the way they carry out the operation. Once the political decision has been made to intervene, the JFC can do little about the legitimacy of that decision, but must adhere to the mandate or policy to retain legitimacy. In addition, CDRs at all levels have an obligation to assert and protect the legitimacy of operations. Restraint and focused application of force are not just legal obligations; they are critical to sustaining the support of both local and US populations. Both restraint and focused application are difficult to apply in IW, or conflicts in which combatants wear no uniforms and operate from population centers. Even so, actions to protect and defend the population must be balanced with legitimacy concerns. Judicious use of force, restructuring the type of forces employed, and ensuring the disciplined conduct of the forces involved may reinforce legitimacy.

e. **Guidance for Maintaining Legitimacy.** Maintaining the legitimacy of the HN and of the joint operation is an ongoing, and overriding, concern for the JFC. The following guidelines apply:

(1) **Conduct interagency coordination on legitimacy expeditiously and at the highest level possible.** Designing joint force and HN legitimacy into operations across all USG activities and understanding the perceptions within the operational environment is an inherently political activity. The JFC should work through and with USAID, under the direction of the chief of mission (COM), to ensure the USG whole-of-government effort is in accordance with the HN government requirements, and complementary to efforts being undertaken by multinational partners, IGOs, and NGOs.

(2) **Conduct Legal Analysis.** Legitimacy has a strong legal component that is not strengthened by workarounds. Understanding the limits of actual legal authority, and the risks if they are ignored, requires fairly sophisticated analysis. As in any operation, the staff judge advocate (SJA) should be an integral part of the planning and decision-making process.

(3) **Recognize that a perceived lack of legitimacy in any one operation will impact operations elsewhere.** How the US is perceived as performing operations in one part of the world has a direct impact on the ability of the US to conduct operations worldwide.

(4) **Leaders at all levels must reinforce that legitimacy is a core consideration for all forces.** Rules of engagement (ROE), guidelines for interaction with the civilian population, and tactical actions should all support the legitimacy of US actions and respect for the legitimacy of the HN authorities. Regardless of whether an operation is conducted under the law of military occupation, or is entirely in support of HN authority, if the HN population does not consent to the authority that is being exercised, they will be less willing partners in enforcing the rule of law.

(5) **Do not overlook non-state security organizations when analyzing the legitimacy of HN authorities and other partners.** Military and other state sponsored security agencies may not be the sole source of civil security in the operational area. Private security contractors and local militias may be present, whether officially sponsored or not. The population may not distinguish between their behavior and that of state security forces.

(6) **Recognize that all of these factors and functions are key components of a communications strategy, and should be pursued as such.** The establishment of the legitimacy of joint force members and actions, and the discrediting of those of the adversary, are critical components of a communications strategy. A conscious comprehensive approach to a communications strategy is necessary to ensure the coherent, effective, and synergistic union of these activities and concerns.

6. **Principles of Stability Operations**

Although the principles of joint operations (see Figure I-4) apply to all aspects of any joint operation, emphasis on certain principles and their applicability during stability operations is appropriate.

For further details on the principles of joint operations, refer to JP 3-0, Joint Operations.

a. **Objective.** *Direct every military operation toward a clearly defined, decisive, and attainable objective.* The objective of a stabilization effort is to achieve and maintain a workable political settlement among the HN government, competing elites, and the wider population. This can be referred to as the primacy of the political purpose and applies at both a local and national level. Military operations are integral to the unified actions required to shape and drive this political settlement.

b. **Offensive.** *Seize, retain, and exploit the initiative.* Failing to act quickly to gain and maintain the initiative in stabilization efforts may create a breeding ground for dissent and possible exploitation opportunities for enemies or adversaries.

c. **Mass.** *Concentrate power at the decisive time and place.* Mass matters in stability operations, particularly when stability operations are conducted in a hostile environment (e.g., during a major operation or in COIN). Deploying a stability force that has the capability to satisfy the concurrent requirements to protect the population and neutralize hostile groups will be a major planning consideration. The problem is compounded when the level of violence or humanitarian need requires joint force participation in stability operations beyond providing civil security. Insufficient mass will often result in loss of the initiative.

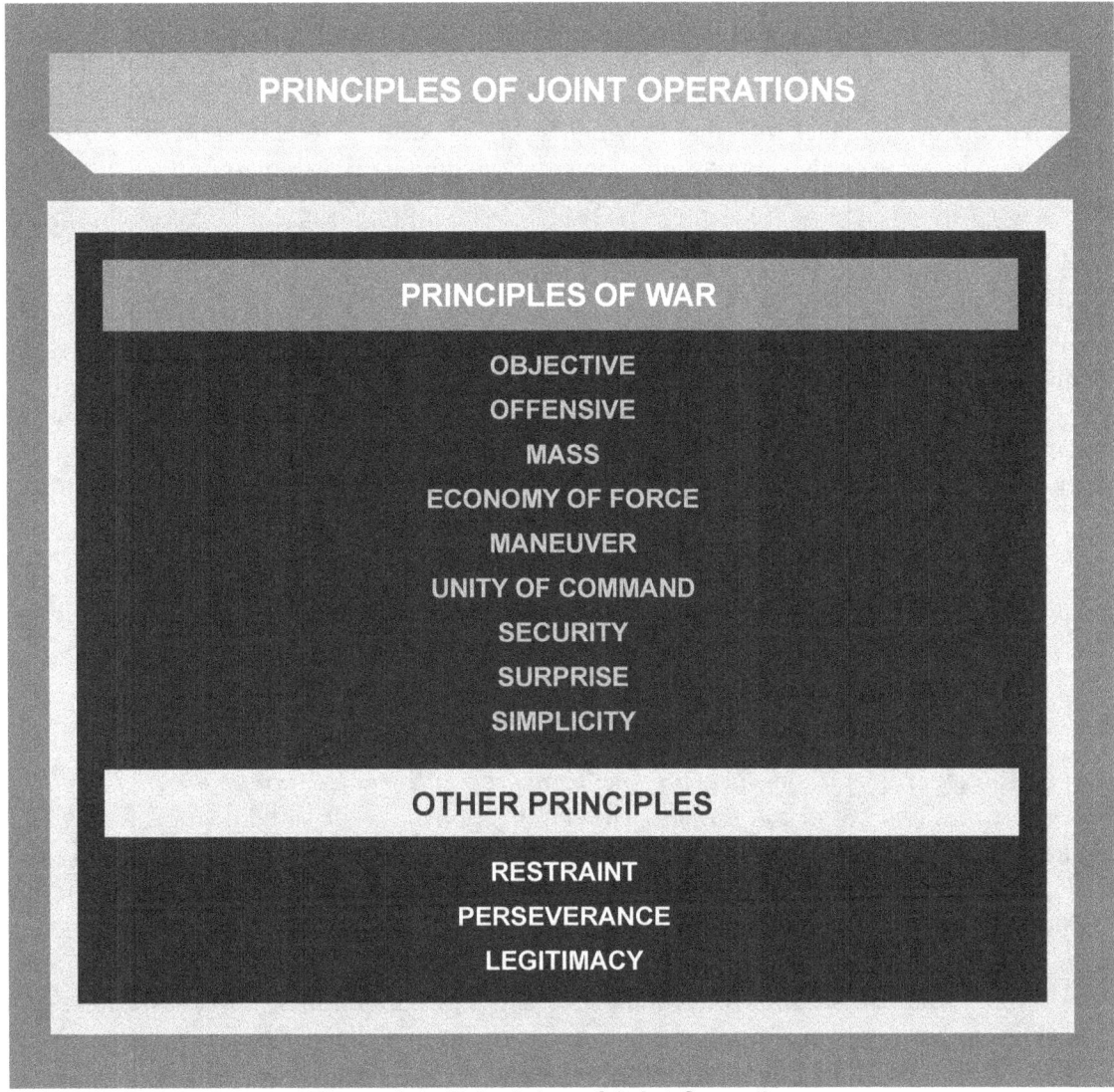

Figure I-4. Principles of Joint Operations

d. **Economy of force.** *Allocate minimum essential combat power to secondary efforts.* Personnel should not presume that stability operations are "secondary" efforts, particularly during major operations and campaigns or even within the context of theater strategic planning efforts. On the contrary, stability operations should be considered across all phases of a joint operation, applying appropriate combat power to support conflict transformation and tying joint operations to the political objectives.

e. **Unity of command.** *Seek unity of effort in every operation.* Unity of command means that all forces operate under a single CDR with the requisite authority to direct those forces employed in pursuit of a common purpose. The threat of force inherent in the employment of the Armed Forces requires that the chain of command for US military forces remain inviolate, flowing from the Secretary of Defense (SecDef) through the combatant commander (CCDR) to the subordinate JFC. Additionally, unity of command will help ensure that stability and combat operations are directed together toward their common objective. Stability operations must be closely coordinated with and through appropriate interagency authorities, as well as HN and other partner nation authorities as appropriate; in many cases, the JFC will be supporting civilian leadership. However, coordination arrangements among military and civilian government agencies, IGOs, NGOs, and other organizations will often be informal, relying largely on personal relationships and trust built over time. In some cases, de-confliction may be the only achievable goal.

f. **Restraint.** *Apply appropriate combat capability prudently.* During stability operations, defending and protecting the population is paramount. It is on this foundation of civil security that the political settlement can be achieved. This, coupled with the need to provide force protection for the joint force (as well as for other organizations, if directed), requires the conduct of offensive and defensive operations alongside stability operations. However, the use of force often antagonizes the population, possibly damaging the legitimacy of both the HN government and the organization that uses force while enhancing the legitimacy of any adversary. Restraint requires the careful and disciplined balancing of protecting the people and infrastructure, conducting military operations, and achieving the overarching objectives of the operation. A single act can cause significant military and political consequences; therefore, when force is used, it must be lawful and measured. Restraint is best achieved when all military personnel understand the political objectives and the potential impact of inappropriate actions and when the ROE are sensitive to political concerns, consistent always with the right and obligation of self-defense.

g. **Perseverance.** *Prepare for the measured, protracted application of military capability in support of strategic aims.* The stabilization of fragile states is, fundamentally, a protracted effort. The long-term focus of transformational stability activities and activities that foster sustainability requires a conviction among the local population that external support for their government will be sufficient and enduring. Indications of half-hearted or transitory engagement by partner nations will undermine the effort. Against this must be set the danger of creating a sense of permanence amounting to dependency and leading to a perception of the external forces as occupiers. With this delicate balance in mind, when military forces conduct initial response activities to fill immediate gaps in assistance, military objectives should be to enable civilian control of stabilization efforts. This facilitates early withdrawal of military forces while preserving the long-term focus of international stabilization efforts. This should not be confused, however, with an imperative to turn over stabilization activities before other institutions, particularly HN security forces, are prepared.

GUIDING PRINCIPLES FOR STABILIZATION AND RECONSTRUCTION

USG [United States Government] civilian institutions that engage in stabilization efforts utilize a broad range of cross-cutting principles that apply to every actor across every area of stabilization. The principles, found in the US Institute of Peace's *Guiding Principles of Stabilization and Reconstruction*, are focused on outcomes. The similarities to the principles of joint operations outlined above are significant and should be considered during planning and execution:

Host Nation [HN] Ownership and Capacity. The affected country must drive its own development needs and priorities even if transitional authority is in the hands of outsiders.

Political Primacy. A political settlement is the cornerstone of a sustainable peace. Every decision and every action has an impact on the possibility of forging political agreement.

Legitimacy. Legitimacy has three facets: the degree to which the HN population accepts the mission and its mandate or the government and its actions; the degree to which the government is accountable to its people; and the degree to which regional neighbors and the broader international community accept the mission mandate and the HN government.

Unity of Effort. Unity of effort begins with a shared understanding of the environment. It refers to cooperation toward common objectives over the short and long term, even when the participants come from many different organizations with diverse operating cultures.

Security. Security is a cross-cutting prerequisite for peace. The lack of security is what prompts stabilization efforts to begin with. Security creates the enabling environment for development.

Conflict Transformation. Conflict transformation guides the strategy to transform resolution of conflict from violent to peaceful means. It requires reducing drivers of conflict and strengthening mitigators across political, security, rule of law, economic, and social spheres, while building HN capacity to manage political and economic competition through peaceful means.

Regional Engagement. Regional engagement entails encouraging the HN, its neighboring countries, and other key states in the region to partner in promoting both the HN's and the region's security and economic and political development. It has three components: comprehensive regional diplomacy, a shared regional vision, and cooperation.

SOURCE: *Guiding Principles for Stabilization and Reconstruction*
US Institute of Peace and US Army Peacekeeping and
Stability Operations Institute

h. **Legitimacy.** *Committed forces must sustain the legitimacy of the operation and of the host government.* The credibility of the HN government and its ability to generate consent is crucial. The population's attitude toward US or multinational forces may be a significant element in this but, ultimately, is of secondary importance. Consent for the presence of US forces conducting stability operations will encompass a spectrum of attitudes and vary from active opposition, through grudging tolerance to active support. The actions of the US and its partner nations must progressively and inexorably convince the majority of the population and wider audiences, including adversaries, that the HN government will prevail and that an acceptable political settlement will be reached.

7. **Unified Action**

a. One of the defining features of contemporary stabilization environments is the array of intervening participants present in the theater of operations. The range of external stakeholders could include various USG departments and agencies, allies—who themselves often have a multiagency presence—IGOs, NGOs, and private sector interests. In many cases, they have been engaged in theater long before the military arrived, and may have a broader historical perspective of the situation. The frictions and difficulties associated with developing a coherent, US whole-of-government approach multiply when stabilization is framed within this broader international context. Despite the differing organizational cultures, experiences, and timelines that inevitably will exist among stakeholders, it is imperative that there be a shared understanding of the national objectives and operational environment, cooperative planning and assessment, and coordinated, integrated when appropriate, actions and activities—unified action.

b. The holistic approach required to implement the comprehensive solutions of the IDAD strategy dictates a subordinate role for the Armed Forces. Other departments and agencies normally have the responsibility, and the COM is most often the lead. Traditional military C2 relationships do not apply in relationships between DOD and USG civilian departments and agencies. Unified action becomes the goal. Achieving comprehensive solutions requires communications and understanding among various centers, commissions, staffs, augmentations, field offices, and agencies. Varying national perspectives regarding mission interpretation complicate these efforts. While the US could interpret the mission in terms of force protection, liaison, and limited direct support, another country could view the same operation in terms of strict neutrality and mediation or one of observation. Additionally, there will be various interpretations of the operational environment and the mission among the military, other government entities, the HN, IGOs, NGOs, indigenous populations and institutions (IPI), and others. The military must understand all of these positions and maintain lines of communications to resolve issues as they arise.

c. Adversaries understand the importance and the fragility of unified action and therefore may decide to use tactics that deliberately target and drive away vulnerable civilian partners. By exploiting this fracture, adversaries aim to prolong the campaign, undermining the collective will and perseverance of the multinational force and the international stakeholders; attacks on civilian targets are often more effective in this regard than attacks on military targets. Attacks on civil capability internal to the HN or externally in countries of partner nations can quickly undermine broad stabilization efforts and are likely to have greater impact on their domestic audiences.

d. **Multinational Operations.** In most cases, the Armed Forces of the United States are likely to be part of either a formal alliance or an ad hoc coalition framework. Even when the US is the lead nation, there will still be a requirement to understand the ways in which other states' armed forces operate. Capabilities, political direction from their capitals, ROE, national caveats, and interoperability issues all need to be considered to ensure cohesion in multinational military operations. If the US is a supporting partner in a coalition, it cannot expect to exert the same degree of control over the conduct of operations. However, the CDR should seek to ensure that US capabilities are used to best effect. Understanding the doctrine, procedures, approaches, and priorities of partner nations, especially the lead nation, and shaping the US contribution optimizes its and the multinational forces' capabilities. Sufficient resources should be expended to ensure that this is practicable. It is also imperative that there is a clear and continually maintained mutual understanding about the level of US capabilities in theater and what can and cannot be expected in terms of operational objectives. Any misunderstanding about this can have a significant detrimental impact on the ability to accomplish the mission or on alliance/coalition relations.

For further details on multinational operations, refer to JP 3-16, Multinational Operations.

e. **Interagency Coordination.** Coordinated and synchronized civilian and military efforts are essential to the conduct of successful stability operations. JFCs should collaborate with other USG agencies as appropriate in a whole-of-government approach to plan, prepare for, and conduct stability operations. As part of this effort, the JFC should support the development, implementation, and operations of civil-military teams and related efforts aimed at unity of effort in rebuilding basic infrastructure; developing local governance structures; fostering security, economic stability, and development; and building indigenous capacity for such tasks.

For further details on interagency coordination, refer to JP 3-08, Interorganizational Coordination During Joint Operations.

f. A comprehensive approach requires more than the cooperation of all players; they must actively apply their full weight in support of one another, with that effort focused in time and space as well as conceptually. The synchronization, coordination, and, when appropriate, integration of military operations with the activities of interorganizational partners to achieve unity of effort are key to success, and military forces need to work competently in this environment while properly supporting the agency in charge. It is vital that the idea of a shared enterprise is continually articulated and promoted. A comprehensive approach requires a coherent and shared logic that binds the participants together.

8. **Civil-Military Operations**

a. Civil-military operations (CMO) involve the interaction of military forces with the civilian populace to facilitate military operations and consolidate operational objectives. Although some CMO may directly support combat operations, such as controlling vehicular traffic during urban operations, many of the missions and tasks associated with stability operations are the essence of CMO. Essentially CMO are how the CDR engages the civilian aspects of the environment in both forging relationships and performing civilian related tasks. As such, planning and organizing for stability operations requires a CMO approach.

b. CMO cannot be separated or stovepiped from common staff functions, processes, and procedures. A CMO staff element (cell, branch, or directorate) and appropriate employment of civil affairs (CA) forces provides connectivity and understanding that enables unity of effort within the headquarters (HQ) and among stakeholders. Other enabling forces such as special operations forces (SOF), engineers, health service support (HSS), transportation, military police, and security forces provide the means to execute CMO-related tasks.

c. CA forces provide military CDRs knowledge and analytical and operational capabilities for CA-related decisions and actions that promote achievement of military objectives and facilitate transition to civil authorities. In stability operations, the military has a supporting relationship to civil authority (if one exists). CA forces provide knowledge to commanders about the civil environment and through engagement with the civilian population and governing authority, support military objectives that influence environmental change and enhance other instruments of national power.

For further details on CMO, refer to JP 3-57, Civil-Military Operations.

CHAPTER II
STABILITY OPERATIONS DESIGN AND PLANNING

> *"The initiation of a campaign before adequate preparations have been made may well be as fatal in a small war as in regular warfare. Prolonged operations are detrimental to the morale and prestige of the intervening forces. They can be avoided only by properly estimating the situation and by evolving as comprehensive, flexible, and simple a plan as possible before the campaign begins."*
>
> **US Marine Corps Small Wars Manual (1940)**

1. Stability Operations Planning

a. The design and development of operation plans that integrate offense, defense, and stability operations and integrate the Armed Forces contribution to stabilization efforts with the activities of interorganizational partners is the responsibility of JFCs and their staffs. JFCs must also ensure that subordinate CDRs executing stability operations understand the overall design of the operation, including, in particular, how various military and civilian stability efforts interrelate and, when possible, integrate with each other and with combat missions, tasks, and activities, if any.

b. It is the responsibility of CCDRs and their subordinate JFCs to incorporate stability operations into the deliberate and crisis action planning processes. In addition to the important role stability operations play in major operations or campaigns and limited contingency operations, stability operations contribute to shaping the operational environment and supporting the GCCs' theater campaign plans.

c. Stability operations are an integral part of the overall joint operation plan (OPLAN) that focuses on achieving both elements essential to strategic success—defeating the adversary and ensuring that in the aftermath that secure and stable conditions are in place that enable reconstruction and development toward a lasting peace. Stability operations are executed continuously throughout operations. Executed early enough and in support of broad national interests and policy goals, stability operations provide an effective proactive tool for building partner capacity and reducing the risks associated with natural disasters and violent conflict in partner states. Effective stability operations do this by preparing HNs for crisis and by anticipating and addressing the possible drivers of conflict long before the onset of hostilities or disaster. As most operations will, therefore, include both combat and stability operations components, there is no separate planning process for stability from that used for combat operations. Rather, there is a single joint operation planning process that applies across the range of military operations. **The balance and simultaneity in execution of offense, defense, and stability operations within each phase of a joint operation demands a similar balance and simultaneity in planning efforts.**

d. While defeating an enemy may remove a physical threat to peace and security, establishing stable conditions that will foster peace and security in the mid- to long term will remain a significant challenge. Therefore, joint planning must also consider the key elements of conflict transformation—of how joint, interagency, and multinational actions can transform the factors producing violent conflict over time to return stability and accomplish strategic ends.

For further details on joint operation planning, refer to JP 5-0, Joint Operation Planning.

2. **Understanding the Operational Environment**

a. A holistic understanding of the operational environment enables the design of complementing offensive, defensive, and stability operations that, together in an appropriate and ever changing balance, achieve operational objectives. A holistic view of the operational environment encompasses physical areas and factors (of the air, land, maritime, and space domains) and the information environment (which includes cyberspace). Analyzing the operational and mission variables provides critical information necessary to develop understanding and frame the complex problems faced in joint operations. CDRs, however, need to remain responsive to the dynamic environment while anticipating the needs of the local populace, as these conditions will impact planning and decision making, including selection of specific course of actions (COAs) and the need to execute a branch or sequel plan.

b. In operations requiring a significant combat component, a holistic understanding of the environment that emphasizes civil factors alongside military factors helps ensure smooth transitions from operational phases that emphasize combat operations to those that emphasize stability operations. In operations with little or no combat, this holistic view is particularly valuable, as there may be no overt adversary military forces, but rather forces of nature, possibly covert adversary forces, and nonmilitary personnel, organizations, and other systems.

c. Particularly in stability operations, subordinate CDRs and staffs at all echelons should interact with the leadership and elements of the lowest tactical units who encounter the local population and local security forces on a daily basis to help the JFC to develop insights about ongoing operational trends.

d. A full understanding of the operational environment typically requires cross-functional participation by all joint force staff elements. The intelligence directorate of a joint staff (J-2) normally manages this effort. As the civilian population is normally the single most important aspect of the operational environment in stability operations, participation by the CA, engineer, and the surgeon staff elements is indispensable.

(1) In response to rapid onset emergencies and other crises that may require short notice military support to stabilization efforts, the GCC may deploy a crisis action team as an initial responder/assessor. Additionally, the GCC may deploy a humanitarian assistance survey team (HAST) to provide a more detailed assessment. The exact composition of these teams and the subsequent follow-on assets will vary depending on the type and severity of the incident and, in some cases, restrictions placed on the number of US military personnel permitted in country by the HN. In all cases, the team must coordinate with the COM and country team prior to deploying. When a joint operation has been or will likely be directed,

the crisis action team can recommend to the GCC priority issues as well as how to organize for the most effective response. The work of these teams will frame the CDR's initial understanding of the operational environment and should be folded into ongoing efforts by the joint force staff, as well as efforts by other USG agencies and international community.

For further details on HASTs, refer to JP 3-29, Foreign Humanitarian Assistance.

(2) Initial assessments, conducted preferably by combined military and civilian assessment teams, should focus on three major areas: threats to the intervening forces, current conditions across all stability sectors (functions), and force support requirements. The use of US country team personnel or mobile training teams can support these assessments.

(a) The assessment of threats is essential to determine requirements for access. This assessment should focus on threats to personnel from criminals, belligerents, and adversaries; the dangers of endemic disease and other health threats; and ongoing natural hazards (e.g., earthquake aftershocks). The assessment should estimate the risks for intervening civilian and military organizations and propose immediate solutions to establish viable working conditions for civilians.

(b) An assessment of conditions across all stability sectors (functions) (e.g., security sector, infrastructure, economic situation/development, justice system, and public health) will be required, and should focus on immediate human security needs as well as the drivers of conflict and instability. These should take as a foundation existing pre-crisis assessments and analysis of the causes of the conflict or crisis.

(c) The assessment of force support requirements should establish what requirements can be met by host-nation support (HNS) and what intervening forces will need to provide for themselves. This may include shelter, food, water, force protection, HSS, and other requirements. This is separate from a determination of forces required to conduct the stability operations themselves; this assessment considers what support that force will need to bring.

(3) To help the JFC and staff visualize and understand the operational environment, the J-2 conducts joint intelligence preparation of the operational environment (JIPOE). The JIPOE process normally forms the backbone upon which the CDR's understanding is built, but it is only one aspect in the development of operational understanding. Other products contribute to this effort, but the J-2 has the overall responsibility for managing the analysis and development of products that provide an understanding of the operational environment.

(a) As part of JIPOE, a systems perspective of the operational environment strives to provide an understanding of significant relationships within interrelated political, military, economic, social, information, infrastructure, and other systems relevant to a specific joint operation. JIPOE support during operations that focus on the civil population as a center of gravity (COG) requires a different mindset and different techniques than a JIPOE effort that focuses on defeating an adversary militarily. For example, some situations (particularly crisis response operations) will require JIPOE analysts to focus primarily upon the effects of terrain and weather, as in the case of natural disasters such as floods or earthquakes, or upon the resulting human catastrophe after a natural disaster. These natural disasters can result in disease or starvation, the alleviation of which becomes the focus of the friendly mission.

(b) JIPOE products for stability operations should be based on a comprehensive understanding of local cultures, people, organizations, and priorities. The opportunities for change, the operational limitations, and any potential obstacles become a collection priority to be fully understood by those conducting stability operations. They must also understand the people, organizations, and institutions that drive change and those that resist it, as well as the factors that may affect the receptiveness of external support for reform.

(c) JIPOE products must describe the impact of ethnic groups and religions, to include their associated leadership, the locations of places of worship and cultural/historical significance, languages spoken, population density, age, living conditions, allocation of wealth, means of income, and influence over the HN government. This information provides the backdrop against which an analysis of social and political factors will allow for successful stability operations to include, when necessary, establishing the process for constituting legitimate governance, and when appropriate, initiating elections. The key social and political factors revolve around understanding previous political systems, parties, formal and informal leaders, affiliations, political and societal grievances, loyalty to former local, regional, and national government officials, patterns of political tolerance or violence, and the presence or absence of a formal education system. Another aspect to consider is influence from neighboring countries on HN border regions, especially if those outside influences are interested in destabilizing the HN government. In many societies, the local and district level government and judicial system are reliant on tribal elders and councils to settle legal disputes and determine the prioritization of development projects. This information will provide an appreciation of the nation's cultural landscape, its previous and potential future leaders, and its expectations of governance and civil institutions. To accomplish this, JIPOE analysts must develop a comprehensive understanding of the society, social structure, culture, power and authority, and interests inside and outside the local population.

For further details on JIPOE during stability operations, refer to JP 2-01.3, Joint Intelligence Preparation of the Operational Environment.

e. Rigorous staff efforts for developing this understanding early in the planning process are important, but not always immediately obtained. Understanding is derived from continuous analysis and engagement with key leaders, organizations, and population segments. Continuity of staff is crucial. The staff and key appointments must become theater specialists, drawing on their knowledge to facilitate continuity and depth of understanding.

f. The CDR's understanding cannot be solely based on the staff's analysis. Input from other stakeholders, such as various intelligence organizations, DOS, USAID, other USG agencies, the HN government, IPI, IGOs, NGOs, and nongovernmental centers of excellence, is essential. The CMO staff, through its linkages and relationships, leverages these competencies from stakeholders to better define the environment and understand the overall capability to address challenges. While the goal in stabilization efforts should be a comprehensive understanding of the operational environment among the HN, the US, and other partner nations, the JFC must strive to achieve a comprehensive understanding among US participants as a minimum.

(1) Participation by the JFC in interagency and multinational forums helps enable this comprehensive understanding. Regular meetings among the JFC, the COM, senior USAID representatives, and other senior agency representatives are important not only for the coordination and deconfliction of activities, but also for developing and sharing a common understanding of the context for ongoing operations.

(2) The JFC should participate in appropriate national level formal and informal discussions among HN, United Nations (UN), and other governmental and nongovernmental participants to share perspectives and develop a common understanding. The UN or HN may establish a humanitarian operations center to provide a senior forum for collaboration.

(3) The establishment of, or participation in, civil-military operations centers (CMOCs), civil-military cooperation centers, a UN on-site operations coordination center, a humanitarian assistance coordination center, or other operational and tactical level collaboration and information sharing organizations by the joint force is essential for developing and sharing a comprehensive understanding among those conducting stabilization efforts in the field.

For further details on civil-military collaboration forums, refer to JP 3-08, Interorganizational Coordination During Joint Operations; *JP 3-29,* Foreign Humanitarian Assistance; *and JP 3-57,* Civil-Military Operations.

(4) Gaining support of the HN government for assessments can be critical to their accuracy. In this case, the assessment process serves two important purposes—to gain clarity of the current situation and to enable the HN government to be aware of the benefits of the transformation process proposed. For all assessments there is a need for initial discussion between the international community and national actors about the scope and objectives of the assessment. These will be determined by a number of factors, including the openness, willingness, and capacity of the key HN leaders. Assessments can provide an important opportunity to build trust between international and local people and organizations and to develop local ownership of assistance programs.

g. Initial assessments may be short and superficial due to pressure to quickly design and implement programs and activities. Political priorities or immediate threats posed by natural disasters and ongoing or threatened violent conflict may obstruct in-depth planning and preparation at the onset of design and planning. If there is too little time to conduct a comprehensive assessment at the outset of stability operations, initial plans should direct the completion of more detailed and comprehensive assessments as soon as possible. If this is not done, there is significant danger of causing more harm than good with ongoing operations based upon incomplete assessments.

h. Maintaining a current understanding of the operational environment and the context for joint operations requires constant vigilance, through the direction and oversight of robust intelligence, surveillance, and reconnaissance (ISR) capabilities, by the CDR, staff, and intelligence operations center. The CDR and staff may be lulled into supposing a predetermined evolution of the operational environment that appears to logically flow from their planned operations. The JFC must be cognizant of the changes in the operational environment or the context for the current operation and the impact those may have on the approach to both combat and stability operations. It may be necessary, particularly after catastrophic events or planned transitions, for the CDR to rigorously reframe his or her understanding, and then to adjust current and future operations and plans as the operation unfolds.

3. Strategic Guidance

a. In preparation for major stabilization efforts, the USG should undertake a conflict assessment in accordance with the Interagency Conflict Assessment Framework (ICAF) and in consultation with other USG departments and agencies, to include DOD. Historically, such assessments are informal at best and usually do not occur.

b. Lead agency determination and intergovernmental relationships will be recommended during this process. The various departmental roles and supported and supporting responsibilities need to be synchronized through the National Security Council (NSC) in a reconstruction and stabilization plan.

4. Designing and Planning Stability Operations

a. Joint force actions to establish stability are a necessary and complementary effort to defeat our enemies. The goal of design and planning is to develop a comprehensive approach that integrates the capabilities and contributions of many diverse participants toward a common purpose of overcoming the destructive effects of instability and violent conflict and serves as a centerpiece for unity of effort in stabilization efforts. In developing this overarching design and plan, the JFC and staff employ the same principles of operational design and planning utilized in JP 5-0, *Joint Operation Planning*. Combat and stabilization are neither sequential nor binary alternatives; the JFC must integrate and synchronize stability operations with other operations (offense and defense) within each phase of any joint operation. The JFC's visualization of the operation will determine the emphasis to be placed on each type of mission or activity in each phase of the operation.

b. At the start of planning, understanding of the situation and task will probably be limited. It follows therefore that identifying the conditions required for success is likely to be difficult. However, as the operation unfolds and understanding develops, so the objectives, and the conditions required to realize them will be refined through learning, adaptation, and anticipation. As the design and plan for the operation evolve, the JFC maintains a constant focus on the objective of political settlement among competing elites in local societies and the need to protect and defend the population.

c. **Operational Approach.** The termination of military operations must be considered from the outset of planning and should be a coordinated whole-of-government effort. The termination of combat operations, if any, generally precedes the termination of stability operations, which normally end only with a transition to complete civilian control rather than true termination.

(1) Normally, Armed Forces participation in stabilization efforts is the result of a gap in civilian capabilities that the military can temporarily fill, for example, combat power for securing the population, the ability to conduct stability operations in a hostile environment, or the capacity for heavy airlift. Whatever the gap, the military end state is tied to the closing of that gap, allowing civilian capabilities (e.g., HN, IGOs, and USG civilian agencies) to assume or reassume that role. It is important during the assessment and planning stages to consider these requirements, and assess how the JFC can terminate or transition operations and redeploy.

(2) The military end state and the termination of military operations are not the only determinants of military objectives. Military objectives must complement and support long-term civilian efforts toward the attainment of the national strategic end state. This requirement may lead to complementing lines of effort. Some lines of effort will drive toward the military end state in building or facilitating a capacity that will permit military redeployment. Other lines of effort will focus on long-term national strategic goals; these lines of effort will be transitioned to other military and civilian institutions when those institutions are able.

(3) Detailed planning requires tying near-term objectives to decisive points along lines of effort and closely coordinating with ongoing civilian efforts. The aim is to provide tangible progress consistent with supporting the USG longer-term objectives in the country. Close civilian and military coordination is required to ensure that short-term actions required to provide security do not undermine long-term political and economic development goals.

(4) Decisive points in stabilization efforts delineate key actions or events required to achieve progress toward increased stability by changing key aspects of the operational environment. Examples of decisive points include changes in the disposition of any adversaries or other drivers of violent conflict and establishment of HN capacity in one of the stability functions.

(5) The JFC and joint force staff should reframe the end state conditions and criteria for termination of military operations as the operation progresses and the operational environment evolves. At the same time, the JFC must guard against an unintentional expansion of tasks and responsibilities, sometimes referred to as "mission creep." A clearly articulated end state, appropriate measures of effectiveness (MOEs), and continuous assessment help the JFC protect against this phenomenon. In particular, the JFC must remember that the decision for the joint force to transition from initial response activities to transformational activities and activities that foster sustainability in an attempt to avert future crises is necessarily a political decision.

EXAMPLE OPERATIONAL APPROACHES IN STABILITY OPERATIONS

The following vignettes are designed to illustrate key points related to operational design involving stability operations. These vignettes are illustrative, not comprehensive.

Joint Task Force (JTF) Able is tasked to train military units of Country X-ray in desert military operations. The US military is conducting this mission due to unique expertise in this training. The military end state is the establishment of the capability within Country X-ray forces. Commander, JTF (CJTF) Able, focuses the military objectives wholly toward this end state, and JTF Able will redeploy once the capability has been established.

JTF Baker is tasked to conduct a foreign humanitarian assistance operation following a devastating earthquake in the mountainous frontier of Country Yoke. The US military is conducting this mission because it has disaster relief supplies, a deployable logistics coordination capability, and helicopters readily available. The military end state is described by the arrival of disaster relief supplies, the establishment of logistics coordination body by Country Yoke, and clear roads that will allow a flow of supplies into the mountains. CJTF Baker establishes the following lines of effort: 1) Support the United States Agency for International Development as it assists Country Yoke in establishing a disaster relief coordination center; 2) conduct immediate humanitarian assistance in the affected area; 3) clear roads into the region to allow the passage of supplies. Once intergovernmental organizations (IGOs) and nongovernmental organizations (NGOs) have facilitated the arrival of disaster relief supplies, Country Yoke has established a coordination center, and the roads are clear to permit the flow of supplies, JTF Baker will redeploy. Note that although JTF Baker focused on providing appropriate humanitarian assistance to disaster victims, the completion of this relief did not describe the end state, and indeed, relief efforts may be ongoing even as JTF Baker redeploys.

JTF Charlie is deployed to Country Zebra conducting a counterinsurgency campaign to try to bolster the newly installed Zebra government. The US military is conducting the mission because Country Zebra security forces are not capable of securing the population against ongoing insurgent attacks; additionally the US military is conducting stability operations because the operational environment is too dangerous for many IGOs and NGOs to conduct stabilization efforts. The military end state is the combination of capable Zebra security forces and declining insurgent forces such that Zebra forces can provide civil security and an operational environment that will permit civilian conduct of comprehensive stabilization efforts. CJTF Charlie establishes the following lines of effort: 1) Conduct operations to secure the population; 2) conduct offensive operations against insurgent groups; 3) Conduct stability operations to help normalize this fragile state; 4) assist in efforts to achieve a political settlement; and 5) build Zebra security force capacity. Once Zebra forces are capable of securing the population and personnel of civilian nation building institutions and conducting sustained operations against the insurgency, JTF Charlie will redeploy. Note that although the defeat of the insurgency did not describe the end state, military objectives designed to defeat the insurgency were a key part of JTF Charlie's operation, and the achievement of a political settlement among competing elites remains a primary objective of the overall US effort.

VARIOUS SOURCES

(6) Experience has shown that cross-cutting, outcome-oriented lines of effort that require coordinated activity from across sectors and functions are critical to success in stability operations. Lines of effort defined around individual sectors or stability operations functions and assigned to separate functional staff elements may result in dangerous stovepiping and an inability to synchronize.

(7) Following provides an example of a set of four complementing lines of effort:

(a) Support an inclusive political settlement.

(b) Assess the drivers of conflict and instability and help build resolution mechanisms.

(c) Build HN capacity in areas that the state needs to survive:

<u>1.</u> Guaranteed territorial security.

<u>2.</u> The ability to provide civil security.

<u>3.</u> A stable revenue base.

<u>4.</u> The rule of law.

(d) Support efforts to respond to public expectations, including delivering essential services, macroeconomic stability and social protection, and supporting voice and accountability (e.g., fair elections, free media, anticorruption).

d. **Arranging Operations.** By arranging operations and activities into phases, the JFC can better visualize, integrate, and synchronize subordinate operations in time, space, and purpose.

(1) **Window of Opportunity.** At the initial employment of the joint force, following a transition from sustained combat operations, or following a public change in strategy, a limited window of opportunity exists to demonstrate progress in a manner consistent with the priorities and expectations of the local population. This interlude may provide a period of political will and opportunity for the international community and HN to take actions that address the drivers of conflict and instability. This window of opportunity is an indeterminate but finite period, the length of which will depend on the circumstances.

(a) Plans and concept of operations (CONOPS) should address this period early and in depth. Failure to act during this period will result in a loss of operational momentum. Regaining the initiative after this period has passed is not impossible, but it is more difficult.

(b) Tasks during this period must ensure security while laying the foundation for the stabilization efforts that will follow. The specific requirements will vary according to the circumstances, but consideration should be given to the following:

<u>1</u>. Physically securing the population, critical infrastructure, and facilities for essential services. When necessary based upon threat, establish population control measures, especially at the borders, to protect and defend the population and detect and reduce the effectiveness of enemy agents. Population control measures include curfews, movement restrictions, travel permits, identification and registration cards, collection of biometric information, and voluntary resettlement.

<u>2</u>. Providing humanitarian assistance to the population. This includes assisting dislocated civilians (DCs) (i.e., refugees or internally displaced persons [IDPs]).

<u>3.</u> Executing quick impact projects (QIPs) at the tactical level that can be started with minimum delay with a streamlined funding process to reestablish essential services and critical infrastructure.

<u>4.</u> Establishing governance, possibly including transitional governance, to immediately establish the rule of law and the provision of essential services.

(c) By nature, achievement of transformation will occur over the longer-term, and attention to transformation activities and activities that foster sustainability competes intensely with the short-term action requirements during this initial period. The JFC, together with the COM and other civilian counterparts, must determine what critical immediate tasks of these longer-term programs must be taken, commit the resources, and begin implementation immediately.

For further details on specific initial actions, refer to Chapter III, "Stability Operations Functions."

(2) **Arrangement of Stability Operations.** The general arrangement of stability operations within an operation is in the four phases described in Figure II-1. These phases may be subphases of a major operation or campaign (e.g., subphases of a stabilize phase) or they may describe the general flow of operations in a crisis response or limited contingency operation involving stability operations. These phases may not be sequential but may occur simultaneously in various parts of the country depending on local circumstances.

(a) **Shaping.** Shaping activities that assist fragile states, preventing them from becoming seriously unstable, or that help build capabilities of partner countries can help create the conditions for the successful conduct of joint operations; or they can prevent the necessity for the conduct of operations in the future. Therefore, allocating adequate resources toward shaping activities focused on stabilization prior to a crisis enables the USG to advance its interests using relatively modest amounts of targeted resources, rather than spending much more substantial, and often massive, amounts of resources to respond to a crisis. Shaping activities also enable joint forces, as well as US civilian agencies and multinational partners, to develop a better understanding of a specific region, which may prove critical for the successful planning and execution of stabilization efforts.

(b) **Crisis Action.** In the crisis action phase, activities normally accomplished by civilian organizations temporarily exceed the capabilities of those organizations. During this phase, the joint force performs those tasks or cooperates with civilian organizations to

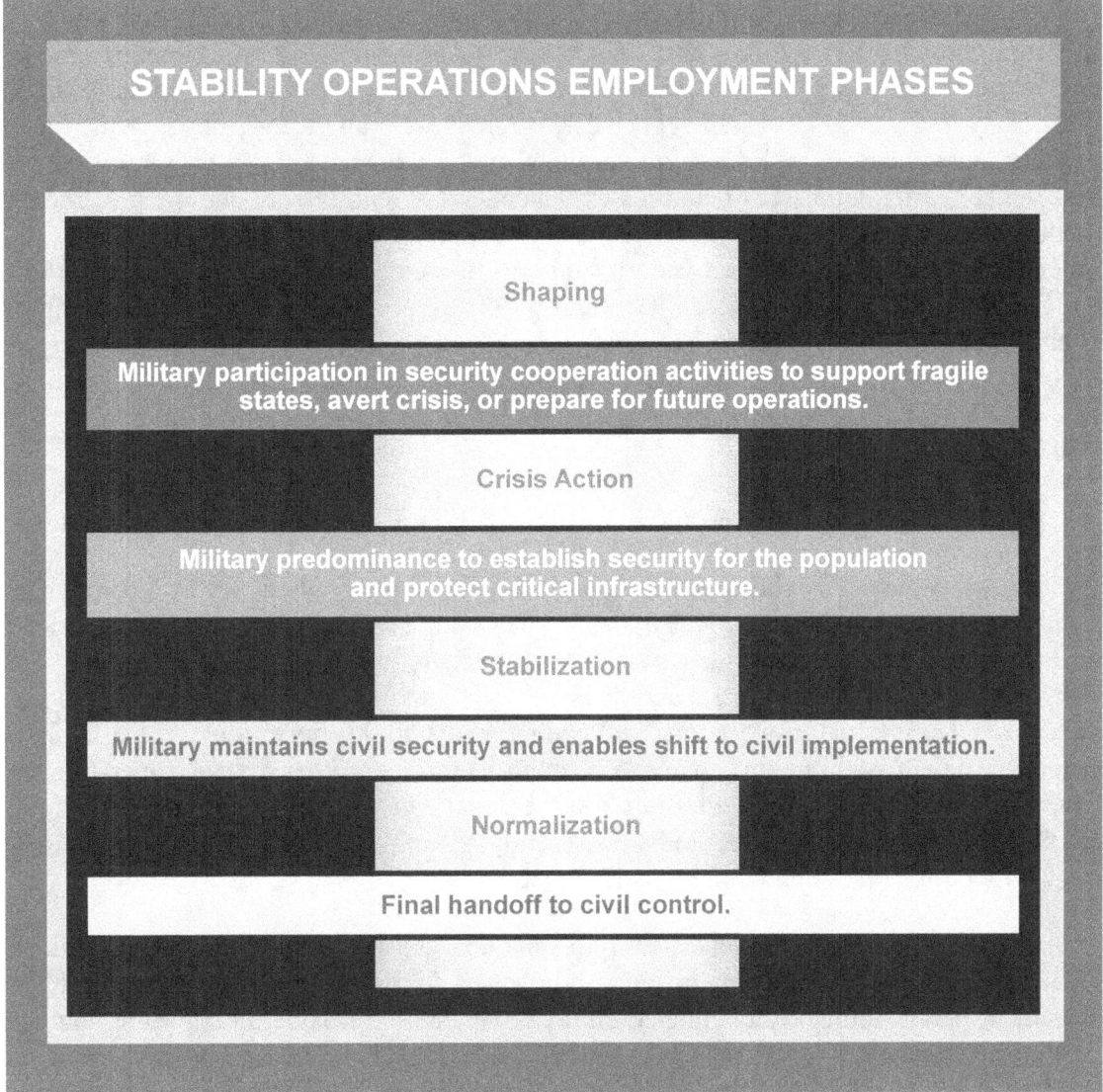

Figure II-1. Stability Operations Employment Phases

ensure that they are accomplished. The joint force should provide immediate relief to save lives and sustain critical infrastructure and provide a secure environment to preempt criminal elements and other adversaries from gaining control over areas of the country. It is important to note that "temporarily" could be months or years in duration.

        (c) **Stabilization.** In the stabilization phase, civil organizations have generated sufficient capability and capacity for the joint force to shift toward facilitating civil implementation.

        (d) **Normalization.** In the normalization phase, the joint force transfers all of the stability tasks, missions, and activities to civilian organizations or the HN and redeploys as required.

(3) **Clear-Hold-Build.** During COIN operations as well as during other operations in which the joint force conducts stability operations in the midst of ongoing sustained combat operations, operations are normally arranged in three phases: clear-hold-build. In the clear phase, security forces conduct primarily offensive operations to remove enemy forces and eliminate organized resistance in an assigned area. In the hold phase, the security forces conduct primarily defensive operations to protect and defend the population, government institutions, and critical infrastructure in the operational area. In the build phase, HN and other civilian agencies, often assisted by military forces conducting stability operations, work to develop the area across all the stability functions, as appropriate, in an attempt to enable a political settlement in the area. United Kingdom (UK) doctrine refers to this process as shape-secure-hold-develop. Typically, clear-hold-build and shape-secure-hold-develop take place in designated localities, supporting a general bottom-up approach to stabilization.

For further details on clear-hold-build, refer to JP 3-24, Counterinsurgency Operations.

(4) **Phasing in Major Operations and Campaigns.** Although JFCs determine the number and actual phases, use of the operational phasing model provides a flexible model to arrange smaller, related operations. Using this model, major operations and campaigns are generally arranged in six phases: shape-deter-seize initiative-dominate-stabilize-enable civil authority. During major operations and campaigns, stability operations are particularly emphasized in the stabilize and enable civil authority phases; however, major operation and campaign plans must feature an appropriate balance between offensive, defensive, and stability operations in all phases. Most importantly, planning for stability operations should begin when joint operation planning is initiated.

(a) **Shaping.** Activities in the shaping phase primarily focus on continued planning and preparation for anticipated stability operations in the subsequent phases. These activities should include conducting collaborative interagency planning to synchronize the civil-military effort, confirming the feasibility of pertinent military objectives and the military end state, and providing for adequate intelligence, an appropriate force mix, and other capabilities. Stability operations in this phase may be required to quickly restore civil security and infrastructure or provide humanitarian relief in select portions of the operational area to dissuade further adversary actions or to help ensure access and future success.

(b) **Deterrence.** Joint force planning and operations conducted prior to commencement of hostilities should establish a sound foundation for operations in the "stabilize" and "enable civil authority" phases. JFCs should anticipate and address how to fill the power vacuum created when sustained combat operations wind down. Accomplishing this task should ease the transition to operations in the stabilize phase and shorten the path to the national strategic end state and handover to another authority.

(c) **Seizing the Initiative.** The onset of combat provides an opportunity to set into motion actions that will achieve military strategic and operational objectives and establish the conditions for operations at the conclusion of sustained combat. Operations to neutralize or eliminate potential stabilize phase enemies may be initiated. National and local HN authorities may be contacted and offered support. Key infrastructure may be seized or otherwise protected. Intelligence collection on the status of enemy infrastructure, government organizations, and humanitarian needs should be increased. Information operations (IO) used to influence target audiences can ease the situation encountered when sustained combat is concluded.

(d) **Dominate.** As the joint force begins to dominate the operational environment and achieves combat objectives, stability operations will begin to transition from planning and preparation to execution. Civil-military teams, such as provincial reconstruction teams (PRTs) or field advance civilian teams (FACTs), supported by joint forces, will begin to enter the operational area if they have not done so already. Even while sustained combat operations are ongoing, there will be a need to establish or restore civil security and provide humanitarian relief as the joint force occupies or bypasses succeeding areas.

(e) The transition from the dominance to the stabilization phase must be carefully planned and executed. Joint force planning and operations conducted prior to commencement of hostilities should establish a sound foundation for operations in the stabilize and enable civil authority phases. The operational momentum achieved by seizing the initiative and dominating the operational environment through combat may be lost if this transition is poorly handled. JFCs should anticipate and address how to fill the power vacuum created when sustained combat operations wind down. Military units conducting combat operations in the dominate phase should have specific follow-on assignments in the stabilize phase that allow for a straightforward transition rather than a complex rearrangement of military and civilian forces. Accomplishing this task should ease the transition to operations in the stabilize phase and shorten the path to the national strategic end state and handover to another authority.

(f) **Stabilize.** As sustained combat operations conclude, military forces will shift their focus to stability operations, even as combat operations are ongoing. Of particular importance will be CMO; initially conducted to secure and safeguard the populace, reestablish civil law and order, protect or rebuild key infrastructure, and restore public services. US military forces should be prepared to lead the activities necessary to accomplish these tasks when indigenous civil, USG, multinational, or international capacity does not exist or is incapable of assuming responsibility. Once legitimate civil authority is prepared to conduct such tasks, US military forces may support such activities as required/necessary.

<u>1.</u> The military's predominant presence and its ability to C2 forces and provide logistics under extreme conditions may initially give it the de facto lead in stability operations normally governed by other agencies that lack such capacities. However, most stability operations likely will be in support of, or transition to support of, US diplomatic, UN, or HN efforts. Integrated civilian and military efforts are essential to success, and military forces need to work competently in this environment while properly supporting the agency in charge. Military forces should be prepared to work in integrated civilian military teams that could include representatives from other USG agencies, foreign governments and security forces, IGOs, NGOs, and members of the private sector with relevant skills and expertise.

2. During stability operations in the stabilize phase, protection from virtually any person, element, or group hostile to US interests must be considered. These could include violent activists or instigators of mob violence, a group opposed to the operation, criminals, warlords, private militias, and terrorists. JFCs also should be constantly ready to counter activity that could bring significant harm to friendly forces and organizations or jeopardize mission accomplishment. If authorized by higher authority, protection may involve the protection of HN authorities, civilian members of the USG, civilian contractors, or members of IGOs or NGOs.

(g) **Enabling Civil Authority.** In this phase, the joint operation normally is terminated when the stated military strategic and operational objectives have been met and redeployment of the joint force is accomplished. This should mean that a legitimate civil authority has been enabled to manage the situation without further outside military assistance. In some cases, it may become apparent that the stated objectives fall short of properly enabling civil authority. This situation may require a redesign of the joint operation as a result of an extension of the required stability operations in support of US diplomatic, HN, IGO, or NGO efforts. Figure II-2 illustrates a notional balance between offensive, defensive, and stability operations throughout a major operation or campaign.

For further details on phasing during major operations and campaigns, refer to JP 3-0, Joint Operations, *and JP 5-0,* Joint Operation Planning.

e. **Force Planning.** Force planning encompasses all those activities performed by the supported CCDR, subordinate component CDRs, and support agencies to select, prepare, integrate, and deploy the forces and capabilities required to accomplish an assigned mission. The size and composition of the force will depend on the mission, the operational environment, and the JFC's CONOPS. However, since stability operations occur in the land domain, joint land forces (to include SOF) will normally provide the majority of the force required supported by joint air, maritime, and space forces.

For further details on joint land operations, refer to JP 3-31, Command and Control for Joint Land Operations.

(1) **Size of the Force.** Stability operations normally require significant forces, particularly when operating in a hostile or uncertain environment. There is no standard template for force level requirements for stability operations; the exact ratio required will depend on a number of variables, most particularly the level of violence. Generating and maintaining these force levels will be a challenge for any intervention force, and so a strategy to develop and integrate an effective and sustainable indigenous security capability is fundamental to success.

(2) **Integration of Conventional and Special Operations Forces.** Success is achieved when operations are designed to optimize the unique capabilities of SOF in conjunction (integrated whenever possible) with conventional forces. The selection of the appropriate ratio of SOF and conventional forces must be a deliberate decision based on thorough mission analysis and a pairing of available capabilities to requirements. The most important factor informing this decision is the capability and expertise required rather than

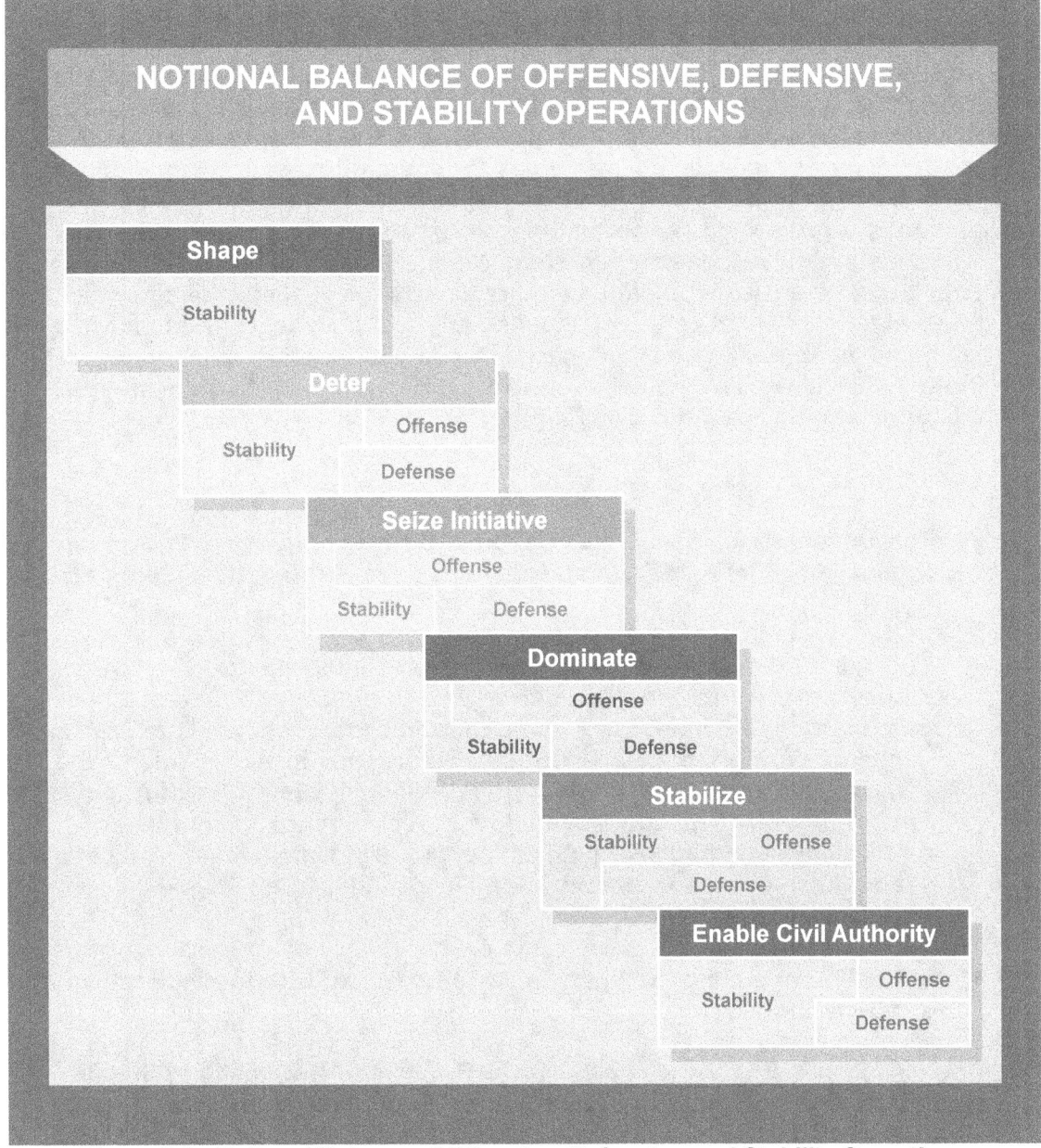

Figure II-2. Notional Balance of Offensive, Defensive, and Stability Operations

the size of the force required. SOF capabilities (e.g., language, cultural awareness, regional focus) are an important consideration when choosing forces to conduct stability operations. Additionally, SOF's ability to operate with little external support makes them adept at initiating programs with indigenous forces. Due to their specialized training, CA personnel and units, both SOF and conventional from all Services, play a key role in stability operations.

f. **Operational Reach.** For any given operation, there is a finite range beyond which predominant elements of the joint force cannot prudently operate or maintain effective operations. Even with forward basing, the force ratios required to operate in and among the

HISTORICAL FORCE RATIOS IN STABILIZATION EFFORTS

As a planning yard-stick, the number of security force personnel per 1000 head of population (expressed as a force ratio) can be a useful mechanism to indicate the mass required. Although numbers alone do not constitute a security strategy, successful strategies for population security and control have required force ratios either as large as or larger than 20 security personnel (troops and police combined) per thousand inhabitants. This figure is roughly 10 times the ratio required for simple policing of a tranquil population. Peaceful populations require force ratios of somewhere between one and four police officers per thousand residents. Recent experience has indicated an approximate benchmark of 20-25 security force personnel per thousand civilians. Where the security environment is particularly hostile, this number may be significantly higher.

For example:

- The United States as a whole has about 2.3 sworn police officers per thousand residents. Larger cities tend to have higher ratios of police to population.

- To maintain stability in Northern Ireland in the 1970s, the British deployed a security force (army troops plus police) at a ratio of 23 per thousand inhabitants. This is about the same force ratio that the British deployed during the Malayan counterinsurgency in the middle of the 20th century. In its initial entry into Bosnia in 1995, the North Atlantic Treaty Organization Implementation Force brought in multinational forces corresponding to 23 soldiers per thousand inhabitants. After five years, the successor Stabilization Force finally fell below 10 per thousand.

- In the 2008 operations against the Tamil Tigers, force ratios were as high as 60 per thousand.

SOURCES: "Burden of Victory: The Painful Arithmetic of Stability Operations," James T. Quinlivan, *RAND Review*, Summer 2003, and Joint Doctrine Publication 3-40 (UK), *Security and Stabilization: The Military Contribution*

people in stability operations, particularly in hostile or uncertain environments, may limit the geographical reach of the joint force.

g. **Simultaneity and Depth.** The interrelationship among different sectors of society and impacts of changes in stability in an area on other localities, the HN, and the region demand the simultaneous application of efforts across the stability functions. For example, building upon efforts to establish effective civil security, the JFC develops simultaneous actions in other areas that advance governance, rule of law, and increase economic opportunity for the populace.

h. **Learn and Adapt.** The complexity and evolving nature of the operational environment requires constant monitoring and continuous assessment to exploit unforeseen opportunities or react to unanticipated events. This situational awareness aids in determining if and when a branch or sequel plan may need to be executed.

5. Integrated Design and Planning

a. Established policy and procedures are designed to support the military chain of command while engendering comprehensive, cooperative planning between military and civilian agencies of the USG to implement stabilization policy and direction. Interagency planning should be an iterative process that synchronizes diplomatic, development, and defense implementation planning and tasks with a view to developing unified action to achieve overall stabilization goals. Whenever possible, the wider international community, including the HN and other multinational partners and NGOs, should be incorporated into this integrated planning process.

b. The Interagency Management System for Reconstruction and Stabilization (IMS) is designed to provide USG policymakers, COMs, and military CDRs with flexible tools to organize the USG civilian response to prevent or prepare for post-conflict situations and to help stabilize and reconstruct societies in transition from conflict or civil strife. Although the IMS has not yet been implemented in an operation, the elements of the guidance as well as the results of exercises and experiments that have used the IMS may help JFCs work with civilian counterparts while conducting stability operations. Though the IMS shows promise, there is no single process model that describes integrated planning between military and civilian agencies of the USG. Whether or not IMS is activated for integrated planning, JFCs should work closely with COMs and other civilian counterparts to establish appropriate structures and processes that will facilitate a shared understanding, integrated design and planning, and coordinated execution and assessment. **The importance of personal relationships between military CDRs and civilian leaders cannot be overemphasized.** Absent formal interagency mechanisms and given the myriad of cultural, funding, C2, and other issues that will arise among partners, these personal relationships are essential to melding a cohesive comprehensive approach to stabilization efforts.

For further details on IMS, refer to Appendix B, "Operating with the Whole of Government."

c. Interagency operational planning takes place over three general phases: initial interagency planning; reassessment and revision of plans; and transition planning, which includes planning for ongoing operations and for when authorities are passed from one entity to another. The integrated planning and execution process which the interagency is working to develop is intended for eventual use in all three of these general phases. This process should identify additional planning requirements, potential impediments, and assumptions regarding the environment. It should establish a timeline for implementation, priority tasks, lead and supporting USG agencies, authorities, and cross-sector linkages and sequencing. This continuous planning process should provide a mechanism to communicate feedback, raise resource and logistic requirements, conduct monitoring and evaluation, and ensure the flexibility of USG activities.

d. It is important that any integrated plan does not become simply an "inventory of activities" that is implemented in a mechanical fashion, but that it embodies a strategy for success. Destabilizing actors may be motivated by ideology, grievance, or greed; the specific motivation, strategy, and tactics employed must be well understood even as they change and evolve. It is critical for operational leaders to take adequate time to reanalyze the overall problem to assure that the integrated plan addresses the essential factors needed to mitigate the destabilizing influences.

e. Flexibility is a vital aspect of the reassessment and revision process. Different agencies and implementing units have differing reporting processes and schedules. Moreover, progress indicators will require varying timeframes for the collection and analysis of data. Noting these challenges, however, does not obviate the need to ensure that the activities and events taking place in the field (whether that is in the host capital, a province within the host country, or in the meeting chambers of our international and bilateral partners), and significant changes in assumptions underlying US plans, are reflected in the integrated plan.

f. The *Post-Conflict Reconstruction Essential Tasks* matrix (ETM), developed by the DOS Office of the Coordinator for Reconstruction and Stabilization (S/CRS) in conjunction with various USG agencies, provides a reference or catalogue of tasks in various sectors. CDRs and their staffs can develop an ETM to identify relevant tasks and to sequence activities within an operation. The ETM found in the document is not itself a planning framework; but it is a reference for thinking systematically about stabilization efforts. Based on the situation, additional tasks not included in the *Post-Conflict Reconstruction Essential Tasks* matrix will likely be required. Many tasks are cross-cutting and require planners to reference other technical sectors. In this respect, the ETM facilitates integration by allowing experts in specific sectoral fields to make and understand linkages with other sectoral activities.

g. The US Institute of Peace's *Guiding Principles for Stabilization and Reconstruction* provides a framework for stabilization efforts that is largely based on the policies, doctrine, and training from civilian agencies across the USG and internationally. Developed in partnership with the US Army's Peacekeeping and Stability Operations Institute (PKSOI), the *Guiding Principles* presents a series of end states in stabilization, conditions describing those end states, and approaches to achieving those end states.

For further details on the Guiding Principles for Stabilization and Reconstruction, refer to Appendix F, "Key Stability Operations Documents."

INTEGRATED PLANNING IN AFGHANISTAN

The Integrated Civil-Military Campaign Plan for Support to Afghanistan provides guidance from the US Chief of Mission and the Commander of US Forces-Afghanistan (USFOR-A) to US personnel in Afghanistan.

In April 2009, the US Government (USG) leadership in Afghanistan commissioned a USG planning team from various civilian and military elements to develop the plan. The core planning team provided planning and assessment expertise and a network capable of reachback to their respective agencies, taking as its guidance the President's Strategic Review, the Afghan National Development Strategy, and existing North Atlantic Treaty Organization (NATO), US Central Command (USCENTCOM), and National Security Council direction. A US Secretary of Defense and NATO-directed assessment also informed the plan's development.

Interagency working groups served as lead agents to develop eleven lines of effort, referred to in the plan as "transformative effects strategies." The working groups comprised stakeholders from relevant USG and NATO International Security Assistance Force (ISAF) civilian and military entities. The core planning team supported each working group in developing the strategies. As appropriate, this included outreach and consultation with the Government of Afghanistan, bilateral partners, the United Nations, and the broader ISAF community.

The embassy and the US military leadership directed the core planning team to work with USG civilians and military and ISAF leadership in each regional command to identify the nationwide concept of operations, as well as regional guidance. Plan development included a series of in-progress reviews with embassy, USFOR-A, and ISAF leadership, as well as with staff and leadership from USCENTCOM and the Department of State's Special Representative for Afghanistan and Pakistan.

The plan was designed to remain a flexible tool designed to incorporate changes in accordance with integrated leadership direction and included the requirement for US leadership in the field to review the plan as needed with a full review (including international and Afghan partners) one year from approval. The annual review takes into account transformation in the operational environment, assessment of all sectors in each region, and changes in the management, resources, and focus of USG and international partner assistance.

Functional appendices and regional annexes to the plan were designed to be living instruments. In addition to the planned annual review, functional appendices were to be updated at least quarterly to reflect the synthesis of best practices, innovative methods, and changing conditions where appropriate. Regional annexes were to be updated on a 6-month basis. Updates were also based on quarterly assessments, in all cases using integrated sources of information to overcome the boundaries imposed by partitioned plans and assessments.

The appendices of the plan are:

A. Resource Requirements

B. Metrics and Measures of Progress

C. Functional Appendices

D. Regional Annexes

E. International Support

F. Regional Support

SOURCE: Condensed from UNITED STATES GOVERNMENT INTEGRATED CIVILIAN–MILITARY CAMPAIGN PLAN FOR SUPPORT TO AFGHANISTAN
10 August 2009

6. Special Considerations

a. In most scenarios, joint task forces (JTFs) will conduct stability operations. The planning and execution of these operations are fully integrated with the planning and execution of offensive and defensive operations, and should not be separated into a separate staff directorate. When the scope of the mission is almost completely focused on stability operations, with little or no combat mission, a JFC may establish a joint civil-military operations task force (JCMOTF) to accomplish that mission. A JCMOTF is a US joint force organization, similar in organization to a JTF, and is flexible in size and composition, depending on mission circumstances. It normally is subordinate to a JTF.

b. **Command and Control.** Traditional military C2 does not apply to relationships with civilian departments and agencies. The JFC must be able to effectively coordinate and, when appropriate, integrate efforts between the joint force and interorganizational partners. This capability also requires the JFC to manage and make available relevant, accurate information to appropriate stakeholders. Inherent in this capability must be the ability to protect and defend information systems by ensuring their integrity, authentication, confidentiality, and non-repudiation. To achieve a holistic approach to stability operations requires communications and understanding among the various centers, commissions, staffs, augmentations, field offices, and agencies. Complicating these efforts are varying national perspectives regarding the mandate and the resulting mission interpretation. The military must understand all of these positions and maintain communications with stakeholders to resolve issues as they arise.

(1) **Leadership and Authority.** Each USG agency has different authorities, which govern the operation of the agency and determine the use of its resources. These authorities derive from several sources: the Constitution, their federal charter, presidential directives, congressional mandates, and strategic direction. It is important that early in stability operation planning, the definition of these authorities be clearly understood and documented. Of note, IGO authorities are based on their formal agreement among member governments.

NGOs are independent of national governments and IGOs; each has it's own unique and individual governance system.

(2) **Commander's Communications Strategy**

(a) Strategic communication (SC) is crucial to success in stability operations. The narrative during an operation is the enduring SC with context, reason/motive, and goal/end state. When stability operations are conducted in areas with significant adversary or belligerent activity, there can be a continuing clash between the competing narratives of the protagonists. This is often what is referred to as the "battle of the narratives." Losing this battle can translate to strategic failure of the operation.

(b) The development of a communications strategy should take cultural sensitivities and perceptions into account. To facilitate this effort, education and training of joint forces should include appropriate linguistic, historical, and cultural elements. Additionally, predeployment exercises and rehearsals should evaluate these skill sets.

(c) Throughout the operation, three primary supporting military capabilities of SC—public affairs (PA), IO, and defense support to public diplomacy—should be continually coordinated and synchronized, both horizontally and vertically. The JFC's communications strategy should support the broader interagency SC effort and closely coordinate support from other agencies and organizations. This strategy must be CDR-driven, proactive, and synchronized with respect to all themes, messages, images, and actions.

For further details on SC, refer to US Joint Forces Command's Commander's Handbook for Strategic Communication and Communication Strategy.

(3) **Command Relationships.** The presence of and coordination with multiple USG and international civilian organizations during stability operations does not preclude the requirement to establish formal relationships among joint forces conducting operations.

(4) **Coordinating with Multinational, USG Agencies, IGOs, and NGOs**

(a) Within the USG, the Armed Forces, other uniformed services, and civilian USG agencies perform in both supported and supporting roles. However, this is not the support command relationship as described in joint doctrine. Relationships between the Armed Forces and USG agencies, IGOs, NGOs, and the private sector cannot be equated to the C2 of a military operation.

(b) Although there may be no formal command relationship between military forces and civilian entities, clearly defined relationships may foster harmony and reduce friction between participating organizations. Formally defined relationships with USG civilian agencies preserve the primacy of civil authorities in their spheres of responsibility while facilitating the full utilization of military forces as permitted by the Constitution, law, and directives of the President.

1. Normally, existing authorities dictate the primary or lead coordinating agency. In cases where the lead is unclear, the President will designate a USG agency. The Secretary of State (SECSTATE) is normally the designated lead of USG efforts to prepare, plan, and conduct stabilization efforts abroad, with US military forces providing support of the broader USG efforts. The COM is normally the designated in-country lead of USG stabilization efforts.

2. An inclusive view and a desire to leverage comparative advantages should guide a JFC's collaboration with civilian colleagues of USG agencies. Each agency has special expertise, authorities, access, and resources that can be brought to bear to support JFC activities. The reciprocal also applies. The contributions of US military forces can reinforce the initiatives undertaken through diplomatic, development, law enforcement, and other activities in support of the USG strategic plan. The challenge lies in leveraging comparative advantages and then integrating efforts under a coherent strategy.

(c) Since US military forces and NGOs will often occupy the same operational space, there is an increased risk of confusion if that space is in a hostile or uncertain environment. To alleviate this potential risk, the use of the CMOC should be considered, where US military forces coordinate any support to NGOs. If possible, NGO liaison officers (LNOs) should be requested to work with the CMOC. Most NGOs are more comfortable working with USG agencies such as USAID than they are working with the military. Some NGOs may choose not to coordinate with the military to avoid the perception of supporting potential combatants. In some cases, US forces may not have a relationship with NGOs in their operational area to ensure the neutrality of that NGO, especially in environments where enemy forces would attack an NGO that was perceived as working with US forces. If this condition is suspected to exist, US forces must immediately cease all contact with that NGO.

(d) Information sharing is critical to the efficient pursuit of a common humanitarian purpose. Although many different groups and authorities can (and should) work in parallel, a collaborative environment facilitates information sharing. Although technology can support the creation of an unclassified collaboration and information sharing space, the challenges are largely social, institutional, cultural, and organizational. These impediments can limit and shape the willingness of civilian and military personnel and organizations to openly cooperate and share information and capabilities.

(e) The components of civil-military coordination consist of information and task sharing, transparency, deconfliction, and cooperative planning—all of which depend on communications and management of data and information. The following issues, however, often complicate effective civil-military coordination:

1. Lack of understanding about the information culture of the affected nation;

2. Suspicions regarding the balance between information sharing and intelligence gathering, as well as the misperception by USG departments that providing information to intelligence personnel transforms them into intelligence collection assets and compromises their mission;

<u>3.</u> Tensions between military needs for classification of data, versus the civilian need for transparency;

<u>4.</u> Differences between C2 of military operations and the cooperation and collaboration of civilian activities; and

<u>5.</u> The compatibility and interoperability of planning tools, processes, and civil-military organization cultures.

For further details and examples of interagency coordination frameworks and mechanisms, refer to Appendix B, "Operating with the Whole of Government," *and JP 3-08,* Interorganizational Coordination During Joint Operations.

(f) To overcome these barriers to effective communications CDRs at all levels must determine what information needs to be shared with whom and when, using the appropriate foreign disclosure guidance classifications and caveats. DOD information must be appropriately secured, shared, and made available throughout the information lifecycle to appropriate mission partners to the maximum extent allowed by US laws and DOD policy. DOD components will share relevant unclassified information among USG agencies, foreign governments and security forces, IGOs, NGOs, and members of the private sector.

(g) CDRs, along with their staffs, need to recognize the criticality of the information sharing function at the outset of complex operations, and not as an afterthought as has occurred so frequently in the past. The "responsibility to provide" mindset needs to be driven by CDR's intent and stated upfront in the "Classification Guidance" section of the various types of operations orders.

(5) **Staff Organization Considerations.** Key staff organization considerations for stability operations should ensure functions are fully integrated with the CDRs' decision-making process.

(a) The operations directorate of a joint staff (J-3) is responsible for the direction of current and future integrated combat/stability plans developed by a plans directorate of a joint staff (J-5). Combat and stability operations are planned and directed in concert. Cross-functional alignment with key staff functions such as CMO, engineer, surgeon, SJA, and comptroller is essential.

(b) The nominations of programs, projects, missions, tasks, and activities that make up stability operations are normally scrutinized for prioritization and approval by a decision board based on the CDRs' priorities, available resources, and staff recommendations. HN input is critical to determining which projects are nominated and in what order of prioritization. CMO-related projects normally require operational level approval under the following conditions: of significant expense, based on stakeholders inability to complete (due to threat level), when resources are limited, or when projects are directly tied to a COA. Staff interdependence enriches the project review process. In addition to the standard roles of the J-2, J-3, J-4 [logistics directorate of a joint staff], J-5, and J-6 [communications system directorate of a joint staff] in cross-directorate processes, the CMO staff element, the comptroller, and the SJA have specific roles in the approval process for stability programs, projects, missions, tasks, and activities. Other staff elements, such as the engineer and the surgeon, may also have important roles depending on the nature of the proposed activities.

1. The CMO staff element makes project recommendations and validates nominated projects based on its analysis of the operational environment.

2. The comptroller identifies available funding programs, accounts for their expenditure, and fulfills budgeting requirements. Finance units will conduct disbursement actions, and acquisition commands will conduct contracting operations to the joint force.

3. The SJA conducts legal reviews of funding caveats.

4. The engineering staff element plays an important role when construction and project management capabilities are required, particularly when timelines, resources, construction standards, and task assessments should be applied.

For further details on engineer staff element support, refer to JP 3-34, Joint Engineer Operations.

5. The surgeon and other staff elements with functional expertise should be a part of the process as required.

6. Once project nominations are fully staffed, the appropriate staff director chairs the decision board for the chief of staff, deputy CDR, or CDR, depending upon approval levels and authority mandated within the various funding programs used.

(c) Consideration should also be given to staff interaction with civilian organizations. Options range from exchange of LNOs between JTFs and civilian agencies to fully integrated staffs. As a minimum, the JFC should include civilian agencies in key battle rhythm events such as boards, bureaus, centers, cells, and working groups to enhance staff integration.

(d) Consideration should be given to highlighting the CMO staff element's expanded role in supporting the overall staff's functions during stability operations.

1. The CMO staff element should develop the analysis of the civil environment serving the informational needs of other staff elements. They should produce CMO staff estimates that enrich other staff planning and assessment products and that can best be integrated into the overall operation.

2. The CMO staff element should provide civil-related expertise and continuous presence to the future operations and future plans event horizons.

3. The CMO staff element should facilitate interactions with non-DOD stakeholders in planning and execution. The CMO staff element facilitates cooperation and assists in developing terms of reference for mutually supportive relationships.

<u>4.</u> The CMO staff should communicate cross functionally throughout the decision cycle and enable inclusiveness by linking with higher HQ CMO, subordinate unit CMO, and stakeholder counterparts. To enable this, the CMO staff requires codified coordinating authority with each level of command and with each stakeholder establishing a clear understanding of representation, authority for the collective sharing and reporting of civil information, and policy for access to HQ processes and procedures.

For further details on staff HQ organization, refer to JP 3-33, Joint Task Force Headquarters.

c. **Intelligence**

(1) **Collection During Stability Operations**

(a) Intelligence production and information gathering in stability operations should be broadly focused and include collection and fusion of information concerning political, military, paramilitary, ethnic, religious, economic, medical, environmental, geospatial, and criminal indicators. The primary intelligence effort must focus on answering the CDR's priority intelligence requirements assisting in the accomplishment of the mission. While normally this will involve assessing potential threats to the mission (from forces external and internal to the affected population), the unique aspects of stability operations may result in significant or even primary emphasis being placed upon logistic, health, or political intelligence and intelligence support to IO and CA.

(b) IGOs, NGOs, USG organizations (e.g., the American embassy), as well as various CA teams may have been in the area for many years and may have area studies, country studies, and other useful resources.

(c) Although the intelligence effort will require input from all intelligence disciplines, human intelligence (HUMINT) and geospatial intelligence (GEOINT) may assume increased importance in stability operations. In combination, HUMINT, GEOINT, and other efforts (e.g., open-source intelligence) enable the creation of products invaluable during stability operations.

(2) **Intelligence Collaboration.** The complexity of the operational environment as well as the multiagency and multinational nature of stability operations calls for intelligence collaboration among military, civilian, and foreign intelligence agencies. This intelligence collaboration relies on unhindered access to and sharing of all relevant information and can take many forms such as competitive analysis, brainstorming, and federation. Successful intelligence collaboration depends on many factors, to include: strong relationship networks, trust and respect among colleagues, sharing a common vision, minimizing territorial issues, continuous communication, and commitment from the leadership of collaborating organizations. An aggressive liaison effort is critical to developing and maintaining unity of effort from initial planning through the execution of operations. However, analysts must base their collaboration on classification, need-to-know, need-to-share, and applicable national, agency, or organizational guidelines.

For further details on intelligence collaboration, refer to JP 2-0, Joint Intelligence.

(3) **Intelligence Sharing.** During stability operations, the joint force will usually operate in a complex international environment alongside other important entities that will have a need for intelligence products. Mission participants such as UN organizations, multinational military and security members, local indigenous military and security forces, NGOs, and private sector companies and individuals providing contract services are also likely to possess valuable information they can provide the joint force that is unique to their own mission and sources. Although the joint force may have organic ISR capabilities assigned and intelligence collaboration may fill many gaps in ISR capabilities, these mission participants may, in fact, provide the bulk of information for analyzing the operational environment during stability operations. The J-2 will find the information coming from these disparate entities just as valuable, or more so, for assessing the overall situation than traditional intelligence sources. Therefore, a robust information sharing process will be required with individuals operating at multiple classification levels. The J-2 must have a process in place to exchange information with external sources and assess the validity of information supplied by mission participants. This process should include foreign disclosure officers, delegated with the proper authority to disclose classified military information to the aforementioned mission participants within the operational area in accordance with legal and policy guidelines. Wherever possible, the J-2 should establish routine procedures to foster a cross-flow of information.

d. **Fires**

(1) Joint forces represent a potent combination of lethal and nonlethal capabilities. Although the presence of military forces may influence human behavior by demonstrating the potential for lethal action, security of the population, HN, or joint force cannot normally be assumed or achieved solely through the physical presence of military forces or the killing or capturing of adversaries. When required, military forces will have to neutralize and isolate irregular actors by winning the contests in both the physical domains and the information environment of the operational area.

(a) Dominance of the operational area may include significant offensive and defensive operations that must be won to establish the HN government's monopoly on the use of force and provide a safe and secure environment for the population. Maintaining order is vital to establishing a safe, secure environment. Even though stability operations emphasize nonlethal actions, the ability to engage potential enemies with decisive lethal force remains a sound deterrent and is often a key to success.

(b) The HN government must provide a more attractive, credible vision of the future than the adversary. Without security, the development of adequate governance, sustainable local economies, and delivery of essential services is significantly impeded and unlikely to succeed.

(2) In any case, combat and stability tasks often occur in the same operational area, requiring close coordination to both deconflict ongoing activities and help create desired effects and avoid undesired effects. There is also a requirement for a thorough understanding of when the escalation of force is necessary and when it might be counterproductive. It

requires sound judgment supported by constant assessment of the security situation and an intuitive sense of timing with respect to the actions of enemies and adversaries.

e. **Protection**

(1) Protection is a fundamental element in stability operations. The ability to provide physical security to the population and those conducting stabilization is often a primary reason for involvement by the Armed Forces of the United States in stabilization efforts. The protection function during stability operations emphasizes force protection, force health protection (FHP), and civil security. The context of the operation will dictate the intensity of protection requirements during stabilization efforts. Protection requirements should be balanced with the military operation's nature and objectives. In some stability operations, the use of certain security measures, such as carrying arms, wearing helmets and protective vests, or using secure communications, may cause military forces to appear more threatening than intended, which may degrade the force's legitimacy and hurt relations with the local population.

(2) **Force Protection.** Even in a permissive environment, the joint force can expect to encounter banditry, vandalism, and various levels of violent activities from criminals or unruly crowds. It is imperative that the joint force be trained and equipped to mitigate threats to US personnel, resources, facilities, and critical information. All deploying members should be provided with threat and force protection briefings prior to and throughout the duration of the operation. Depending upon the mission, the operational environment, and directives from higher level CDRs, force protection may also extend beyond the joint force to encompass protection of civilian personnel and systems from the USG, the HN and other partner nation governments, IGOs, and NGOs. Particularly in hostile security environments, protection of civilians participating in stabilization efforts may be vital to their continued presence in the operational area. However, due to organizational mandates, some NGOs may refuse the protection offered by military forces to not compromise their reliance on the humanitarian principles of independence, impartiality, and neutrality. The extent to which joint forces can protect civilian partners should be addressed in the ROE.

(3) **Force Health Protection.** Public health threats do not discriminate between individuals. When planning for and conducting stability operations, JFCs should consider the factors that threaten the health of the indigenous population, multinational forces, USG employees, contractors and, as appropriate, IGOs and NGOs. Personnel likely to serve in areas where stability operations are conducted may enter with very little, if any, natural immunity to endemic diseases. The degree of cultural and social interaction required to support the mission, as well as the sharing of food, quarters, and recreational facilities with local nationals, may increase the exposure of personnel to diseases endemic to the host country. Stability operations may last for extended periods of time (months or years, not days or weeks), increasing the risk of contracting endemic disease. The enforcement of proper FHP measures is critical to minimize the risk to personnel.

For further guidance on FHP, refer to JP 4-02, Health Service Support.

(4) **Civil Security.** By protecting the population in fragile states, intervening forces and their interagency partners enable daily life to continue. This, in turn, helps stimulate economic activity and supports longer-term development and governance reform. Importantly, it generates confidence in local people in their security situation and an economic interest in ongoing stability, and denies adversarial groups one of their principal strategies for expanding their support base.

f. **Sustainment**

(1) Stability operations are often logistics and engineering intensive. Therefore, the overall logistic concept should be closely tied into the operational strategy and be mutually supporting. Planning also should consider the potential requirements to provide support to nonmilitary personnel (e.g., USG civilian agencies, NGOs, IGOs, IPI, and the private sector).

(2) Cultural and religious considerations are particularly important for logistic planners supporting stability operations. Inappropriate foods, materials, and methods will not only prolong the requirement to provide assistance and increase cost and risk, but may also have a dramatic negative impact on the local population's perceptions of the joint force and the stability operations at large. Additionally, local hires and contractors may need to be divided between multiple population groups (i.e., religious sects, nationalities, or tribes) to demonstrate impartiality.

(3) Theater support contracting and some external support contracting actions can have a positive (and sometimes negative) effect on the civil-military aspects of the overall operation or campaign. Since the majority of theater support contracts are awarded to local vendors, these actions can have a tangential positive benefit by providing employment opportunities to indigenous personnel, promoting goodwill with the local populace and improving the local economic base. In some operations, there may be a high degree of local unemployment that can lead to local unrest and cause local nationals to support an insurgency simply for monetary compensation. Maximizing local hires through theater support contracting or civil augmentation programs can help alleviate this situation. However, consideration should be given to mitigating possible inflationary effects of local hiring and unintended adverse consequences, such as reduction in the number of qualified personnel to serve in HN institutions, due to variations in levels of compensation. US forces must carefully determine appropriate labor rates, so as to not set a rate that would promote nepotism or that is unsustainable after US forces leave the region. In addition, US forces must carefully determine the ethnic makeup of their local workforce and use labor from within villages and districts rather than from provinces or other urban areas, especially if they are different from where the actual work is being conducted.

(a) Integrating the contracting support plan into a joint operation is especially important where there are significant reconstruction requirements.

(b) HNS can be a significant force multiplier. Whenever possible, available and suitable HNS should be considered as an alternative to deploying logistic support from other locations outside of the operational area. HNS can dramatically increase the timeliness of response to a developing situation and reduce the strategic airlift and sealift requirements necessary to deploy forces to the operational area.

For further detail on contracting and HNS, refer to JP 3-34, Joint Engineer Operations; *JP 4-0,* Joint Logistics; *and JP 4-10,* Operational Contract Support.

7. Continuous Assessment

a. Continuous and timely assessments of the operational environment and the progress of operations are essential to measure progress toward mission accomplishment. Assessment occurs at all levels and across the entire range of military operations. Assessment in stability operations is as important as assessment in combat operations and can be more complex than traditional combat assessment. The results of stabilization activities will be very difficult to achieve, or indeed, to measure, and the CDR may therefore need to devote greater effort to this area if he is to gain a clear picture of progress. Normally, the entire staff assists the J-3 or J-5 in coordinating assessment activities.

b. Assessments of stability operations should encompass a broad range of conditions. JFCs should encourage collaboration and consultation between military and civil actors. Establishing an agreed picture across military, development, and diplomatic lines of effort will be by consensus and may necessitate the establishment of a dedicated assessments cell to which all USG agencies contribute.

c. The greatest challenge in stability operations is to select suitable measures that enable shorter-term assessment of longer-term effects, as it is crucial to maintain focus on the campaign objectives rather than on their supporting activity. Responsiveness is a particularly important consideration for selecting measurement tools in this type of environment. In this context, responsiveness is the speed with which a measurement tool can detect a desired change. In practice, responsiveness varies greatly among potential MOEs.

d. Planning for data collection (what is to be gathered, when, by whom, and for what purpose) is conducted collaboratively between each participant, and an assessment framework should be used to support this. Information developed across USG agencies, or from raw data provided by the IPI, IGOs, NGOs, or other sources, requires special care to ensure consistency of reporting criteria, to avoid skewing comparative results over time if the data set is modified. Gathering and maintaining disaggregated data can be particularly important to support analysis of population subgroups. Civil information management, a CA core task, will play a key role in data collection. If a JFC is employing distributed units, they can become important sources of accurate and timely local information.

For further details on civil information management, refer to JP 3-57, Civil-Military Operations.

e. MOEs during stability operations should be based on impact indicators that measure the change in the lives of the people, rather than process indicators that calculate USG efforts and their immediate outputs.

f. The ultimate purpose of assessment is to inform a CDR's judgments on the progress of operations and support subsequent decisions. Events can change opinions and perceptions of relevant populations disproportionately, and reverses from previous successes should be expected. Accordingly, assessment must periodically review any changes from previous positions, rather than assuming that once objectives are met they will be enduring and require no further maintenance activity. The identification and direction of trends are more informative than absolute measurements of activity.

g. A comprehensive assessment framework, identified at the beginning of operational planning and agreed to across as many actors as possible, will help all aspects of operational assessment. There is no single all-encompassing checklist for MOEs. MOEs and measures of performance (MOPs) will vary according to the circumstances. Three example frameworks that may be useful in assessment planning are found in Appendix A, "Assessment Frameworks."

For further details on assessment, refer to JP 5-0, Joint Operation Planning.

8. Transitions

a. Because the national strategic end state may be general or broad in nature, it may be difficult to determine whether and when military operations should be terminated. A requirement, therefore, exists, to determine the military end state and the termination criteria. The military end state is the set of required conditions that defines achievement of all military objectives. It normally represents a point in time or circumstances beyond which the President does not require the military instrument of national power as the primary means to achieve remaining national objectives. Establishing benchmarks tied to measurable conditions is normally more effective in determining when and where a transition from military to civil efforts and lead agent responsibilities should begin. The termination criteria, on the other hand, describe the relevant and measurable standards that must be met before a joint operation can be concluded. The actual success of military operations will be measured against the national strategic end state and not just attainment of the military end state. The JFC must remain aware that the national strategic end state may change. The termination criteria should be developed through a collaborative planning process with both military and civilian agencies. They should relate to the national strategic as well as the military end state and the local and cultural realities of the HN. Transitions can occur at different times in the operation and in different parts of the HN. The JFC, in synchronization with civil agencies, must manage these transition events. The JFC must also be prepared to recommend a change in the strategic end state to political and military leadership if the original goals are no longer achievable.

b. The relationships established in the initial stages of operations, coupled with accurate assessments of progress achieved in civil-military implementation, are crucial to affecting a smooth transition to civil authority. A transition plan should be based on an accurate and shared understanding of the capabilities, responsibilities, and resources of all participants. The result should be an agreed plan, including MOEs and resources, which results in decreasing military involvement and increasing civil involvement. Transitions can occur at different times in the operation and in different parts of the HN. The JFC, in synchronization with civil agencies, must manage these transition events.

c. Stability operations may include transitions of authority and control among military forces, civilian agencies and organizations, and the HN as HN capacity increases (see Figure II-3). Each transition involves inherent risk. The risk is amplified when multiple transitions must be managed simultaneously or when the force must quickly conduct a series of transitions. Planning anticipates these transitions, and careful preparation and diligent execution ensures they occur without incident. Transitions are identified as decisive points

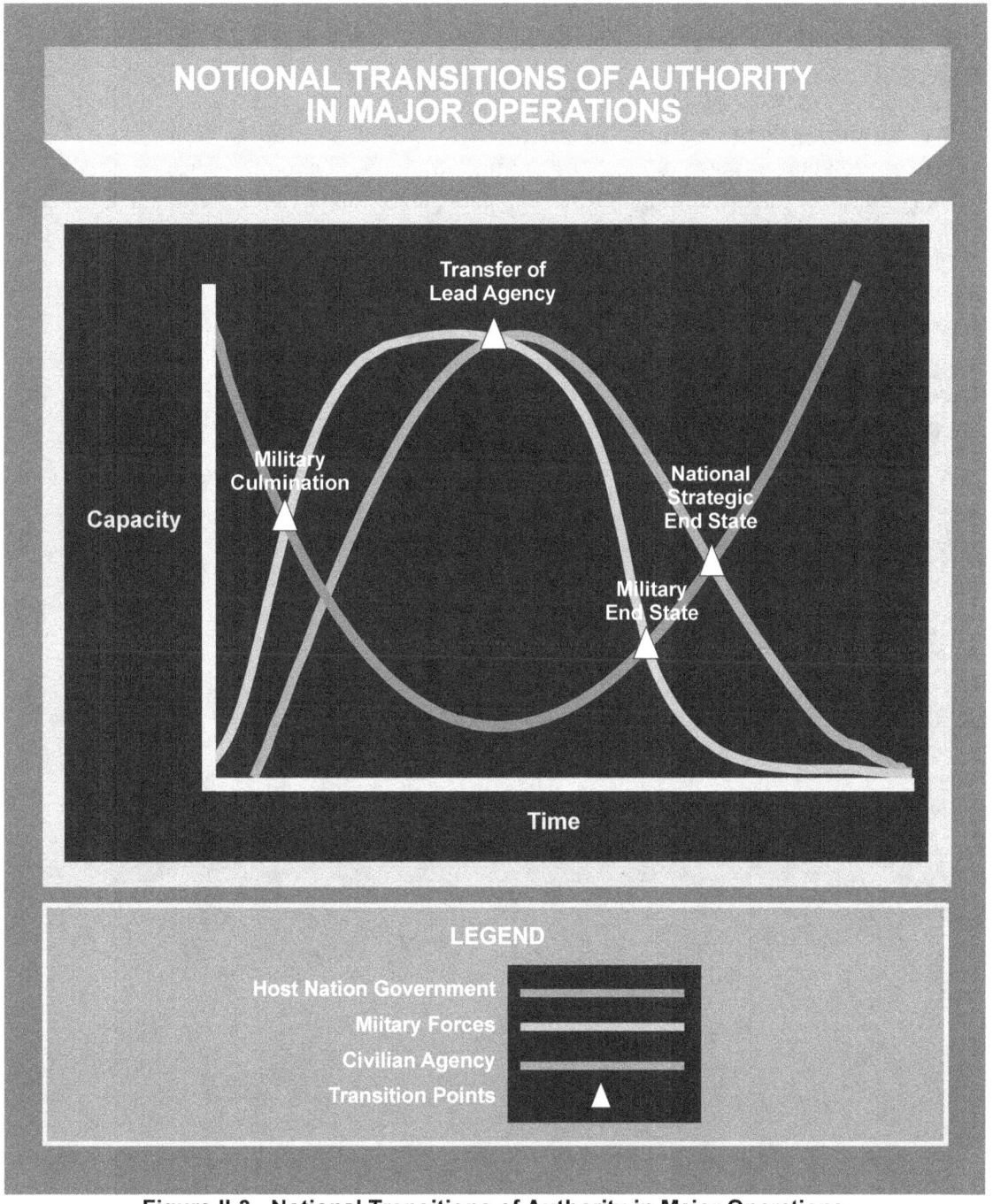

Figure II-3. Notional Transitions of Authority in Major Operations

on lines of effort; they typically mark a significant shift in effort and signify the gradual return to civilian oversight and control of the HN.

9. Training for Stability Operations

a. **Joint and Interagency Training and Exercises.** Joint force stability operations training should provide for individual military and civilian instruction, military unit and civilian agency instruction, and combined military and civilian agency training in formal joint programs. While numerous humanitarian and complex crises during the previous several years have provided opportunities for military and civilian agencies to perform their mission skills, there is a clear requirement for joint forces to train to better integrate with interagency, IGO, and NGO planning and training to synchronize all components of a US response to a crisis.

b. **Training Prior to Deployment.** CCDRs should schedule interagency, IGO, and NGO coordination training as a part of routine training and exercise participation, and as training for a specific operation. The training audience should include members of the entire JTF HQ staff and relevant NGOs, the UN, and USG civilian agencies willing to participate. JFCs may also cross-train select staff elements through other willing government agencies, IGOs, and the humanitarian assistance community. Joint force training for interagency, IGO, and NGO interaction during stability operations should focus on identifying and assessing military and agency capabilities and core competencies, and identifying procedural disconnects. Such training also serves to build personal relationships and the trust so important to achieving unity of effort.

CHAPTER III
STABILITY OPERATIONS FUNCTIONS

"The Department shall have the capability and capacity to conduct stability operations activities to fulfill DOD Component responsibilities under national and international law. Capabilities shall be compatible, through interoperable and complementary solutions, to those of other US Government agencies and foreign governments and security forces...."

Department of Defense Instruction 3000.05
Stability Operations
16 September 2009

1. Introduction

a. While the assignment of specific tasks and prioritization among them depends on the mission and conditions of the operational environment, the stability operations functions, as a framework, are a tool to help visualize the conduct of an operation, sequence necessary activities within an operation, and develop appropriate priorities for those activities and resource allocation. Individually, the functions encompass the distinct yet interrelated tasks that constitute stability activities in a functional sector. Collectively, they are the pillars upon which the USG frames the possible tasks required in a stabilization effort. The tasks within each function are crosscutting, generating effects across multiple sectors.

b. Although some tasks are executed sequentially, success necessitates an approach that focuses on simultaneous actions across the operational environment. These tasks are inextricably linked; positive results in one area of stabilization depend upon the successful integration and synchronization of activities across the other areas. The JFC may establish lines of effort around the stability functions, but must ensure coordination and synchronization across them. Preferably, the JFC should use them simply as a guide to action, ensuring broader unity of effort across all sectors of the HN. In hostile environments, joint forces may be tempted to utilize all available capacity on security efforts. However, security is usually conditional on a degree of popular consent and this, in turn, is conditional on the restoration of basic governance functions. Accordingly, the CDR should not presume that others could implement, for example, governance functions once the joint force has managed to reduce the level of violence. In the same way, partners in the governance and economic sectors should not expect security as a prerequisite for their activities. All are interdependent and a minimal level of governance, rule of law, and economic stability will be necessary to facilitate early stabilization.

c. The functions described here are security, humanitarian assistance, economic stabilization and infrastructure, rule of law, and governance and participation. These functions are based upon the sectors developed in the ETM by S/CRS as interagency guidance on stability and reconstruction activities across the USG. Figure III-1 generally depicts how stability operations, used to establish civil security and civil control, restore essential services, repair and protect critical infrastructure, and deliver humanitarian assistance, are nested within this framework.

d. **Strategic Communication.** Although not discussed specifically in any given functional area, SC themes and messages, fully coordinated with other operational activities, enhance the legitimacy of HN forces and ultimately the stability of the HN. Information must be synchronized with operations. PA and IO provide the "words," supported by the "deeds" of stability operations and CMO. Joint force staffs must carefully ensure that messages are consistent with actions and vice versa.

(1) Implementation of SC guidance encompasses national-strategic level and non-DOD activities that are not under the direct control of the JFC. This adds to the complexity of adapting and applying themes, messages, images, and actions at each level within military operations to create desired and avoid undesired outcomes in selected audiences. DOS has responsibility for coordinating public information efforts by the USG during stabilization efforts.

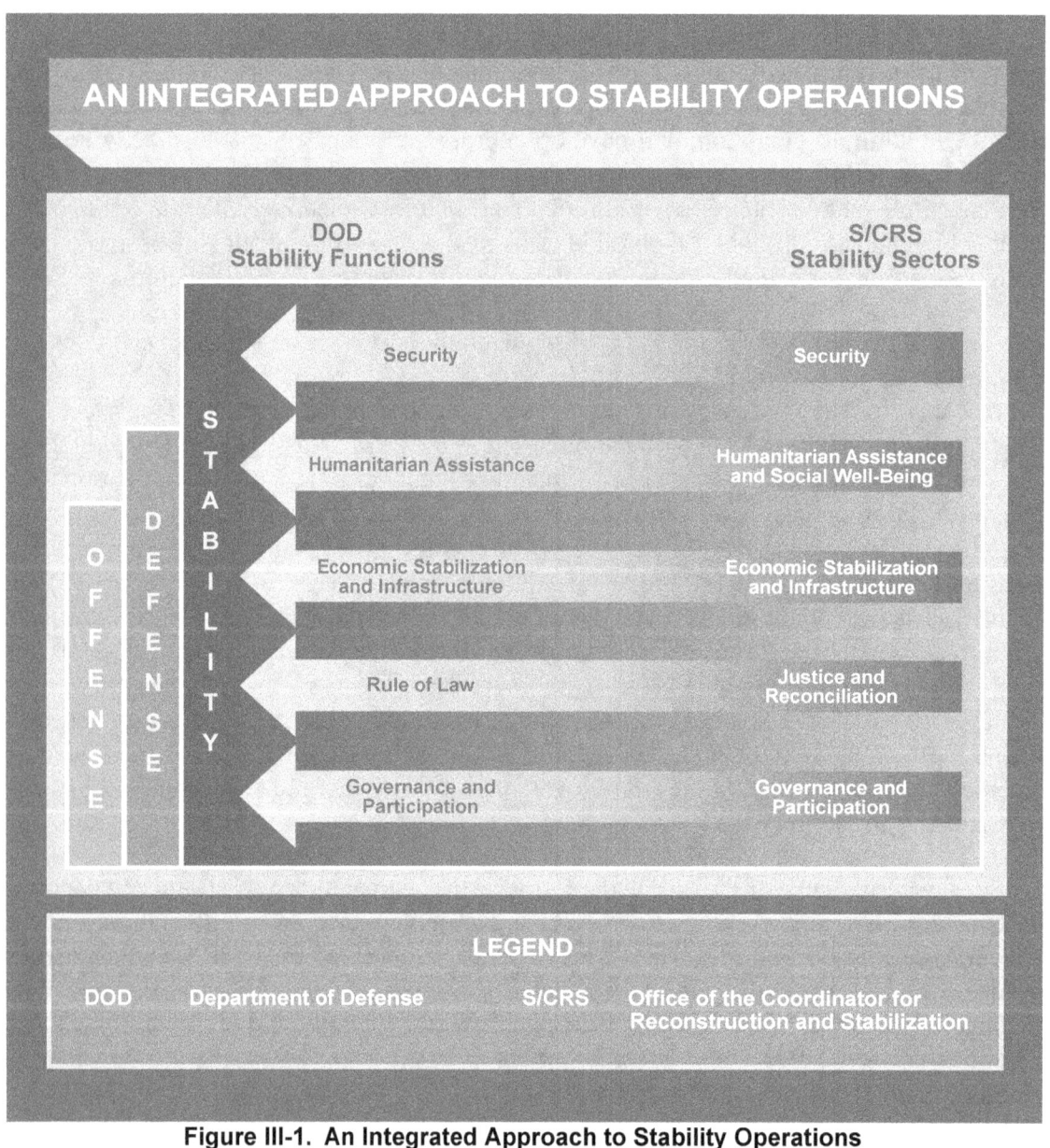

Figure III-1. An Integrated Approach to Stability Operations

INTERDEPENDENCE OF FUNCTIONS

On 14 August 1992, US forces were committed to emergency airlift food to Somalia. The largest and most difficult problem was security for the food once it arrived in Somalia. Armed looters and thieves made it difficult to get the food to the hungry. On 2 December, US forces commenced Operation RESTORE HOPE, with UN [United Nations] authorization, to create the secure environment necessary for the provision of humanitarian relief and promotion of national reconciliation and economic reconstruction in Somalia. The UN resolution required that soldiers be withdrawn once order was restored. By April 1993, major installations were secured and open, and free passage of relief supplies was established. Humanitarian relief was provided and a larger disaster was averted. However, with no political reconciliation among competing elites and no functional security apparatus, incidents of violence continued as US forces turned over leadership to UN forces in May 1993.

UN operations at this point focused on transformational stability activities that would establish the institutions necessary to alleviate suffering in Somalia. These activities included efforts to build local and national governance, re-establish local and national security forces, develop food, health-care, agricultural, and water systems, foster an open and working economy, and re-establish an education system. US participation persisted as Operation CONTINUED HOPE.

Despite the appearance of political resolution, including a signed agreement among all Somali political movements, attempts by UN military forces to implement disarmament led to increasing tensions and to open conflict among the clans and UN forces beginning in June. Notwithstanding the ongoing violence, civilian organizations made significant progress in transformational stabilization in the fields of public health, education, agriculture, and other areas, and the UN attempted to build institutions that could govern Somalia and enforce the rule of law, but the protracted political impasse created a vacuum of civil authority and governmental structure in Somalia, leaving no function on which to build. With no political settlement in sight that might help bring an end to the escalating violence, the US and other nations withdrew military support to the operation in early 1994. UN military forces withdrew completely one year later.

This intervention demonstrated the vital link between humanitarian assistance and national political reconciliation. The former was geared towards the immediate amelioration of emergency situations, while the latter was necessary to ensure stability in the long term so that the positive results of humanitarian assistance could be preserved and a recurrence of the tragedy avoided. Even as intervening military forces and emerging Somali security institutions were able to establish security to enable humanitarian assistance activities, security was untenable in the long term without a political reconciliation.

SOURCE: Joint Military Operations Historical Collection
The Blue Helmets: A Review of United Nations Peacekeeping

(2) JFCs, through PA officers, should provide factual, accurate information to the media to control rumors and disinformation, conducting interviews, managing social media initiatives, highlighting success stories, and issuing timely and clearly worded press releases in local languages. Efforts should include assisting HN authorities with public information programs.

For further details on SC, refer to US Joint Forces Command's joint force commander's handbook, Strategic Communication and Communication Strategy.

SECTION A. SECURITY

2. General

a. Security activities seek to protect and control civil populations, property, and territory. They may be performed as part of a military occupation during or after combat, to help defeat an insurgency, or in response to a humanitarian disaster. They seek ultimately to reassure rather than compel. Security activities conclude successfully when civil violence is reduced to a level manageable by HN law enforcement authorities. A safe and secure environment is one in which the population has the freedom to pursue daily activities without fear of politically motivated, persistent, or large-scale violence. Such an environment is characterized by an end to large-scale fighting; an adequate level of public order; the subordination of accountable security forces to legitimate state authority; the protection of key individuals, communities, sites, and infrastructure; and the freedom for people and goods to move about the country and across borders without fear of undue harm to life and limb.

b. The military provides the security on which stability can be built. The goal must be pragmatic: not a complete absence of violence, but its reduction to levels containable by indigenous forces and where normal life can be resumed.

c. The provision of a safe and secure environment is one of the fundamental ingredients in establishing human security, along with the provision of humanitarian assistance. Meeting the basic human security needs of the population is fundamental to the development of HN government authority and ultimately security of the state.

d. Initial response activities in security focus on the actual provision of security to establish a safe and secure environment. Transformational activities focus on developing legitimate and stable security institutions in the HN. Activities that foster sustainability focus on consolidating that indigenous capacity to enable long-term security. Although joint forces may help establish or reestablish a safe and secure environment for a limited time and even assist in the development of HN security forces, it is the transformative nature of stability operations focused on development and not ongoing security operations that make peace sustainable. For this reason, the achievement of a lasting political settlement among competing elites remains the overarching objective of stabilization efforts.

e. The actual provision of security is not, in the strictest sense, a stability operation. It is generally a defensive operation, though offensive operations may play a key role as well. Nonetheless, the security of the population is so central to the success of stabilization efforts that the provision of security warrants discussion here. Securing vital national infrastructure and implementing measures to reestablish and maintain control of key populations, such as significant ethnic minorities, through the provision of rule of law and basic public services, is central to HN legitimacy.

f. The security requirements vary greatly across the range of military operations, and the JFC should consider security actions based on the mission and his understanding of the operational environment.

(1) During major operations or campaigns, the law of war calls for occupying forces to provide security for local populations. The provision of population security also enables force protection in operational areas by helping to deny safe havens to adversary forces that may have blended into the population to continue covert attacks. JFCs should provide population security through a combination of CMO and policing efforts, as required.

(2) During crisis response and limited contingency operations, the operational environment largely dictates the security requirement, which varies fundamentally from operation to operation. During some operations, security may be well established by local security forces and cultural norms in place, while in other operations, joint forces may be operating among warring factions battling for control.

(a) In a hostile environment, the joint force's first priority is to secure the operational area, then to hold it while stability activities focused on development attempt to build on those security gains. This is normally conducted area by area, rather than in a single sweeping operation.

(b) In an uncertain environment, offensive operations to clear and secure an area may not be required, but the joint force must still focus on holding the area. In this case, US forces normally provide direct support to HN security forces working to establish security.

(c) In a permissive environment, security considerations focus almost solely on force protection, relying on HN security forces and local cultural norms to secure the population.

(3) During military engagement, security cooperation, and deterrence activities, security is not normally a significant impediment to stability operations. HN security forces and local cultural norms ensure a secure environment, and US security considerations focus almost solely on force protection requirements.

g. **Security Sector Reform.** In addition to providing security as required, a major joint force role in stabilization may be to provide support for SSR. Beyond simply providing security, SSR includes the broad set of policies, plans, programs, and activities that a government undertakes to improve the way it provides safety, security, and justice. Transformational activities and activities that foster sustainability in the security sector generally fall under the rubric of SSR.

SAFE AND SECURE ENVIRONMENT
NECESSARY CONDITIONS

Cessation of Large-Scale Violence

- Large-scale armed conflict has come to a halt
- Warring parties are separated and monitored
- A peace agreement or cease-fire has been implemented
- Violent spoilers are managed

Public Order

- Laws are enforced equitably
- The lives, property, freedoms, and rights of individuals are protected
- Criminal and politically motivated violence has been reduced to a minimum
- Criminal elements (from looters and rioters to leaders of organized crime networks) are pursued, arrested, and detained

Legitimate State Monopoly Over the Means of Violence

- Major illegal armed groups have been identified, disarmed, and demobilized
- The defense and police forces have been vetted and retrained
- National security forces operate lawfully under a legitimate governing authority

Physical Security

- Political leaders, ex-combatants, and the general population are free of fear from grave threats to physical safety
- Refugees and internally displaced persons can return home without fear of retributive violence
- Women and children are protected from undue violence
- Key historical or cultural sites and critical infrastructure are protected from attack

Territorial Security

- People and goods can freely move throughout the country and across borders without fear of harm to life and limb
- The country is protected from invasion
- Borders are reasonably well-secured from infiltration by insurgent or terrorist elements and illicit trafficking of arms, narcotics, and humans

SOURCE: *Guiding Principles for Stabilization and Reconstruction*
US Institute of Peace and US Army Peacekeeping and
Stability Operations Institute

For further detail on SSR, refer to Appendix C, "Security Sector Reform." For further details on security and population security, refer to JP 3-10, Joint Security Operations in Theater, *and JP 3-24,* Counterinsurgency Operations.

3. Evaluation, Analysis, and Assessment

a. To plan for and execute an intervention CDRs and their staffs conduct an in-depth analysis to provide relevant background concerning existing dynamics that could trigger, exacerbate, or mitigate violent conflict. The key lies in the development of shared understanding among all agencies and countries involved about the sources of violent conflict or civil strife. This requires both a joint process for completing the assessment and a common conceptual framework to guide the collection and analysis of information. This conflict diagnosis should deliver a product that describes the context, core grievances and resiliencies, drivers of conflict and mitigating factors, and opportunities for increasing or decreasing conflict.

b. Initial evaluation and assessments for security should determine the level of security present as well as the difficulty of establishing or reestablishing security, identifying possible obstacles to success. Analysis should include a broad political, economic, and sociological analysis to understand the drivers of possible or actual conflict and mitigating factors. Specific threats to the establishment of a safe and secure environment must also be assessed. The following list of questions, while not comprehensive and dependent on the circumstances, may guide in the development of a security assessment.

(1) What is the current level of conflict? Is there a basic level of population security that will permit the conduct of stabilization activities by civilian organizations? If not, what conditions are required before civilian organizations can be employed?

(2) If there is ongoing conflict, are there unsatisfied aims for which disputants remain willing to fight? Even if warring parties sign a peace settlement, do unresolved conflicts persist? Are there factions that remain opposed to the peace settlement? Will the signatories respect the settlement?

(3) Is there an HN government with legitimacy among the population? If not, has this created a power vacuum that is likely to lead to a bitter internal struggle for power? What conditions must be met before peaceful means, such as elections, can effectively substitute for force in determining who governs?

(4) Can the rights of minority or disenfranchised populations be reliably guaranteed, or is majority rule likely to be perceived as a continuation of a life-and-death, zero-sum form of politics by at least one of the parties to the conflict? Do citizens, and in particular minorities and women, enjoy adequate guarantees for fundamental civil and political rights of speech, movement, and assembly?

(5) Are security threats conventional and military or subversive and criminal in nature? Do informal linkages involving political extremists, paramilitary formations, intelligence operatives, or the criminal underworld remain potent forces? Are there networks of criminals, warlords, or corrupt or extremist ruling elites that must be broken?

(6) Who is providing security—HN security forces, external intervention forces such as a UN peacekeeping force, or non-state entities? What indigenous security capacity must be developed to ensure that the threat of political violence ends? Did indigenous security forces disintegrate? Were they responsible for brutality and repression that led to conflict?

(7) Who wins and who loses economically if peace prevails? Does illicit wealth determine who wields political power, fueling continued conflict? What revenue streams flow to major obstructionists that sustain their capacity for coercion, terrorism, paramilitary activities, and intelligence operations?

(8) What is the likely impact of the presence of US or multinational forces? Will foreign forces be viewed as occupiers or as propping up an illegitimate government, regardless of their role in ongoing stabilization efforts?

c. Ongoing assessment of the security situation can be problematic because of the time involved for the effects of operations to become apparent. During a crisis intervention, the levels of outcome-based security metrics (e.g., numbers of attacks, civilian deaths, military casualties) may increase as a result of operations as security is implemented. During this period, intelligence and ongoing threat analysis will normally provide better indications of success. MOPs are an important link to the long-term use of MOEs.

4. Military Contribution

a. Separation of Warring Parties

(1) Separating warring parties involves establishing distinct areas of control that keeps factions apart and allows the joint force to monitor their actions. The establishment of security fundamentally requires a monopoly on the use of force by a single entity. In stabilization efforts, the goal is normally to support a legitimate HN governmental authority that holds this monopoly, using it to protect the population, or to help that authority attain the monopoly. Toward this goal, joint forces take action to support efforts to end ongoing conflict, build HN security force capacity, and disarm adversary forces. When the joint force is providing security, DOD will normally have the lead role in this area; otherwise, this area is generally led by USAID's Bureau of Democracy, Conflict, and Humanitarian Assistance (DCHA). DOS's Bureau of Political-Military Affairs and various intelligence services could also play significant supporting roles.

(2) **Supporting the Peace Process.** Understand that stopping armed conflict and securing peace requires political, not military, solutions. A robust political settlement is the cornerstone for sustainable peace that enables warring parties to share power within an agreed framework and resolve their political differences in peaceful ways.

(3) **Peacemaking and Peace Enforcement.** The cessation of hostilities among belligerents is critical to providing effective security for the local populace. These may take the form of cease-fires, peace agreements, or other formal and informal settlements. Establishing these agreements is a diplomatic effort, but military support to PM includes provision of military expertise to the PM process, military-to-military relations, security

assistance, peacetime deployments, or other activities that influence the disputing parties to seek a diplomatic settlement. The joint force may conduct PKO or PEO, such as the enforcement of cease-fires or buffer zones, in support of this process.

For further details on PM, PKO, and PEO, refer to JP 3-07.3, Peace Operations.

(4) **Disposition and Constitution of National Armed and Intelligence Services.** Stability operations that initiate the rebuilding of national armed and intelligence services help to establish the conditions for successful SSR. These tasks focus on the security and intelligence institutions that form the underpinnings of an effective security sector based in a clearly defined legal framework. They provide the broad guidance and direction for the training and advising effort central to SSR.

(5) **Disarmament, Demobilization, and Reintegration.** Disarmament, demobilization, and reintegration (DDR) attempts to stabilize the operational environment by disarming and demobilizing armed groups and by helping return former combatants to civilian life. DDR can potentially provide incentives for combatants and their leaders to facilitate political reconciliation, dissolve belligerent force structures, and present opportunities for former belligerents and other DDR beneficiaries to return to their communities. A successful DDR program helps establish sustainable peace. The objective of the DDR process is to contribute to security and stability in post-conflict environments so that recovery and development can begin. The DDR of former combatants is a complex process, with political, military, security, humanitarian, and socioeconomic dimensions. It aims to deal with the post-conflict security problem that arises when former combatants are left without livelihoods or support networks, other than their former comrades, during the vital transition period from conflict to peace and development. Disarmament and demobilization refer to the acts of releasing or disbanding an armed unit and the safe collection, inspection, transportation, inventory, disposal, and control of weapons, ammunition, and explosive ordnance. Reintegration helps former combatants return to civilian life through benefit packages and strategies that help them become socially and economically embedded in their communities. DDR must be carefully coordinated and consistent with SSR plans and programs.

For more information on DDR, refer to JP 3-24, Counterinsurgency Operations; *JP 3-07.3,* Peace Operations; *and S/CRS's* Lessons-Learned: Disarmament, Demobilization, and Reintegration (DDR) in Reconstruction and Stabilization Operations.

b. **Territorial Security.** Side-by-side with the monopoly on the use of force, the HN government must also be in control of its borders, and must be able to reasonably monitor and control movement within its borders, particularly movement by adversaries. Territorial integrity is a necessary condition in which ordinary citizens and legitimate goods are able to move in relative freedom within the country and across its borders, while illicit commodities and individuals that present threats to security are denied free passage. As with all security concerns, territorial security must balance security requirements for restriction with the political and economic requirements for openness. Again, DOD will normally lead this effort, but may share that lead with DOS's Bureau of International Narcotics and Law Enforcement Affairs (INL) and Department of Justice (DOJ) International Criminal

Investigative Training Assistance Program (ICITAP). The Department of Homeland Security (DHS), particularly US Coast Guard and US Customs and Border Protection, may also play significant supporting roles.

(1) **Border Control and Boundary Security.** A central component of security is the ability of the state to monitor and regulate its borders and ports of entry, including land boundaries, airports, coastlines, and seaports to prevent arms smuggling, interdict contraband, prevent trafficking of persons, regulate immigration and emigration, and establish friendly control over major points of entry (e.g., border crossings, airports, and seaports). Generally, border and coast guard forces secure national boundaries while customs officials regulate the flow of people, animals, and goods across state borders. The control of approaches to borders, such as sea lanes, rivers, and airlanes also contributes to border security.

(2) **Freedom of Movement.** Refers to the free flow of people and goods throughout the country without fear of physical harm or disruption, while spoilers, illicit commodities, and other sources of instability are restricted in movement. Enabling freedom of movement has wide-reaching benefits, promoting economic growth and social normalization among communities. Freedom of movement allows children to travel to school without fear of attack and farmers to take their goods to market. The ability to move about also promotes social integration of communities that might otherwise remain isolated. Checkpoints, curfews, and rules relevant to movement help security forces control the movement of adversaries within the operational area. At the same time, dismantling of adversary roadblocks and other impediments helps the population to resume everyday activities. Security forces must strike a balance between ensuring the freedom of movement necessary for the regular activities of governance and economics and the control of movement necessary for security.

(3) **Identification.** Identification programs complement efforts to vet HN personnel, encourage participation in representative government, resolve property disputes, and validate professional credentials. Although vital to other programs for rebuilding a functioning civil society, identification programs are equally important to security. After the collapse of an authoritarian or hostile regime, these programs help prevent potential adversaries from reintegrating into society without notice. Thus, they are deprived of the ability to provide the seeds for future organized sabotage, subversion, or insurgency. The use of biometrics in identification programs is vital to establishing and verifying identities with confidence. Biometrics enables the vetting process, limits the ability of potential adversaries to assume false identities, and can be used to tie individuals to crimes or acts of terrorism. The collection of biometric data will also locate, track, and identify an individual during tactical operations, manage local populations during military operations, control physical access, and allow for the collection of forensic evidence.

c. **Public Order and Safety.** Public order is one of the functions of governance that affects early perceptions of the legitimacy of the state and thus will almost always be one of the first and most important public tasks. Public order is a condition characterized by the absence of widespread criminal and political violence. Under this condition, the people of the country can conduct their daily movement and business without fear of violence.

Without public order, people will never build confidence in the public security system and will seek security from other entities like militias and warlords. Public order is the responsibility of police or other policing agencies, courts, prosecution services, and prisons. The population cannot be protected by security forces that remain on operating bases or in central police stations. The security of the population depends on active participation by police forces. Although the Armed Forces of the United States are not designed or trained, by and large, to be a constabulary force, the joint force may be called upon to conduct certain constabulary functions on a temporary basis until HN or other security forces can assume those responsibilities. This requirement is largely driven by the size and presence of the joint force, particularly in the immediate aftermath of war or other devastating events. Lead roles in this area are generally shared by DOD, INL, and DOS's Bureau of Population, Refugees, and Migration (PRM), while ICITAP and DCHA may play significant supporting roles.

(1) **Protection of Civilians.** The joint force may be called upon to provide protection for civilians if the HN is unable or unwilling to provide such protection. The protection of civilians from physical violence, including genocide, ethnic cleansing, war crimes, and crimes against humanity, is vital. Civilians and international workers, refugee camps, and other facilities for DCs may provide attractive targets for adversaries, particularly in areas of historic ethnic or cultural conflict. Security forces are charged with the protection of such facilities, while also enabling access by NGOs, IGOs, and others providing humanitarian assistance to DCs.

(2) **Policing.** Foot and mounted patrols by military forces with an eye toward preventing violent acts from adversaries may be an important part of establishing security. While local police forces are becoming established, the joint force may provide security to those police forces conducting regular policing activities.

(3) **Clearance of Explosive Ordnance and Chemical, Biological, Radiological, and Nuclear (CBRN) Hazards**

(a) In an area already burdened by collapsed institutions of central government, the presence of landmines and explosive remnants of war (ERW) and CBRN hazards inflicts stress that the surviving institutions may not be able to bear.

1. Unsecured explosive ordnance in the form of landmines, unexploded explosive ordnance (UXO), or abandoned explosive ordnance (AXO) can be used by terrorists, criminals, or insurgents to disrupt public order, impede economic development, or continue the conflict. These hazards restrict freedom of movement, negatively affect income producing activities such as agriculture, hinder international trade, and detract from the ability of a fragile state to secure its borders and boundaries.

2. CBRN hazards include chemical, biological, radiological, and nuclear elements; toxic industrial material (toxic or radioactive substances in solid, liquid, aerosolized, or gaseous form); chemical and biological agents; radioactive material; and hazards resulting from the employment of weapons of mass destruction.

(b) Securing and disposing of these munitions facilitate the safety, security, and well-being of the local populace. This may include the rendering safe or disposal of explosive ordnance which has become hazardous by damage or deterioration, when the disposal of such explosive ordnance requires techniques, procedures, or equipment which exceed the normal requirements for routine disposal.

For more information on clearing explosive ordnance and CBRN hazards, refer to JP 3-34, Joint Engineer Operations; *JP 3-15,* Barriers, Obstacles, and Mine Warfare for Joint Operations; *and JP 3-11,* Operations in Chemical, Biological, Radiological, and Nuclear (CBRN) Environments.

d. **Protection of Indigenous Infrastructure.** Both the short -and long-term success of any stabilization effort often relies on the ability of external groups to protect and maintain critical infrastructure until the HN can resume that responsibility. When required, military forces may extend protection and support to key HN personnel, infrastructure, and institutions to help ensure their continued contribution to the overall joint operation or stabilization effort. In the interest of transparency, military forces specifically request and carefully negotiate this protection. Examples of infrastructure that may require protection include government, religious, or cultural persons or sites of importance, HN military facilities, medical treatment facilities, and power generation and distribution systems. DOD and INL normally lead this effort, with significant supporting contribution from ICITAP.

e. **Protection of Personnel Involved in the Stabilization Effort.** The joint force may be called upon to provide protection for civilian personnel from the US or other nations that are assisting in the stabilization effort. Interagency or international memorandums of agreement will be required in this instance, laying out specific rules and responsibilities as well as ROE. Only on the rarest of occasions will military forces provide protection for NGO personnel, and only when directly requested; many NGOs feel that their reputation for neutrality, that is their independence from US or any other political and military influence, forms the basis of their security—joint forces must be careful not to impinge upon this reputation. DOD and INL normally lead this effort, with support from ICITAP.

5. **Threats and Vulnerabilities**

a. **Participants.** Everyone present during stabilization efforts has the potential to influence the course of events in ways which may be positive or negative. The CDR will strive to understand the full range of participants and their motivations, aspirations, interests, and relationships. Generically, the participants can be divided into six categories based on their aims, methods, and relationships: adversaries, enemies, belligerents, neutrals, friendlies, and opportunists. However, the category to which an individual belongs may not be immediately obvious, and over time some participants may change categories. These generic categories can be tailored to reflect the specific groups and interests in fragile and failed states.

(1) **Adversaries.** Terms such as insurgents, irregulars, terrorists, warlords, and criminals are commonly used in stabilization and COIN literature; each nation and organization has different understandings of these terms. Here they are all covered by the

term adversary. Although the term adversaries can also be used broadly to include enemies, adversaries may be distinguished from enemies by the fact that they may be susceptible to suasion or co-option to neutralize their hostility, or at least their violence. Adversaries may oppose either the HN government or the international forces, or both. Some of them can be actively and violently hostile, while others will be merely antagonistic. Not all violence will be perpetrated by adversarial groups; in many societies low level violence has long been a characteristic of politics. Equally, many less ardent adversaries will stop short of significant violence against foreign forces or government authorities in their day-to-day behavior, but may provide materiel or moral assistance to more hostile elements. Their reasons for providing such support will not necessarily be personal antagonism toward the HN government but may, for example, be based on traditional understandings of hospitality and obligation (e.g., Pashtunwali) or coercion, or fear of reprisals. Motivation and commitment will be variable across and within groups, and some adversaries will be irreconcilable. Many may be receptive to concessions, or a path back into the mainstream, in the form of limited or national settlements and confidence building measures. Constant assessment and probing will reveal fault lines within and between adversarial groups which can be exploited to change the conflict geometry.

(2) **Enemies.** An enemy is a person, group, force, state, or other authority that can wage war that is unalterably, implacably, and violently opposed to the HN government, friendly forces, or the United States. Unlike adversaries, enemies are not susceptible to suasion or co-option to neutralize their hostility, or at least their violence. Enemies, therefore, unlike adversaries, must be eliminated, or otherwise isolated from the population. Over time, enemies may be induced to become adversaries, and vice versa.

(3) **Belligerents.** Belligerents are primarily hostile to each other. Their motivations, intentions, and relationships may be influenced by historical grievance, self-interest, ideology, religion, or ethnicity. While belligerent hostilities are usually not directed toward intervening forces, they contribute to the societal conflict in destabilizing ways. Examples include competing tribes and warlords, nationalist groups, or religious organizations attempting to influence local or national power structures through the use of violence. In recent operations adversaries have attempted to mobilize belligerent groups by focusing their existing ideological, religious, or ethnic tensions toward the international force. An example of this is al-Qaeda's attempt to mobilize Sunni tribes to oppose coalition forces in Iraq by playing on preexisting Sunni–Shia tensions, and claiming that coalition forces were supporting a general de-Sunnification of Iraq's political elite.

(4) **Neutrals.** Neutrality covers those who may stop short of active opposition to the HN government at the one end, through passive consent, to those who support it but with reservations at the other. The conflict produces uncertainty for neutral groups with the potential for both risk and reward. Groups in this category will often play a critical role in the campaign, especially if they constitute a large proportion of the population. Historically, the passive acquiescence of neutrals has proven to be vital to the success of an insurgency. This group cannot be expected to support the HN government until it has clearly shown that it is likely to prevail.

(5) **Friendlies.** Friendly groups broadly support the HN government and the international force. They may include members of HN government institutions (including the security forces), dominant groups within the political settlement under contest and, if fortunate, large sections of the population. Building and then maintaining a broad coalition of friendly participants (which may be in competition with one another) is part of the operational art in stabilization.

(6) **Opportunists.** Opportunists, sometimes referred to as "spoilers," exist in all conflict-affected countries. They tend to be highly enterprising and adaptable, making use of the conflict environment to further their interests. In some cases opportunists have an interest in maintaining the status quo and may attempt to frustrate progress or to prevent any change harmful to their interests. Examples include: arms dealers, pirates, and smugglers. Some opportunists may not have a decisive impact on the situation, but criminal gangs operating in organized networks, possibly across national borders (for example, narco criminals), can have a significant destabilizing effect. Criminal opportunists and adversaries will exploit the nexus of interests, sharing lines of communication and exploiting instability for their own ends. In addition to criminal opportunists, foreign governments may be opportunists, attempting to exploit ongoing conflict or fragility in a state to further their own political goals; this may be particularly true when the US is involved in a controversial role. Opportunists can be helpful in changing the conflict geometry, but as with all the above groups, should be constantly re-evaluated, not least for long-term rather than declared goals.

b. **Shifting Allegiances.** Assessment based on observed behavior is useful, but can be misleading. Applying labels such as adversary or irreconcilable is a way to organize our thinking when dealing with a complex problem. However, they should be used with care. Groups are rarely fixed and bounded entities, and seeing them as such can inhibit the CDR's understanding of social interactions and deprive him of opportunities for influencing key participants. People have many, shifting identities and allegiances, and the categories cross-classify each other in complex ways. Belligerents may be friendly on some issues and hostile on others; adversaries today may be neutral tomorrow (or vice versa). Warlords, for example, may start as belligerents, squabbling amongst themselves, but then be drawn into the conflict and act as adversaries, or, alternatively, may partner with the HN government and, as a legitimized local government, become friendly. Any categorization must balance the need to organize our approach to a problem with building walls to compartmentalize and using labels to describe things that are in reality porous and ambiguous.

c. **Insurgency.** When the Armed Forces of the United States are required to help establish security, insurgency is normally the most significant security threat. Insurgencies are primarily internal conflicts that focus on the population. An insurgency aims to gain power and influence, win a contest of competing ideologies, or both.

For more detail on insurgency, refer to JP 3-24, Counterinsurgency Operations.

d. **Mass Atrocities.** Large-scale, deliberate attacks on civilians of a particular racial, political, or cultural group are a direct assault on universal human values, and genocide fuels instability, particularly in fragile states. Under extreme circumstances, such group persecution can develop into ethnic cleansing, which attempts to kill or forcibly relocate the population of entire cities or regions. History has shown that genocide and mass atrocities manifest themselves in highly variable ways, and future perpetrators should not be assumed to follow old patterns.

(1) Genocide is not the inevitable result of "ancient hatreds" or irrational leaders; rather it requires planning and is carried out systematically. The emphasis of USG efforts to counter genocide lies in prevention and detection of early warning signs.

(2) DOS leads efforts to detect and prevent genocide around the globe. Preventing or halting genocide, however, may require the employment of a joint force to deter or halt ongoing atrocities. Any such intervention will require a significant stability operations component. Additionally, when operating in fragile states, joint forces may be critical to detecting early warning signs, preventing or deterring genocide.

(3) Military ISR assets and the JIPOE process can help identify early warning indicators and describe important contextual factors, such as the nature of belligerents and the status of the civilian population, connections between leaders and followers, and the means of violence.

(4) Development of security institutions, including vetting of security and intelligence personnel as well as training and other assistance, should include some emphasis on preventing and countering mass atrocities and genocide. Key leader engagement is particularly important in this area.

(5) JFCs should ensure ROE specify guidance to units or individuals that encounter genocide or other mass atrocities, as well as human rights violations that could lead to such atrocities.

6. Security Response

a. **Population Security.** To provide protection to the population, JFCs employ a range of techniques. Not all will be popular.

(1) Static protection of key sites (e.g., market places or refugee camps).

(2) Persistent security in areas secured and held (e.g., intensive patrolling and check points).

(3) Targeted action against adversaries (e.g., search or strike operations).

(4) Population control measures (e.g., curfews and vehicle restrictions).

b. **Countering Adversaries.** Direct military action against adversaries may be a central component of a stabilization effort. In which case, setting the conditions for a negotiated political settlement will entail breaking the ideological, financial, or intimidatory links within and among different adversarial and belligerent groups, as well as between them and the broader population. Developing and maintaining an understanding of the motivations of different adversarial and potentially violent groups allows the JFC to tailor his approach to each. It may be that the most effective way of countering some of these groups is to reach an accommodation from a position of strength through formal accords or local bargains. However, there may be a number of actively hostile and irreconcilable adversarial groups, and countering these requires a balanced mix of the use of force, incentives, and detention.

For further detail on countering adversaries during stabilization, refer to JP 3-24, Counterinsurgency Operations.

c. **Tailored Approaches.** A well-targeted, differentiated strategy for engaging the various participants can transform the strategic geometry of the conflict. Such a strategy may allow the CDR to co-opt once adversarial or belligerent groups into the emerging political settlement. Consequently, efforts should be focused on:

(1) Supporting, protecting, empowering, and reassuring friendly groups and neutrals; for example, by giving public credit for changes in force posture.

(2) Persuading, providing incentives, or compelling belligerents, opportunists, and reconcilable adversaries.

(3) Marginalizing, disempowering, and targeting irreconcilable and actively hostile adversaries and enemies.

d. **Security Force Organization.** The JFC may organize joint forces into a number of different composite units for the purpose of establishing security in and among the population; these include framework forces, strike forces, surge forces, and specific focus task forces. Additionally, local non-regular militia may be incorporated into security operations.

(1) **Framework Forces.** Framework forces enable and conduct the bulk of the routine security operations. They will largely be focused on securing key installations, locations, and population centers. Units will normally have their own operational areas for which they are responsible and should be capable of autonomous action. Likely tasks include:

(a) **Population Security.** Some elements of the force will conduct operations that directly protect the population. This means living among the people. Involvement over time provides enhanced knowledge of, and an intuitive feel for, their specific area. The aim is to become as confident and competent when operating in this environment as the adversary. The integration of indigenous security forces as quickly as possible is essential.

(b) **Infrastructure Security.** Another element will conduct the control activities necessary to secure essential infrastructure and facilities.

(c) **Maneuver Outreach.** A maneuver element will attempt to create security throughout the operational area by their presence within it. The maneuver element should conduct routine presence patrolling, normally from secure locations, and should be capable of gathering information for intelligence.

(2) **Strike Forces.** Strike forces are used against high-value military, critical, infrastructural, and high-visibility leadership targets. They should be resourced and trained according to the task and will need to act on verified intelligence. Although these strikes are usually lethal, they should be supported by IO (e.g., electronic warfare, military information support, or operations security).

(3) **Surge Forces.** Surge forces are deployed to reinforce framework forces. They can be a separate part of the overall force package and can be deployed, employed, and redeployed where needed. They can be used in support of strike forces, or as a reserve for a specific operation. Although good for achieving temporary localized mass, they lack the finely tuned awareness of framework forces and will require LNOs or local security forces attached to them to provide local knowledge.

(4) **Specific Focus Task Forces.** Depending on the complexity of the threat, there may be a need to develop specific focus task forces that target narrow aspects of the conflict. These task forces will usually include cross-government representation, possibly including the security services. For example, if the adversary has a dynamic improvised explosive device (IED) capability, then developing a specific task force that targets the whole of the network and IED system may be necessary to bring the threat under control. Areas that could attract the creation of specific focus task forces with a diminishing military involvement may be: biometrics collection, counter-IED, counterterrorist, counternarcotics, and counter-corruption operations.

(5) **Local Militias and Cadres.** As a short-term expedient to free up other security resources or to generate sufficient mass, the CDR may consider the use of locally recruited militias and other cadres. Being lightly armed, they can provide point security and guard vital installations such as government buildings and businesses. They should not be trained or empowered to conduct offensive operations or arrest and detain people. These militias may be drawn from armed civilian groups including concerned local citizens; former irregular parties to the conflict; or they may be the remnant of the previous indigenous security forces that have remained outside of the SSR process. Should the option be considered, the competing advantages and disadvantages will have to be carefully weighed and judged; the key criterion is that these home guard units must be brought under HN control. Over time, these groups should be either formally incorporated into the HN security infrastructure through the SSR process, or be given new skills and returned to civilian occupation through the DDR process.

e. **Security Force Assistance (SFA).** Providing protection for civil society and expanding security and development zones has historically involved greater security force ratios and been more difficult than first expected. Often, there will be hard choices to be made between allocating troops for concurrent capacity building and operations to isolate and neutralize adversaries, recognizing that the demands of these tasks require different skills and structures. Ultimately, success will involve recruiting, training, possibly equipping indigenous security forces, and embedding with them. It may also entail the creation of nonstandard security forces, such as village or neighborhood guards, to reach the critical mass which population protection demands. In addition to bolstering security force numbers, indigenous forces lower the profile of intervening organizations and reinforce the security capacities of the state. In contrast, sectarian or poorly disciplined forces may fuel the conflict. The HN government may require firm advice, as well as financial support, to sustain the capabilities required. The generation and subsequent training of indigenous security forces should be conducted in a coordinated manner with broader SSR initiatives such as the development of civilian oversight bodies, judiciary and detention institutions, as well as transitional justice mechanisms and DDR programs.

For further details on SFA, refer to Appendix C, "Security Sector Reform," and JP 3-22, Foreign Internal Defense.

7. **Transitions**

a. The JFC should consider moving from an international military security lead to an indigenous lead as soon as practicable. The ability to transfer this responsibility will be a function of two inputs: the threat and the capacity of indigenous security forces. If the joint force is required for the establishment of security in support of a stabilization effort, it is likely that local security forces do not have the capacity to counter ongoing threats. Some combination of a lowering threat and a buildup of local security force capacity will result in an appropriate transition point. This will be a political as well as security judgment. There are at least two options: transition from international forces to an indigenous military security lead; or transition direct to a civil (police) lead (i.e., police primacy). In either case, the international community is likely to be asked to assist the HN government to generate basic policing capacity so that the rule of law can be seen to apply.

b. Police primacy should be the ultimate goal as it can bolster the perception of progress and reinforce the impression of hostile groups as criminals rather than freedom fighters. It demonstrates the HN government's commitment to governing through the rule of law. However, police primacy will often be unachievable until relatively late in the campaign and may even be an alien concept in some societies. Premature police primacy can be disastrous.

SECTION B. HUMANITARIAN ASSISTANCE

8. **General**

a. The humanitarian assistance function includes programs conducted to meet basic human needs to ensure the social well-being of the population. Social well-being is characterized by access to and delivery of basic needs and services (water, food, shelter, sanitation, and health services), the provision of primary and secondary education, the return or voluntary resettlement of those displaced by violent conflict, and the restoration of a social fabric and community life.

b. Civilian development agencies generally break humanitarian assistance into three categories: emergency humanitarian and disaster assistance; shorter-term transition initiatives; and longer-term development assistance. These generally parallel the military approach of initial response activities, transformational activities, and activities that foster sustainability; however, in the civilian agencies, each category has distinct operational approaches, staff, and resources.

c. With civil security, the provision of humanitarian assistance fulfills the basic requirements of human security—food, personal security, health, and survival. Human security includes protection from deprivation and disease as well as protection from violence. The assistance provided is designed to supplement or complement the efforts of the HN civil authorities and various IGOs and NGOs that may have the primary responsibility for providing humanitarian assistance.

(1) During major operations and campaigns, sustained combat operations or atrocities committed by adversary forces may cause humanitarian disasters or near-disasters in the operational area. The presence of joint forces and the dangerous security environment in these situations often drive the JFC to take immediate action to conduct humanitarian assistance missions to save lives, reduce suffering, and establish the conditions for civilian humanitarian assistance provision. OPLANs should include the provision of humanitarian assistance to establish the human security required to maintain operational momentum.

(2) During crisis response and limited contingency operations, the JFC may conduct humanitarian assistance as a stabilizing influence, particularly when lack of security could undermine other objectives of the joint operation.

(3) During military engagement, security cooperation, and deterrence activities, humanitarian assistance may be conducted to assist in development in an unstable or potentially unstable area, to enhance US IO goals, or train foreign forces in humanitarian assistance operations. Such missions, in particular, must be closely coordinated with the local COM and country team to ensure that efforts by the joint force are aligned with development goals established by the US.

d. Armed Forces of the United States participation in humanitarian assistance generally falls into one of two categories. Humanitarian assistance that provides support to alleviate urgent needs in an HN caused by some type of disaster or catastrophe falls under the rubric of FHA; FHA includes the provision of humanitarian relief to affected civilian populations following combat operations in a campaign or major operation conducted by joint forces. Humanitarian assistance conducted as part of programs designed to increase the long-term capacity of the HN to provide for the health and well-being of its populace typically falls under the rubric of NA.

(1) FHA consists of DOD activities, normally in support of USAID or DOS, conducted outside the US, its territories, and possessions to relieve or reduce human suffering, disease, hunger, or privation. FHA is conducted to relieve or reduce the results of natural or man-made disasters or endemic conditions such as human suffering, disease, hunger, or privation that might present a serious threat to life or that can result in great damage to or loss of property. FHA may be conducted as a stand-alone mission (e.g., relief following an earthquake or other natural disaster) or as one component of a larger operation (e.g., relief provided during PO).

(a) With the exception of immediate response to prevent loss of life, military forces conduct FHA only upon the request of USAID's Office of US Foreign Disaster Assistance (OFDA), located within DCHA, and in coordination with the COM and DOS.

The use of military assets to provide humanitarian assistance should be by exception. However, where civilian and humanitarian capacities are not adequate or cannot be obtained in a timely manner to meet urgent humanitarian needs, military assets, including military aircraft, may be deployed.

(b) Typical supporting roles include: providing prompt aid, such as military airlift (i.e., heavy lift helicopters) support, that can be used to alleviate the suffering of foreign disaster victims; making available, preparing, and transporting nonlethal excess property to foreign countries; transferring on-hand DOD stocks to respond to unforeseen emergencies; providing funded and space available transportation of humanitarian and relief supplies; conducting some DOD humanitarian demining assistance activities; and conducting foreign consequence management.

For further detail on FHA, refer to JP 3-29, Foreign Humanitarian Assistance.

For more information on clearing explosive ordnance and CBRN hazards, refer to JP 3-34, Joint Engineer Operations; *JP 3-15,* Barriers, Obstacles, and Mine Warfare for Joint Operations; *JP 3-11,* Operations in Chemical, Biological, Radiological, and Nuclear (CBRN) Environments; *JP 3-40,* Combating Weapons of Mass Destruction; *and JP 3-41,* Chemical, Biological, Radiological, and Nuclear Consequence Management.

(2) Humanitarian assistance conducted as part of NA is normally either HCA or MCA. HCA provides humanitarian assistance to the HN population, while MCA is a training tool to enable indigenous military forces to provide humanitarian assistance. The use of HCA or MCA generally depends on the mission and the capacity of HN military forces for conducting humanitarian assistance.

(a) HCA is assistance to the local populace provided in conjunction with authorized military operations. Assistance provided under these provisions must promote the security interests of both the US and the HN and the specific operational readiness skills of the members of the armed forces who participate in the activities. HCA programs are typically preplanned military exercises designed to provide assistance to the HN populace while also meeting the above requirements to promote operational readiness skills and mutual security. Usually these are planned well in advance and are usually not in response to disasters, although HCA activities have been executed following disasters. When at all possible, the assistance provided in HCA should be designed to increase the long-term capacity of the HN to provide for the health and well-being of its populace. Assistance is limited to:

1. Medical, surgical, dental, and veterinary care provided in areas of a country that are rural or are underserved by medical, surgical, dental, and veterinary professionals, respectively, including education, training, and technical assistance related to the care provided;

2. Construction of rudimentary surface transportation systems;

3. Well drilling and construction of basic sanitation facilities;

4. Rudimentary construction and repair of public facilities; and

5. DOD may provide information and communications technology capabilities and associated unclassified data and voice services for US task forces to support civil-military partners in stabilization and reconstruction, disaster relief, and HCA when it is determined to be in the best interest of the DOD mission, and when the access is not in conflict with HN post, telephone, and telegraph ordinances.

(b) MCA programs offer the JFC an opportunity to improve the HN infrastructure and the living conditions of the local populace, while enhancing the legitimacy of the HN government, when requested. These programs use predominantly HN military forces at all levels in such fields as education, training, public works, agriculture, transportation, communications, health, sanitation, and other areas that contribute to the economic and social development of the nation. These programs can have excellent long-term benefits for the HN by enhancing the effectiveness of the HN by developing needed skills and by enhancing the legitimacy of the HN government by showing the people that their government is capable of meeting the population's basic needs. MCA programs can be helpful in gaining public acceptance of the military, which is especially important in situations requiring a clear, credible demonstration of improvement in host-military treatment of human rights. MCA can also help eliminate some of the causes of civilian unrest by providing economic and social development services. MCA may involve US military supervision and advice, but the visible effort should be conducted by the HN military.

For further detail on HCA and MCA, refer to JP 3-57, Civil-Military Operations, *and JP 3-22,* Foreign Internal Defense.

e. Humanitarian assistance is often considered as a high-impact SC tool—an important tool in winning "hearts and minds" in populations around the globe. The use of military forces to conduct humanitarian assistance has, in many examples, proven to bolster local public opinion in favor of both the US in general and the Armed Forces of the United States in particular. JFCs should be mindful, however, that it has also proven to irreparably harm the US image, particularly when such missions have failed to meet larger expectations for stabilization.

(1) Humanitarian assistance missions should have limited scope that is clearly articulated via public communications. The axiom to under-promise and over-deliver is especially appropriate during humanitarian assistance missions.

(2) JFCs should be mindful of the potential for mission creep and should plan for transition and redeployment from the outset.

(3) Military delivery of aid may politicize humanitarian assistance and is not always welcome by external agencies, particularly IGOs and NGOs that conduct humanitarian assistance every day and consider political neutrality to be their primary means of security. The Armed Forces of the United States, regardless of intentions, may also be either an information target or a physical target for local or global adversaries.

(4) The efficiency and effectiveness with which US forces can deliver humanitarian assistance, particularly medical and dental care, can have the unintended consequence of decreasing the population's confidence in the HN's ability to provide basic care. Possibly even worse, excessive US humanitarian assistance may delay and undermine the reconstitution of existing medical and other basic needs infrastructure in the HN. To mitigate these possibilities, primary consideration should be given to supporting and supplementing existing infrastructure and to ensuring that associated IO and PA efforts focus on the legitimacy and effectiveness of the HN.

9. Evaluation and Assessment

It is normally appropriate to base MOEs for humanitarian assistance on *The Sphere Project Humanitarian Charter and Minimum Standards in Disaster Response*. The Sphere Project, developed by IGOs and NGOs involved in humanitarian assistance, recommends key indicators for provision of water, sanitation, food, health, shelter, and non-food items in disasters, and establishes voluntary minimum standards for each sector.

**SOCIAL WELL-BEING
NECESSARY CONDITIONS**

Access to and Delivery of Basic Needs Services

The population has equal access to and can obtain adequate water, food, shelter, and health services to ensure survival and life with dignity.

Access to and Delivery of Education

The population has equal and continuous access to quality formal and nonformal education that provides the opportunity for advancement and promotes a peaceful society.

Return and Resettlement of Refugees and Internally Displaced Persons

All individuals displaced from their homes by violent conflict have the option of a safe, voluntary, and dignified journey to their homes or to new resettlement communities; have recourse for property restitution or compensation; and receive reintegration and rehabilitation support to build their livelihoods and contribute to long-term development.

Social Reconstruction

The population is able to coexist peacefully through intra- and intergroup forms of reconciliation—including mechanisms that help to resolve disputes non-violently and address the legacy of past abuses—and through development of community institutions that bind society across divisions.

SOURCE: *Guiding Principles for Stabilization and Reconstruction*
US Institute of Peace and US Army Peacekeeping and
Stability Operations Institute

---

10. Military Contribution

a. **Dislocated Civilian Support Missions.** These missions are specifically designed to support the assistance and protection for DCs. A "dislocated civilian" is a broad term primarily used by DOD that includes a displaced person, an evacuee, an IDP, a migrant, a refugee, or a stateless person. These persons may be victims of conflict, natural, or man-made disaster. Typically, the UN or other IGOs and NGOs will build and administer camps, if needed, and provide basic assistance and services to the population. However, when the US military is requested to provide support, DC support missions may include camp organization (basic construction and administration); provision of care (food, supplies, medical attention, and protection); and placement (movement or relocation to other countries, camps, and locations). An important priority for the management of DCs should be to utilize the services and facilities of non-DOD agencies when coordination can be accomplished, as DC operations are often long term and require enormous resourcing normally not immediately available through DOD sources. Relief providers must take care not to construct camps with a sense of permanence that discourage return, repatriation, or resettlement. Within DCHA, OFDA will normally lead efforts in support of IDPs, while PRM leads efforts to support refugees. Such efforts are supported by DOD's Office of Humanitarian Assistance, Disaster Relief, and Mine Action (OHDM).

b. **Trafficking in Persons (TIP).** Trafficking victims are persons subjected to sex trafficking (i.e., recruitment, harboring, transportation, provision, or obtaining of a person for the purpose of a commercial sex act) in which a commercial sex act is induced by force, fraud, or coercion, or in which the person induced to perform such act has not attained 18 years of age; or the recruitment, harboring, transportation, provision, or obtaining of a person for labor or services, through the use of force, fraud, or coercion for the purpose of subjection to involuntary servitude, peonage, debt bondage, or slavery. Simply stated, TIP is modern-day slavery, involving victims who are forced, defrauded, or coerced into labor or sexual exploitation. Ongoing TIP in an area undermines ongoing stabilization efforts, as well as US and HN legitimacy. DOS's Office to Monitor and Combat Trafficking in Persons normally leads efforts in this area, with support from USAID, ICITAP, DOJ's Office of Overseas Prosecutorial Development, Assistance, and Training (OPDAT), and the Department of Labor's Bureau of International Labor Affairs.

(1) Ongoing security activities, such as border protection and freedom of movement activities, should support the HN's battle against TIP. In particular, the protection of vulnerable populations, such as women and children, from TIP activities is a key part of population security.

(2) Additionally, CDRs should deter activities of Service members, civilian employees, indirect hires, contract personnel, and command-sponsored dependents that would facilitate or support TIP, domestically and overseas.

c. **Emergency Food Assistance and Food Security.** IGOs such as the World Food Programme, NGOs such as Cooperative for Assistance and Relief Everywhere, and USG agencies such as USAID can be expected to provide for the food needs of the relevant population. In some cases, military involvement may consist of providing security for food aid warehouses and delivery convoys in uncertain and hostile environments. It may be appropriate for military planners to consider effects on food production and distribution among affected populations when developing operation plans. One approach to estimating the degree of hunger in a population is the household hunger scale, a rapid assessment methodology used by USAID. Food security activities are normally led by DCHA, with support from OHDM; OFDA; USAID's Bureau of Economic Growth, Agriculture, and Trade (EGAT) and Food for Peace; and the US Department of Agriculture's Foreign Agricultural Service (FAS).

d. **Shelter.** Although the basic need for shelter is similar in most emergencies, considerations such as the kind of housing needed, the design used, what materials are available, who constructs the housing, and how long it must last will differ significantly in each situation. More particularly, materials and design should meet the minimum technical standards for the different climatic conditions.

(1) Although the general perception is that shelter must be available before other services can be developed properly, the proposed way forward would be to install other services concurrently with shelter.

(2) The best way to meet emergency shelter needs is to provide materials similar to those used by the displaced population or the local population. Only if such materials cannot be adequately acquired locally should emergency shelter material be brought into the country. If possible, materials should be provided which can be reused later in permanent reconstruction. Whenever practical, maximum use should also be made of materials which can be salvaged from damaged buildings.

(3) "Temporary housing" (usually prefabricated) should be avoided. These units are often very expensive, involve transport problems, and absorb resources, which might be better directed toward permanent reconstruction. Such units or the sites chosen for them have often been found unsuitable for local patterns of family life and cultural traditions. Moreover, prefabricated units tend not to be replaced.

(4) Tents may address emergency shelter needs, especially when local materials are not available, but provide no long-term solution either. In case of natural disasters, only the necessary minimum time, efforts, and resources should be committed to temporary emergency shelter. Permanent reconstruction should be promoted as soon as possible.

e. OFDA's Technical Assistance Group (TAG) provides OFDA with a skilled cadre of technical experts in a variety of fields relevant to its disaster response mechanism. It is divided into a number of subgroups that include food security, health, most vulnerable populations, and natural hazards groups. The JFC should coordinate through OFDA to obtain relevant expertise from the TAG in evaluation and assessment, as well as the design of humanitarian assistance operations.

f. **Other Non-Food Relief.** Disaster-affected households and those displaced from their dwellings often possess only what they can salvage or carry, and the provision of appropriate non-food items may be required to meet their personal hygiene needs, to prepare and eat food, and to provide the necessary thermal comfort. The most individual level of response is the provision of bedding (blankets, mats) and clothing. Non-food relief, including shelter, is led by DCHA/OFDA, with support from OHDM.

g. **Humanitarian Demining Assistance.** Humanitarian demining assistance is defined as activities related to the furnishing of education, training, and technical assistance with respect to the detection and clearance of land mines and other ERW. ERW includes both UXO and AXO. Humanitarian demining assistance is a form of humanitarian assistance and normally does not support military operations; humanitarian demining assistance must not be confused with tactical countermine operations. Within DOS, the Office of Weapons Removal and Abatement serves as the lead organization in coordinating all USG humanitarian mine action activities worldwide. DOD humanitarian demining programs are coordinated by the designated CCDR humanitarian mine action program manager, funded by the Defense Security Cooperation Agency (DSCA) Overseas Humanitarian, Disaster, and Civic Aid (OHDACA) funds, and coordinated with interagency partners by the office of the Assistant Secretary of Defense for Special Operations and Low-Intensity Conflict and Interdependent Capabilities. The clearance of landmines and ERW as part of humanitarian or population security measures should be carefully considered in light of US law. In accordance with Title 10, US Code (USC), Section 407, no member of the Armed Forces of the United States, while providing humanitarian demining assistance, will engage in the physical detection, lifting, or destroying of land mines or other ERW (unless the member does so for the concurrent purpose of supporting a US military operation); or provide such assistance as part of a military operation that does not involve the Armed Forces of the United States.

For further details on humanitarian demining assistance, refer to Chairman of the Joint Chiefs of Staff Instruction (CJCSI) 3207.01B, Military Support to Humanitarian Mine Actions; *JP 3-15,* Barriers, Obstacles, and Mine Warfare for Joint Operations; *the United Nations Electronic Mine Information Network: http://www.mineaction.org; and the DOD Humanitarian Demining Research and Development Homepage: http://www.humanitariandemining.org.*

h. **Public Health**

(1) Joint force operations to rebuild and protect infrastructure, potable water, proper sewage disposal, and essential health services that contribute significantly to the health of the HN population must be closely planned and coordinated with the HN ministries and USG agencies responsible for health sector redevelopment assistance. USG public health stabilization and reconstruction efforts are normally led at the country level by a USAID mission with technical and program assistance from USAID regional and technical bureaus (e.g., the Bureaus for Global Health), the Centers for Disease Control and Prevention, and DOS. Military health forces can play either a lead or support role in health sector reconstruction operations.

(2) The JFC may employ forces to conduct medical HCA to support local military and civilian health systems or provide direct public health care to include primary medical, dental, veterinary, and other needed care. Medical civil-military operations must always be

coordinated closely with USAID/OFDA health advisors, other USG agencies, HN medical authorities, NGOs, and IGOs. Primary consideration must be given to supporting and supplementing existing medical infrastructure. The JFC must avoid operations that supplant existing public health and medical infrastructure or subvert longer-term plans.

(3) During stability operations the military may need to provide public health services for humanitarian reasons as well as to build community trust in the HN government. When authorized, US forces may provide short-term health care to foreign civilian populations on an urgent or emergent basis (within resource limitations). The JFC and joint staff surgeon, in consultation with legal authorities, must develop written guidance for the treatment and disposition of non-emergent and non-military patients that are consistent across the theater. Such care will be terminated as soon as the foreign civilian population can be returned to its national health system. Medical personnel may be called on to assist in reestablishing and supporting indigenous medical infrastructure, particularly those affected by disaster. However, while improving the HN public health systems fosters self-sufficiency and may contribute to accomplishing the US military mission sooner, care must be taken to ensure that health care standards are appropriate for the local population and at a level that can be maintained by the existing HN medical infrastructure.

(4) Health sector planning in stability operations requires identifying objectives that link the initial response activities of humanitarian relief, transformational activities, and activities that foster sustainability.

For further details regarding the provision of aid in public health, refer to JP 4-02, Health Service Support; *JP 3-29,* Foreign Humanitarian Assistance; *and JP 3-57,* Civil-Military Operations.

i. **Education.** Military activities to support education programs generally focus on physical infrastructure. In some cases, trained personnel with appropriate civilian backgrounds provide additional services such as administrative or educational expertise. The efforts of civilian organizations aim to improve adult literacy, train teachers and administrators, develop curricula, and improve school-age access to education. As with any infrastructure support, military planners must ensure that schools or other contributions from the joint force are closely coordinated with HN authorities to ensure long-term sustainability. USAID's EGAT normally leads stabilization efforts in education.

11. **Transitions**

a. Because humanitarian assistance is largely a civilian endeavor, with the military in a supporting role, the termination of US or multinational military humanitarian assistance activities will not normally coincide with the termination of international efforts. Generally, military forces operate in the initial stages of disaster relief to fill immediate gaps in assistance; military objectives will be to enable civilian control of disaster relief efforts (HN, international, or USG agency).

b. The transition of humanitarian efforts to HN authorities will not occur by default. Planning of humanitarian assistance must involve extensive international and interagency coordination from the very beginning to ensure a successful transition. Humanitarian efforts by the joint force should support the lead USG agency in restoring the capacity of the HN. The goal is to transition all efforts to HN, USG civilian agency, IGO, or NGO ownership to permit an orderly reduction of the joint force's involvement and presence. All MOE, end state, transition, and termination planning should reflect this goal.

For more information, refer to JP 3-29, Foreign Humanitarian Assistance.

SECTION C. ECONOMIC STABILIZATION AND INFRASTRUCTURE

12. General

a. The economic stabilization and infrastructure function includes programs conducted to ensure an economy in which people can pursue opportunities for livelihoods within a predictable system of economic governance bound by law. A sustainable economy is characterized by market-based macroeconomic stability, control over the illicit economy and economic-based threats to the peace, development of a market economy, and employment generation.

b. Though meeting the needs of the population—both in terms of the provision of physical security and humanitarian assistance—lays the foundation for the stabilization of fragile states, economic stabilization and development help to consolidate gains made in human security and enable political solutions. Although security and governance reform remain priorities, early attention to economic growth increases the likelihood of success. Accordingly, while economic measures and reconstruction are not the panacea for stability, they should constitute a significant component of the solution. Priorities for international agencies and forces include measures designed to stabilize the economy, protect and reconstruct critical economic infrastructure, generate employment, and address any underlying economic drivers of conflict.

c. Economic stabilization consists of restoring employment opportunities, initiating market reform, mobilizing domestic and foreign investment, supervising monetary reform, and rebuilding public structures. Infrastructure restoration consists of the reconstitution of power, transportation, communications, health and sanitation, fire fighting, education, mortuary services, and environmental control. This includes restoring the functioning of economic production and distribution.

d. Economic and infrastructure security and development are inherently civilian undertakings; however, the presence of US forces will almost always have an impact, even indirectly, on this area. There may be times when more direct military involvement in economic development will be necessary: for example, when conditions restrict civilian movement or when civilian agencies have not yet arrived in the area.

(1) The protection and, when necessary, restoration of economic foundations and critical infrastructure, particularly during the "stabilize" and "enable civil authority" phases of a major operation or campaign, are a necessary part of OPLANs. In all phases of the operation, planning for targeting and other areas must be closely coordinated with plans for stabilizing the operational environment following sustained combat operations.

(2) During crisis response and limited contingency operations, participation in economic stabilization activities by the joint force will normally occur in PO or other interventions where the joint force had little influence on the conflict and post-conflict environment. The level of participation by the joint force will largely depend on the operational environment, civilian capacity, and the mission.

(3) During military engagement, security cooperation, and deterrence activities, the military will rarely directly participate in stabilization activities involving enhancing the economy and infrastructure. The conspicuous exception may be the conduct of stability operations to rebuild certain critical infrastructure facilities.

e. It is important to emphasize that creating or repairing infrastructure is not the overarching goal; the ultimate goal is to assist the HN to set up the means for the provision of fundamental government services to a target population, with a view toward long-term sustainability of the economy. The importance of this approach and these projects cannot be overstated. As they are planned and come on line, service and infrastructure projects will have a direct impact on grass-roots entrepreneurship, the overall economy, and people's daily lives.

f. When considering economic stabilization and infrastructure, the JFC should be mindful of the fundamental differences in both approach and timeframe between stabilization and development. Conflict is a significant driver of poverty and vice versa. Consequently, US forces will often find themselves working in theater alongside, supporting, or being supported by targeted development programs from the US and other sources.

(1) Stabilization focuses on violence reduction, while addressing the drivers of conflict; it has greater immediacy and visibility in the short term. This lends itself to in-conflict or post-conflict reconstruction. CDRs will face strong pressure for immediate results; many requirements will appear urgent, but can ultimately detract from developing more permanent solutions. In virtually all circumstances, the JFC's ultimate goal, in close coordination with USG civilian agency partners, should include setting viable conditions for transition of responsibility to the HN, both for services and for managing the supporting infrastructures.

(2) Development activity focuses on poverty reduction and addresses the drivers of poverty over the longer term. Development initiatives may be less considerate of current conflict dynamics, while stabilization efforts may be less considerate of long-term sustainability of projects. The CDR should develop an understanding of the drivers of societal conflict and be an advocate for those development activities that best address the causes of local instability. The JFC should consider the use of joint force development funds and activities to avoid creating additional societal conflicts. The JFC should coordinate with the COM and other agency in-country leads to avoid undesired effects.

g. In an ongoing conflict or post-conflict environment, economic stabilization tasks should normally be conducted by a PRT or some other interagency field-based team, such as a FACT with military support and participation. These interagency teams combine expertise with operational capacity to directly support HN local institutions in establishing legitimate and effective governance, including the stabilization of economic activity. Where these interagency teams are not established, local CDRs should attempt to work with USG and other civilian agencies to assess, plan, and conduct economic stabilization and infrastructure reconstruction stability operations.

For further details on economic stabilization and infrastructure, refer to US Joint Forces Command's joint force commander's handbook, Military Support to Economic Normalization.

13. Evaluation and Assessment

a. Each country has a unique economic structure based on its resources, the needs of the people, laws, customs, traditions, and level of development. The four steps performed in an assessment are designed to support the planning process and development of economic goals, measures, and general COAs specifying who, what, when, and why economic actions are to be taken. The assessment should describe the situation, end state, CDR's intent, and national strategic objectives to stabilize a post-conflict economy, reduce the economic

---

SUSTAINABLE ECONOMY
NECESSARY CONDITIONS

Macroeconomic Stabilization

- **Monetary and fiscal policies are established to align the currency to market levels, manage inflation, and create transparent and accountable systems for public finance management**

Control Over the Illicit Economy and Economic-Based Threats to Peace

- **Illicit wealth no longer determines who governs**
- **Predatory actors are prevented from looting state resources**
- **Ex-combatants are reintegrated and provided jobs or benefits**
- **Natural resource wealth is accountably managed**

Market Economy Sustainability

- **A market-based economy is enabled and encouraged to thrive**
- **Infrastructure is built or rehabilitated**
- **The private sector and the human capital and financial sectors are nurtured and strengthened**

Employment Generation

- **Job opportunities are created to yield quick impact to demonstrate progress and employ military-age youths**
- **A foundation is established for sustainable livelihoods**

SOURCE: *Guiding Principles for Stabilization and Reconstruction*
US Institute of Peace and US Army Peacekeeping and
Stability Operations Institute

---

drivers of conflict, and increase institutional capacity. The four steps in conducting an economic assessment are:

(1) **Compile a country economic profile** to understand the policy, strategy, environment, and performance of the economy. The profile provides the facts and conditions used during mission analysis and a baseline level of knowledge to share understanding with other USG departments. In addition to providing key economic data, the profile includes the country's economic strategy, economic and social policies, and the extant economic system.

(2) **Develop a country economic implementation plan,** based on the data collected in step one, that explains the country's economic situation and includes the interests of significant economic entities. This plan provides additional facts for mission analysis and includes assumptions. It should identify:

(a) Pre-conflict problems;

(b) The impact of ongoing conflict on the course of the economy;

(c) The impact of the actual or anticipated post-conflict security environment on the economy;

(d) Ongoing or planned post-conflict stabilization and reconstruction programs by the HN, USG, international and other donor organizations; and

(e) HN country willingness and capacity to implement such programs.

(3) **Identify and analyze the economic drivers of any ongoing conflict** so actions can be planned to mitigate the drivers and reduce the risk of a return to conflict. This analysis should identify the economic COGs, critical factors for mission analysis, and support developing potential COAs. This identification and analysis should provide answers to the questions:

(a) What were the economic drivers of conflict? Ideally, this information would be available from the completed collaborative interagency conflict assessment.

For further details on the interagency conflict assessments, refer to Appendix A, "Assessment Frameworks."

(b) How have the drivers been affected by the conflict's outcome?

(c) What are the economic interests of conflict stakeholders and power brokers, and how did those interests influence the course of the conflict?

(d) What potential measures and COAs can be taken to reduce these economic influences so that the conflict will not reignite?

(4) **Prepare an economic section for inclusion in an initial staff estimate.** This provides a description of the situation, a mission statement, and outlines potential general COAs for military support to economic normalization. This section should include:

(a) Summary of the structure and performance of the economy, environment, country's economic strategy, the anticipated post-conflict economic conditions, and problems;

(b) USG policy goals, both multilateral and bilateral, if available;

(c) Desired end state; and

(d) Potential general COAs.

b. Infrastructure analysis should emphasize what currently exists and what is a critical shortfall locally, regionally, and nationally. Analysts should also assess the vulnerability of critical infrastructure to sabotage, direct attack, or other interference by adversaries or natural disasters. Infrastructure analysis must be tailored to orient CDRs and planners on the priorities for US military, interagency, NGO, and IGO relief immediately and over time so as to prevent humanitarian crises and to reinforce a secure and stable environment.

14. Military Contribution

Civilian agencies have the lead responsibility for this mission sector, but the joint force may render support, particularly in the conduct of initial response activities of infrastructure restoration.

a. **Employment Generation.** Providing employment is an immediate peacekeeping task, a post-conflict objective, and a means of establishing the foundation for future economic growth and political stability. The initial primary emphasis is to provide employment quickly, even if those jobs are temporary and not sustainable. The joint force paying young men to pick up shovels provides a better alternative to being paid by the enemy to pick up guns. Even though the military focus will be on quickly implementing short-term efforts, it is essential that the military and civilian agencies have a common understanding of the problems and risks, and work to align short-term efforts to support civilian agency longer-term economic and political development strategies, as soon as practical. Key determinants of the appropriate nature of the military role in employment generation include the general security environment, the condition of the economic-related infrastructure, the scope of the need for employment generation programs, and the access of civilian responders to the area. The **USAID EGAT** will normally lead USG efforts in employment generations.

(1) The JFC should engage all USG early to request flexible and immediate funding for work initiatives similar to the Commanders' Emergency Response Program (CERP) in Afghanistan and Iraq to quickly implement programs.

For further details on DOD funding considerations, refer to Appendix E, "Legal and Fiscal Considerations."

(2) Creating the security conditions needed to facilitate employment is a key military contribution. The joint force should assist with providing security for all employment activities, not just US projects, as conditions and resources permit. Additionally, joint force efforts to enable freedom of movement for the population, particularly to and from potential employment, are an essential part of establishing security that facilitates economic growth. The JFC, together with other USG leaders, may consider establishing a secure economic zone, a secure area where civilians can engage in commerce and activity.

(3) Military forces can directly generate employment opportunities for the civilian population by hiring local labor to provide sustainment support to the joint force or by funding local QIPs that will employ local labor. JFCs should take care, particularly when directly hiring local labor, to consider local labor market forces to avoid causing inflationary pressure on wages or draining skilled labor from local industry.

(4) Employment generation schemes, as part of political and economic recovery plans, should be closely coordinated with DDR programs to help enable the reintegration of combatants.

b. **Monetary Policy.** Establishing a central bank system and basic monetary policy is foundational to a recovering economy. The military contribution to this establishment is peripheral and should be thought of strictly in terms of providing required security, supporting resources (e.g., USG office equipment, specific CA expertise). Should a transitional military government be required, establishing monetary policy should be among the initial actions. Efforts in the area of monetary policy are normally led by the Department of the Treasury's Office of International Affairs office of Technical Assistance (OIA/OTA).

c. **Fiscal Policy and Governance.** Fiscal policy is an important link between legitimate governance and economic stabilization. The military will contribute to HN fiscal actions by providing security for financial institutions and for cash distribution, including salary or contractual payments, as required. The support of customs policy while conducting border security also contributes to HN fiscal development. Additionally, military input may be required when establishing priorities for public spending, particularly on security programs such as DDR and critical security infrastructure. When civilian assistance is unavailable, the JFC may need to facilitate microcredit and other financial programs, including the use of JFC funds, when authorized. Finally, ensuring that US forces set an example for transparency in contracting provides indirect influence on HN government agencies. OIA/OTA and EGAT will lead fiscal and governance efforts for USG, with support from the US Trade and Development Agency, FAS, and the Department of Commerce's Commercial Law and Development Program.

d. **Critical Infrastructure.** The joint force may be called upon to support infrastructure development by providing security, funding and materiel, CA functional expertise, or construction. Perhaps the most challenging requirement for large stabilization efforts is to conduct an infrastructure design and planning process that determines the priorities and sequencing of critical infrastructure construction, based on the broader planning priorities and resource availability. The restoration of essential services such as sewer, water, and energy is clearly a priority for infrastructure construction, based on both humanitarian and governance considerations. Similar considerations drive the requirement for infrastructure projects in essential industrial sectors, such as transportation, communication, agriculture, and production, though the emphasis on any one will depend on the circumstances. Reconstruction of critical infrastructure may be a labor-intensive activity that also contributes to reducing unemployment. Critical infrastructure programs are normally led by EGAT and the US Army Corps of Engineers (USACE), with appropriate support from the Department of Transportation, the Federal Communications Commission, and the Department of Energy.

(1) **Water and Sanitation.** Water is always a priority to sustain life. It is especially a requirement for DCs. Temporary water infrastructure can be important even to meet short-term requirements. One constraint which will likely be common in water supply systems in crisis states is the imperfect state of the water distribution system. Rebuilding or restoring water facilities as part of long-term reconstruction efforts is usually necessary. Restoring water systems is constrained by the availability of electric power to drive the pumps. During military engagement, security cooperation, and deterrence activities, well drilling or well digging is a popular activity for communities lacking easy access to potable water. In addition to knowing water table accessibility, there are considerations that need to be examined in an assessment: for example, is there the potential for the activity to cause conflict, does the community have the capacity to maintain a pump that is installed or to public works maintenance services, and are there any environmental considerations (i.e., aquifer depletion, wastewater flow). Attention must also be paid to the tensions and linkages between water as a life resource, water as an economic commodity (for personal or industrial use), and water as part of a sanitation system.

(2) **Agriculture.** Restoration of agriculture production is an absolutely necessary recovery activity. Infrastructure requirements in support of restoring agriculture production and delivery are generally neither an immediate nor a high priority. Agriculture production is usually not badly affected by conflict, unless there is a major population displacement or a deliberate scorched earth campaign. Marketing of agriculture products requires access to roads and is examined as part of the transportation assessment. Agriculture requirements, however, should also be included in the infrastructure assessment. The more sophisticated the agriculture production system, the closer the infrastructure restoration requirements need to be examined. Production (including irrigation systems), transportation, storage, processing, and marketing infrastructure requirements may exist.

(3) **Transportation.** Repair of roads and bridges will be a top priority when access to locations with at-risk populations is limited due to damage caused by natural disasters or conflict. The capacity of railroads to meet relief requirements will be part of the assessments. Railroads have the potential to permit high-volume surface transportation that may be critical to long-term economic viability. Additionally, repair and maintenance of the rail services provide employment opportunities. Ports and airports will also need to be assessed. In particular, if ports are necessary to support delivery of emergency commodities or to facilitate the restoration of economic activity, they could be a priority in reconstruction. For the mid- to long term, road reconstruction may be a recovery priority. In addition to integrating national economic activity, expanding the influence of centralized government

can be facilitated by having better roads. The high cost and longer times for delivery of transportation infrastructure, however, must be considered when prioritizing transportation reconstruction activities.

(4) **Information and Communications Technology.** All post-conflict recovery experiences have placed a high priority on both restoring communications systems and assessing the opportunity for upgrading and modernizing communications infrastructures. Restoring land-line and microwave systems to revive previously existing capacities is the first step. The process of assessing requirements needs to include building an effective public-private sector partnership, because private sector investment generally comes more rapidly. Assessing the regulatory environment is a critical part of the process to determine if policy reform and new institutional requirements should be put in place to ensure an effective communications system. While transition to a market-based system that allocates resources economically is preferred over a system of political allocation of resources, care must be taken with regard to winners and losers of political power to avoid sowing the seeds of the next conflict. Media infrastructure requirements will often be a high priority, in conjunction with building effective participative governance. The JFC should be particularly attentive to the requirements of the modern wireless communications sector, to include Internet access, even in regions where the advanced technology would seem to be out of place. Recent experience has shown that the commercial sector puts its earliest post-conflict emphasis on creating a viable wireless network for the full range of wireless applications. Accordingly, planners must anticipate that electromagnetic spectrum management in particular will be an immediate commercial and economic issue, demanding a high degree of coordination between military users, and civilian partners in USAID and the Department of Commerce, and the HN government.

(5) **Energy.** Except for transportation and some industrial and commercial process heat applications, virtually all modern economic, social, and medical services (e.g., handheld and network telecommunications infrastructure, medical equipment, water pumps, commercial and industrial equipment) are powered at the retail or local level by electricity. In all environments, sufficient electrical capacity to power this equipment will impact the ability of local populations to move on with their lives and thus the efficiency of stability operations. Destruction or degradation of power generation and distribution facilities are considerations analyzed during the targeting process. This will include consideration of the extent of reconstruction efforts in relation to the anticipated benefits of destruction or degradation.

(6) **Production Enterprises.** Restoration of certain production enterprises is essential in support of reconstruction activities. Cement and brick-making plants, for example, supply critical construction materials. Metal working enterprises are necessary for normal economic activity. Assessments include the status of production facilities and requirements to restore their productive capacities. In some countries with economies dependent on an extractive industry, like oil production in Iraq and aluminum ore mining in Guinea, restoring the production operations will be a high priority. Restoration of revenue-earning enterprises can contribute to accelerating recovery.

15. Quick Impact Projects

a. QIPs are relatively short-term, small-scale, low-cost, and rapidly implemented stabilization or development initiatives that are designed to deliver an immediate and highly visible impact, generally at the local provincial or community level. Their primary purpose is to facilitate political and economic progress, promoting the legitimacy and effectiveness of the HN government. In areas where the HN government lacks legitimacy (possibly because it has not existed previously or is perceived as corrupt and ineffective), it may be necessary for the joint force to support QIPs without the presence of the HN government until initial trust can be established and relationships built that will help enhance the legitimacy of the HN government as progress continues. In uncertain environments, where it is deemed that the project is critical for early stabilization and cannot wait until the security situation improves, the joint force might implement QIPs. In more permissive environments, it is only where there is a capability gap that cannot be filled by another actor, or where the military possesses particular specialist skills that QIPs are likely to be implemented by the joint force.

b. It is useful to distinguish between two types of QIPs: direct and indirect.

(1) Direct QIPs are critical, rapidly implemented, security, governance, or development projects that directly support a goal on the path to stability. Direct QIPs tend to focus on key elements of security (such as the repair and refurbishment of police stations and vehicle check points), critical enabling infrastructure (such as market places, roads and bridges), or the delivery of essential services (such as schools and health clinics).

(2) Indirect QIPs are rapidly implemented security, governance, or development projects that serve primarily as instruments of influence and are designed to generate legitimacy for the HN government or international forces, thereby indirectly contributing to stability. Indirect QIPs tend to focus on influencing perception and gaining consent. They may be used to communicate positive messages, provide incentives for compliance, facilitate key leader engagement, or demonstrate tangible benefits from peace. Indirect QIPs are particularly effective where lack of demonstrable progress is seen as an important driver of instability. Examples include the construction or refurbishment of parks, the clearance of waste or drainage systems, and broader infrastructure refurbishment programs. Often, the most appropriate indirect QIPs are ones which cluster projects by visibly rolling out initiatives in sufficient numbers to create the perception of systematic change.

c. Where PRTs or other interagency field-based teams (e.g., FACTs) exist, much of this activity will be funded, planned, and implemented by development agencies coordinated through the PRT or interagency team. In these circumstances, development and security activities will need to be mutually reinforcing within a civil-military integrated plan. In other circumstances, however, the JFC should understand the various sources of funding himself to capitalize on opportunities for QIPs as they arise. The sources of funding for QIPs are varied and change frequently. QIPs should always be planned with lead civilian agencies accountable for transition and development assistance to avoid unintended negative impact on longer-term assistance, such as building clinics in areas that cannot maintain their operations.

For further details on funding and authorities for stability operations, refer to Appendix E, "Legal and Fiscal Considerations."

d. **Guidelines for the Effective Use of Quick Impact Projects.** As previously noted, joint force action should be assessed by its actual or potential contribution toward influencing the key conflict relationship within the society and shaping the eventual political settlement. It is on this basis that the utility of each QIP must ultimately be assessed. To help the CDR balance short -and long-term imperatives and avoid unintended consequences, a number of guidelines for the effective use of QIPs are provided:

(1) **Participation.** Ensure that the host community and local government are involved in selecting, planning, design, and delivery.

(2) **Influence.** Ensure that there is a strategy for communicating the positive benefits of the project that politically significant communities are included and that appropriate HN and local community leaders are engaged. Use the project to promote understanding, if not reconciliation, across sectarian divides and shape the emerging political settlement.

(3) **"Do No Harm."** Ensure that the project is conflict-sensitive and avoids creating or exacerbating conflicts, jealousies, or rivalries by the selection of beneficiaries.

(4) **Efficiency.** Ensure resources are used in the most efficient and cost-effective way and that the project is not diverting resources from more important ones.

(5) **Timeliness.** Ensure that the project will be implemented or completed in a time frame relevant to the JFC's overall campaign.

(6) **Sustainability.** Address recurrent costs associated with the project, and when possible, link the project to longer-term HN development initiatives.

(7) **Coordination.** Ensure the project coheres with national priorities and is coordinated with the activities of other relevant participants.

(8) **Delivery.** Ensure that the most appropriate agency delivers the project, favoring local expertise and civilian agencies whenever practicable.

(9) **Monitoring and Evaluation.** Ensure there is a plan for assessing the project's effectiveness as well as its impact on the overall conflict dynamics.

(10) **Technology.** Ensure the project is technologically appropriate for the community.

16. **Other Considerations**

a. **Ownership Issues.** A fundamental question that must be addressed as infrastructure projects are planned will be public versus private ownership of the project. USAID's broad experience in this area concludes that in most circumstances, private ownership is the desired end state. This involves a transformation from a culture where revenue to pay for utility infrastructure is acquired politically and utility services are likewise allocated among political allies, to a culture where investors pay for utility infrastructure and users of utility services pay fees that recover, at a minimum, the cost of construction, operations, and maintenance. Joint planners supporting civilian agencies that are implanting regulatory reforms must be wary of old political structures reemerging in almost-new forms.

(1) **Full Privatization.** The shift to privatization in infrastructure and utility operation represents a profound reassessment of conventional public policy. The old and deceptively simple model of state ownership is rife with underinvestment, under-pricing (revenue inadequacy), high costs, low productivity, poor service quality, theft of service, political interference, and a general lack of transparency. USAID has found that privatization, if accompanied by unbundling of assets and regulatory reform, offers the highest potential for increased investment, cost-reflective tariffs, incentives for efficiency, access to superior management and service quality, political insulation, and greater transparency. All of these factors are crucial for long-term effectiveness of the utility or infrastructure project. Key stakeholders in any privatization plan will include: shareholders, politicians, boards, regulators, business managers, and, at the end of the chain, the customers who will both consume the service and pay the tariffs.

(2) **Partial Privatization.** In some circumstances, the joint force may find that local political leaders or the prevailing political culture may be unwilling to risk the certain controversy and possible loss of support that privatization may entail. In this case, joint force infrastructure planners must look at the option of improving, as far as possible, the performance of a state-owned utility, particularly as it relates to the relationship between the business itself and its government "owners." The underlying issue will be improving, and in some cases developing from scratch, a climate of highly professional corporate governance. Assuming there are credible local authorities with whom to consult or negotiate, it will be critical for the host government to make a viable commitment to cost-covering tariffs (or a cost-covering combination of tariffs and subsidies). Without such a commitment, private investors will most likely not buy into the utility. Strong consideration must also be given to reducing the government's fundamental conflict of interest in being both the owner and manager of the utility.

b. **Cost Recovery.** In the realm of stabilization-related infrastructure development, particularly regarding utilities, JFCs must keep in mind the long-term nature of the project, which by necessity means that the local population must, in one way or another, act as true customers, and actually pay for the services they receive from the utility. As part of the larger reform of a utility, cost recovery is often less an issue of willingness to pay and more an issue of willingness to charge. Operating costs will include, among others: salaries, energy, costs of goods or services sold, maintenance, information technology, capital costs including debt and equity, etc. Long-term success for a complex project demands contract agreements and operating plans designed from the start to create a system that is financially solvent. The old adage, "There is no free lunch," must apply. JFCs should work with local authorities and civic leaders to help develop a "culture of payment" with the recipient population. Achieving a culture of payment will necessitate a break with prior political arrangements. Planners will need to assess whether publicly emphasizing such a break will calm or incite the political environment, but regardless, the new approach must be perceived to be a fair and just break with the past. Project costs may be direct, as noted above, or hidden. Security concerns in particular have been shown to add up to 20 percent to an enterprise's operating expenses. In this regard, military planners may not even be aware of the extent to which their normal force protection posture would add to a utility's budget once the intervention force is re-deployed, assuming concomitant security requirements remain steady. Turnover plans should factor this into the equation.

c. **Getting Services to Those in Need.** A key subset of cost recovery will be designing a system that will help ensure continued delivery of utility services to those in need. Direct subsidies should be avoided, where possible, as they will generally create a situation where customers and managers will lose the will to work toward actual cost recovery. A subsidized "safety net" of sorts can be designed, but can only be effective if the households are legally connected to the system and accurately metered. Poorly designed subsidies will often have the unintended consequence of encouraging inefficient consumption by the household and provide disincentives for the utility to reduce costs or expand its service.

d. **Contracting as a Management Tool.** Planners will need to distinguish between contracting for construction services and creating operating contracts to manage re-established utility services. In many post-conflict and natural disaster scenarios, simply rebuilding the infrastructure and turning it back to local authorities will not ensure improved services. USAID has learned over the years that the use of incentive-based operating contracts will often mitigate the original weak capacity of the utility staff. If operating contracts are used, planners need to factor in indigenous capacity building so that local staffs will ultimately be able to manage their own assets.

e. **Business, Legal, and Regulatory Environment.** Infrastructure is not just physical facilities. It is often a set of businesses that own, operate, and renew infrastructure facilities. A joint force is likely to be required to reform an existing enabling environment under which the infrastructure operates. This will involve "fixing" corporate form and governance, laws, regulation, public funding, capital markets, infrastructure institutions and facilities. It is the **business** that operates and maintains the system. As such, a "bankable" utility has enough cash to pay all its costs, including operational and capital costs; has a predictable means of recovering its revenue requirements; has sufficient financial controls to meet high standards of creditworthiness; and can deal with the financial risks that happen in the normal course of business. It is important that statutory authorities for government operation exist before expectation of government performance can be realized. Infrastructure and services practitioners will be highly affected by the larger environment of a fragile or recovering government structure.

f. The joint force may be intervening in a societal environment where some level of regulation was already in place, but is now at some other level dysfunctional. In that case, reforms to existing structures must begin at the beginning, fixing the corporate form and governance, getting the sector structure and enabling environment right, with the recognition that costs will ratchet up as the full nature of the service-infrastructure system builds to maturity. Sequencing the reconstruction is vitally important and runs from the cheap (e.g., enacting law and establishing regulation and private sector participation); to the mixed costs of credit enhancements, improved bureaucratic efficiency, and access for the poor; to the expensive (e.g., physical utility construction, distribution systems, renewable energy). Key indicators of an effective business environment include: improved mechanisms for enforcing contracts; improving employment law; simplifying tax administration; and improved political governance (i.e., improved accountability of the government to its citizens).

g. JFCs who are facing the task of establishing a reformed regulatory environment should begin with a thorough review of the Organization for Economic Cooperation and Development's (OECD) *OECD Principles of Corporate Governance (2004)*. The OECD Principles focus on governance problems that result from the separation of ownership and control. Corporate governance involves a set of relationships between a company's management, its board, its shareholders, and other stakeholders. Corporate governance also provides the structure through which the objectives of the company are set and the means of attaining those objectives and monitoring performance are determined. Good corporate governance should provide proper incentives for the board and management to pursue objectives that are in the interests of the company and its shareholders and should facilitate effective monitoring. The principles are:

(1) Design and plan through regulatory and governance structures before taking physical actions;

(2) Consult with local leadership and higher-level political players;

(3) Consult with USG civilian agencies, especially USAID EGAT in coordination with the US embassy; and

(4) Study the full OECD Corporate Governance document, which can be found online at: www.oecd.org/daf/corporateaffairs/principles/text.

h. **Maintenance Standards.** From the moment a project or piece of equipment comes into being, it begins an inexorable process of deterioration. During a crisis response operation, normal long-term maintenance requirements for facilities and equipment are often rightly put aside in favor of more immediate operational results. Additionally, the majority of joint force interventions will likely be into areas and cultures where Western standards of maintenance are only honored by exception. Therefore, for joint force efforts to have lasting effect the programs and systems must be designed with the expectation of inadequate maintenance. Project managers can accomplish multiple goals by enlisting local populations for ongoing maintenance efforts. In addition to keeping projects functioning, employing locals can create over the long-term a small business or team of businesses that supports broader economic growth in the community.

i. **Security.** Construction of security boundaries and other force protection infrastructure is a well-understood military mission. If physical security for facilities and local populations is not assured first, very little else can be constructively accomplished. In the absence of physical security, workers can be driven away, facilities destroyed, and local populations terrorized into submission to, or even cooperation with, adversaries. That said, civilian-oriented services and infrastructure operations demand attention to the latent security situation, particularly when undertaken in an unstable intervention scenario. It is cost prohibitive to erect enough dedicated security infrastructure to protect all essential services facilities. As a result, cost-effectiveness calculations are required. For facilities with high-value assets (e.g., power plants, or facilities that provide crucial resources such as water pumping facilities that can be protected with point-specific security protection infrastructure), it is cost-effective to protect those assets. However, for facilities that have extensive distribution systems (e.g., power transmission lines, underground water pipes) where protection infrastructure becomes far more expensive than simply replacing damaged property, total security infrastructure will not be cost-effective. The greatest security in many cases is provided by sympathetic local populations. If these can be kept secure against external threats, they can multiply the effectiveness of other security precautions, and also degrade the effectiveness of most adversary threats. At times it can be cost-effective to construct parallel, redundant, or "looped" systems to thwart the effects of damage (e.g., road systems or electrical transmission lines that connect at geographic intervals or at the extremities so traffic or electricity can flow back around the damaged loops.)

j. **Accountability, Auditing, and Financial Oversight.** Infrastructure reconstruction work brings with it significant amounts of resources to implement major works. However, without the proper legal authorities and regulatory institutions in place, it also brings the propensity for inefficiencies, exploitation, substandard work, and the reestablishment of economic conditions not conducive to stability and improved governance. Attention must be paid therefore to assisting the HN build the appropriate policies and effective institutions to deter criminality and corruption right from the outset. A conscious and deliberate effort is needed to design accounting systems into reconstruction operations and assign them sufficient priority to assure that they are effectively employed. It is advisable to consult with the inspector general office to get advice on how to do this without detracting from operations. Professional accounting organizations are less concerned with the occasional inconsistency than with systemic neglect or abuse of accounting practices. Initial counseling and following good advice goes far to prevent bad reports and weak credibility of the operations.

17. Transitions

a. JFCs must anticipate the transition from military to civilian program management and plan actions supportive of the long-term strategy. Joint forces can provide immediate support for economic stabilization, but the programs are frequently not viewed as long-term solutions. To maximize project effectiveness, these projects should be sequenced with the work of international civilian agencies and with the private sector to ensure continuity of effort with employees, functions, and support. The military's role is to help restore normalcy and fill the gap until civilian-led, longer-term programs commence.

b. Cooperative planning with other agencies is needed to link short-term emergency programs and transition them to long-term HN and private sector economic initiatives. Recent experience in Iraq and Afghanistan has shown that not nesting local projects with larger strategies often results in projects in one sector having unintended effects in another sector, sometimes in seemingly unrelated areas. Mitigating this risk entails, among other things, continuous communication with HN officials at all levels and USG agencies.

SECTION D. RULE OF LAW

18. General

a. The rule of law function refers to programs conducted to ensure all individuals and institutions, public and private, and the state itself are held accountable to the law, which is supreme. The rule of law in a country is characterized by just legal frameworks, public order, accountability to the law, access to justice, and a culture of lawfulness. Rule of law requires laws that are publicly promulgated, equally enforced, and independently adjudicated, and that are consistent with international human rights principles. It also requires measures to ensure adherence to the principles of supremacy of law, equality before the law, accountability to the law, fairness in applying the law, separation of powers, participation in decision making, and legal certainty. Such measures also help to avoid arbitrariness as well as promote procedural and legal transparency.

b. The rule of law is fundamental to legitimate governance. Perceived inequalities in the administration of the law, and real or apparent injustices, are triggers for instability. It is of paramount importance that all actions taken by a government and its agents in attempting to restore stability are legal. Though human security may be established through physical security and humanitarian assistance, and economic stabilization may be initiated, long-term stabilization requires the establishment of the rule of law. Indeed, it is often the establishment of the rule of law, and a security sector that can enforce it, that will permit the redeployment of the joint force when supporting a stabilization effort in a failed or failing state.

c. In general terms, the establishment of the rule of law helps ensure:

(1) The state monopolizes the use of force in the resolution of disputes.

(2) Individuals are secure in their persons and property.

(3) The state is bound by law and does not act arbitrarily.

(4) The law can be readily determined and is stable enough to allow individuals to plan their affairs.

(5) Individuals have meaningful access to an effective and impartial justice system.

(6) The state protects basic human rights and fundamental freedoms.

(7) Individuals understand and respect judicial institutions and develop a belief in their equity and fairness that guides the conduct of their daily lives.

d. The rule of law in the HN should normally be based on the existing legal framework, in whatever state it exists. However, if the existing legal framework is manifestly unjust and repressive, a source of grievances, and driver of conflict, the joint force should be prepared to take allowable steps to address such problems. The COAs that may be available will depend on the nature of the presence of the US forces in the HN, as well as the policy guidance for the operation.

e. Planning for stability operations to support the strengthening of the rule of law can be complex. However, by adhering to a commonly accepted set of definitions and engaging with appropriate civilian and multilateral partners early in the planning process, military planners should be able to identify those issues that are critical to understanding the operating environment and formulating viable, sustainable strategies and concrete tasks. Efforts in rule of law can generally be categorized as structural, strategic, or functional. Examples of structural, strategic, and functional activities are listed in Figure III-2.

(1) **Structural.** Structural activities in rule of law articulate the components of national and local institutional structures and institutions, and the public knowledge and participation in them that are essential to enabling the rule of law.

(2) **Strategic.** Strategic rule of law activities deal primarily with the substantive political goals and strategic context required to enable or sustain the rule of law. Operations to strengthen rule of law and SSR should be aligned with this larger context if they are to be successful and sustainable. All four are closely intertwined. Sovereignty must be based on legitimacy and respect for human rights. SC is essential in promoting the values expressed by the other three activities.

(3) **Functional.** Functional areas of interest focus on specific types of short -and long-term rule of law-related tasks and missions that the JFC commonly supports.

f. "Traditional," "customary," or "informal" justice are simply terms applied to the broad range of ways in which communities resolve their disputes nonviolently using their customs and leadership structures other than those imposed by formal government systems. In many parts of the world, including those where unstable conditions may require military intervention, traditional and informal justice systems play an important role in adjudicating disputes and providing social order. These systems generally have long histories and a high degree of acceptance by the populace. Often, they function parallel to formal justice systems; in some cases, they are competing. In other cases, the formal justice system of the HN government has broken down, and traditional/informal systems are the only effective mechanisms. These systems should not be romanticized as a panacea for a broken justice system, but in many cases, they can contribute substantially to stability by providing orderly, nonviolent methods of dispute resolution, and, in some cases, can serve as a mechanism to reconcile formerly hostile groups. There are important caveats: sometimes such systems may be inconsistent with internationally recognized human rights standards or may in some cases be a driver of the conflict. Military support to traditional justice systems may mirror that provided to more formal systems, including security for judicial officials and comprehensive reform of criminal and civil laws and their enforcement.

g. **Security Sector Reform.** SSR centers not only on the security forces of the HN, but also on broader rule of law initiatives. The overall objective of SSR is to provide an

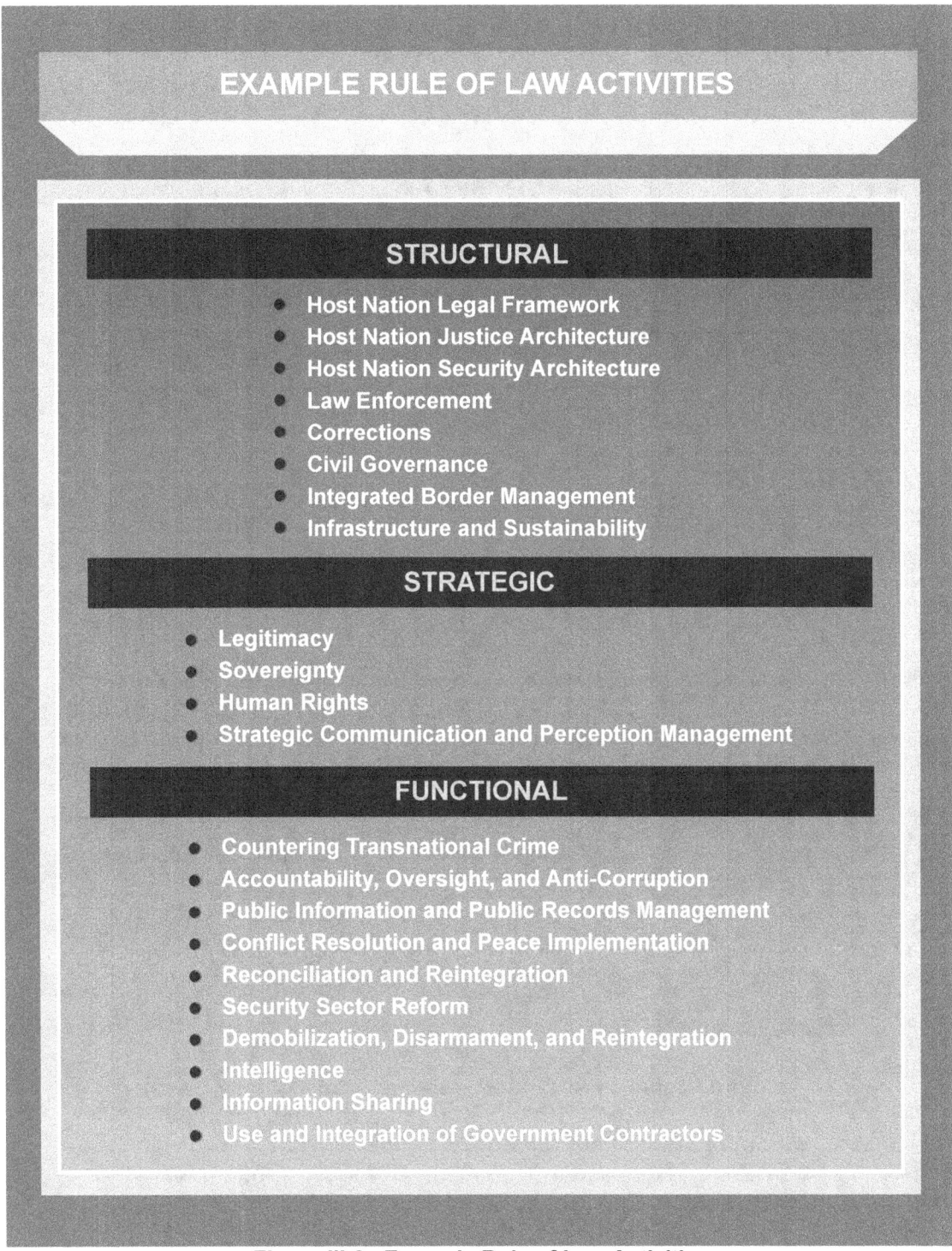

Figure III-2. Example Rule of Law Activities

effective and legitimate public service that is transparent, accountable to civilian authority, and responsive to the needs of the public. Transformational activities and activities that foster sustainability in rule of law generally fall under the rubric of SSR.

For further details on SSR, refer to Appendix C, "Security Sector Reform."

h. **SJA review of rule of law programs.** Programs to influence the legal systems of the HN are not above the law. Apart from US policy considerations, stability operations in the rule of law must themselves be governed by the rule of law; actions must be reviewed to ensure that they comply with applicable provisions of US law, international law, and HN

RULE OF LAW
NECESSARY CONDITIONS

Just Legal Frameworks

- Laws are consistent with international human rights norms and standards; are legally certain and transparent; are drafted with procedural transparency; are equitable; and are responsive to the entire population, not just powerful elites

Public Order

- Laws are enforced equitably
- The lives, property, freedoms, and rights of individuals are protected
- Criminal and politically motivated violence has been reduced to a minimum
- Criminal elements (from looters and rioters to leaders of organized crime networks) are pursued, arrested, and detained

Accountability to the Law

- The population, public officials, and perpetrators of past conflict-related crimes are held legally accountable for their actions
- The judiciary is independent and free from political influence
- Horizontal and vertical accountability mechanisms exist to prevent the abuse of power

Access to Justice

- People are able to seek and obtain a remedy for grievances through formal or informal institutions of justice that conform with international human rights standards
- A system exists to ensure equal and effective application of the law, procedural fairness, and transparency.

Culture of Lawfulness

- The general population follows the law and seeks to access the justice system to address its grievances

SOURCE: *Guiding Principles for Stabilization and Reconstruction*
US Institute of Peace and US Army Peacekeeping and
Stability Operations Institute

---

law, as well as any UN or other international mandate governing the intervention. Such reviews must be done by or under the supervision of a military judge advocate or other attorney duly authorized to give legal advice to military CDRs.

For further details on the rule of law, refer to US Joint Forces Command's joint force commander's handbook: Military Support to Rule of Law and Security Sector Reform.

19. Evaluation and Assessment

a. The necessary first step is an effective assessment that is comprehensive enough to provide situational understanding of the status of rule of law and that describes the deficiencies in a country's justice and security systems and does so holistically. It must take into account the various activities for rule of law and the interaction between them so that as one activity is improved, a positive synergistic impact might occur on another activity, or perhaps even degradation in still another might be an unintended consequence.

b. One of the most important initial steps in conducting rule of law programs is determining what law applies in the HN. Such a determination is essential to assist the HN government in building security capacity; to conduct joint security operations with HN forces; and, when required, to restore, administer, and reform those laws and systems or temporarily administer the HN laws and legal systems as part of CMO either during conflict or in the immediate post-conflict period. Regardless of the type of operation, it is critical that planners understand that the law of the HN will be one of the most important factors during operations to restore or strengthen the rule of law and increase stability.

c. It is essential that the JFC understand the actual state of the legal system. It is not enough to know constitutions, codes, and regulations. It is important to understand the processes for creating, changing, applying, and enforcing the law, as well as understanding the public's perception, understanding, and acceptance of the systems. If the JFC lacks understanding of the HN legal system and how it functions, it will be difficult to make informed decisions about how US forces can or should operate in relation to that system.

d. Understanding the justice system at work requires looking beyond the formal structures of courts and laws. The political and social dimensions of the justice system must be closely understood to strengthen the rule of law. A comprehensive understanding of the justice system includes the identification of key leaders, along with political, societal, tribal, or other relationships that play key roles in the operation of the justice system as a whole.

e. The Criminal Justice Sector Assessment Rating Tool (CJSART) developed by DOS is designed to assist civilian and military leaders prioritize and administer HN criminal justice sectors needing assistance. Once the assistance programs are under way, the CJSART is a systematic tool designed to measure progress and accomplishments against standardized benchmarks. Used in its entirety, the CJSART holistically examines a country's laws, judicial institutions, law enforcement organizations, border security, and corrections systems as well as a country's adherence to international rule of law standards such as bilateral and multilateral treaties.

For further details on CJSART, refer to Appendix A, "Assessment Frameworks."

20. Military Contribution

a. **Establishing an interim criminal justice system.** When conditions require the restoration of governance, establishing an interim justice system is a prerequisite. This restoration requires a wide range of skilled professionals working under a clearly defined legal authority: judges, prosecutors, court administrators, defense lawyers, corrections personnel, law enforcement, and investigators. Civilian agencies normally support the development of an interim criminal justice system; however, when operating in a failed state, especially during and immediately after conflict, the joint force may be required to supply military police, legal, CA, and other personnel to fulfill these roles. The focus of these efforts should be to ensure a basic rule of law with the objective of providing a temporary respite allowing the HN to restore its capacity. The JFC should avoid implementing long-term changes to the justice system, but rather focus on immediate needs to deal with crime while minimizing pretrial confinement. Efforts to establish an interim criminal justice system are led by DOS together with DOD.

(1) **Indigenous police forces.** Integral to establishing rule of law is the support military forces provide to law enforcement and policing operations. HN civilian law enforcement agencies and organizations should provide this capability if the security environment permits; however, in a fragile state, these institutions may have become corrupt or failed altogether. While local civilian police forces are established, the joint force may provide security to police forces conducting regular policing activities and to police institutions. USG efforts to develop indigenous police forces are led by INL, with assistance from ICITAP and DOD.

(2) **Legal framework.** Establishing effective rule of law typically requires an international review of the HN legal framework, a justice reform agenda, and general justice reform programs. Many societies emerging from conflict will also require a new constitution. All efforts to establish and support the rule of law must take into account the customs, culture, and ethnicity of the local populace. Efforts to reform the HN legal system are led by DCHA, with support from INL, and OPDAT.

(3) **Judicial system.** Initial tasks in the judicial system include establishing legal mechanisms for criminal and civil trials. The support provided to judicial institutions parallels efforts with police and security forces to enhance the state's capability to maintain civil control and security. Of particular importance, the joint force may be required to provide security for judges and other officials and their families in order to ensure an independent and fair judiciary. Efforts to establish or reestablish judicial systems are led by INL, with support from OPDAT and USACE.

(4) **Penal system.** The joint force may be required to support the establishment of appropriate penitentiary facilities to support the criminal justice system. Such facilities should be separate from military detention facilities, tying them to the criminal justice system rather than ongoing military operations. Immediate efforts should be taken, particularly in a post-conflict environment, to conduct a comprehensive assessment of the current prisoner population to help reintegrate political prisoners and others unjustly detained

or held without due process. Efforts in corrections are led by INL, with support from ICITAP, USACE, and the joint force.

b. **Personal property.** One of the most vital services provided by the judiciary branch is the resolution of property disputes. In a fragile state, long-standing disputes over ownership and control of property are common. Authorities must implement dispute resolution mechanisms. This prevents the escalation of violence that can occur in the absence of the rule of law as people seek resolution on their own terms. Typically, the military's role in resolving disputes is limited unless the joint force implements these mechanisms in the absence of a functioning HN government. CA arts, monuments, and archives personnel can support the immediate recovery and securing of personal property documentation. Efforts in the area of personal property are led by USAID's DCHA Office of Conflict Management and Mitigation (CMM), with support from DOJ.

c. **War crimes tribunals and truth commissions.** While a military governing authority may operate military commissions and provost courts, the international community oversees the conduct of war crimes courts, tribunals, and truth commissions. As part of the broad processes that represent justice system reform, military forces should identify, secure, and preserve evidence for courts and tribunals of war crimes and crimes against humanity. However, military forces also provide support in other forms, to include helping to establish courts and tribunals, supporting the investigation and arrest of war criminals, providing security to courts and tribunals, and coordinating efforts with other agencies and organizations. USG efforts to support war crimes tribunals and truth commissions are led by DCHA/CMM, with support from DOS, DOJ, and DOD.

21. Transitions

a. The military's role in ensuring rule of law, other than providing security, is normally limited; however, when operating in a failed or failing state, especially during and immediately after conflict, the joint force may be required to play a direct role in capacity building of justice systems and security sectors. As soon as the security situation warrants, these programs should be transitioned to civilian agencies, either from the US or multinational partners, or those of the HN.

b. Efforts to implement rule of law programs are closely coordinated with governance programs. Both programs will transition together as the situation and the mission allows.

SECTION E. GOVERNANCE AND PARTICIPATION

22. General

a. Governance and participation refers to programs conducted to help the people to share, access, or compete for power through nonviolent political processes and to enjoy the collective benefits and services of the state. Stable governance is characterized by a government that provides essential services and serves as a responsible steward of public resources; government officials who are held accountable through political and legal processes; and a population that can participate in governance through civil society organizations, an independent media, and political parties. Stable governance is the mechanism through which basic human needs of the population are largely met, respect for minority rights is assured, conflicts are managed peacefully through inclusive political processes, and competition for power occurs nonviolently.

b. Stable governance provides a foundation on which rule of law and economic activity can thrive and become drivers of security and stability. Support to effective governance involves establishing rules and procedures for political decision making, strengthening public sector management and administrative institutions and practices, providing public services in an effective and transparent manner, and providing civil administration that supports lawful economic activity and enterprise.

c. Effective and legitimate governance and functional, efficient, and transparent public administration cannot be imposed on a nation by external forces, no matter how well-intentioned. Sustainable civil society can only be implemented by the HN. Stabilization efforts that seek to build local governance and participation capacity must ensure their initiatives encourage HN responsibility for these processes and align with long-term USG objectives concerning the HN and the region. Although perhaps counterintuitive and initially inefficient, citizens who have been habitually disenfranchised, marginalized, and even oppressed must be encouraged to take the lead in building their own government. Their leadership is essential to establishing successful, enduring HN government institutions. Even when external organizations, such as the UN or regional coalitions, perform certain governance functions temporarily, the processes to build HN capacity—complemented by comprehensive technical assistance programs—are vital to long-term stability.

d. Developing good governance in fragile states requires improvements in every sector, including the military, the legislature, judiciary, and the various arms of the administration. Given limited resources of time, money, troops, and organizational capacities, an understanding of what constitutes "good enough" governance in each particular context, and prioritization become essential. Common activities include initiatives to draft a constitution, institute political reform, and create an effective civil administrative framework to foster civil society.

e. Establishing legitimate HN government generally occurs in graduated stages. First, the contending forces must be disarmed, demobilized, and reintegrated. Then civil society and independent media are given resources and time to grow. Political parties organize under new rules. Ministries are organized and staffed with professionals. Security forces are reorganized and trained. Local elections are held, and grassroots democracy takes hold. Then, as the capstone, national elections are held, and full sovereignty is returned to a freely elected government.

f. To create a durable political system under the new regime, new participants may be needed. The intervening authorities can encourage the development of new local leaders by devolving responsibility for the provision of government services to local authorities and by encouraging local input into decisions. The joint force must also ensure that leadership develops among all factions. NGOs can be especially useful in developing leadership in local communities and among women and minority groups. Members of the diaspora can also be useful in developing or supplementing local talent.

g. As the goal of a stabilization operation is ultimately to return the control of the territory to a legitimate government, stabilization operations should be carried out in such a way as to create and empower legitimate national agencies wherever possible, rather than substitute for them. Not all local governing bodies are necessarily legitimate in the eyes of the population, and so care must be taken not to empower illegitimate groups, without bringing them within a framework of rule of law and accountability for use of power.

h. Levels of local security will invariably dictate the extent of the military contribution in governance. Where possible, the bulk of this assistance, including SSR, will be led, planned, and implemented by USG or international civilian agencies. However, the joint force must be prepared to establish or assist HN public administration, or to provide short-term support to an established HN government or interim government. Where civilian access is limited, the joint force will inevitably be drawn in to those key governance functions essential for early progress. Nonetheless, military substitution for absent international civilian leadership should be considered a temporary solution, and civilian expertise and advice integrated into the planning process through appropriate reach-back or in-theater advisors. DOS, USAID, and, to a lesser extent, DOJ and other USG agencies direct US efforts to encourage and enable the HN to develop a functional government.

For further details on governance and participation, refer to US Joint Forces Command's joint force commander's handbook, Military Support to Governance, Elections, and Media.

23. Evaluation and Assessment

a. The Democracy and Governance Assessment is an assessment framework developed by USAID, designed to assist civilian and military leaders prioritize and administer HN governance areas needing assistance. Data collection and analysis may involve a combination of research and interviews or focus group sessions with key country stakeholders. Particularly when combined with the ICAF assessment of any ongoing conflict, the Democracy and Governance Assessment helps identify and assess key issues, key people, and key institutions in HN governance.

For further details on the Democracy and Governance Assessment, refer to Appendix A, "Assessment Frameworks."

b. The joint force should gather information about the state of the media prior to and after the conflict, including media facilities. Television and radio studios, presses, and communication systems are often targeted and damaged during conflict. Civilian agencies and IGOs require knowledge about who controls or supports the media, including outside countries, political parties or factions, warlords, and criminal organizations. These assessments need to take into consideration what is being broadcast from outside the state and from where.

24. Military Contribution

a. **Support national constitution processes.** When the HN has no government, as may be the case during immediate post-conflict reconstruction or interventions in failed states, developing a national constitution is typically an important first step to establishing a foundation for governance and the rule of law. This may also be a key part of the process for achieving political settlement. An inclusive and participatory constitutional process that helps build broad based consensus on the country's political future may help prevent the reemergence of violent conflict. The military can support this process both with CA functional expertise, as required, and the provision of security and logistic support for key constitutional processes such as debates and balloting. Efforts to support national constitution processes are led in the USG by DCHA, with support from DOS Bureau of Democracy, Human Rights, and Labor (DRL).

b. **Support transitional governance.** Prior to the return or establishment of viable HN control over UGAs, a transitional, interim government may be required. This transitional government may be a transitional military authority, normally established following the military defeat of the adversarial government, a transitional civilian authority, normally established in failed states in which security is not the overriding concern, or a transitional HN government. The military may support transitional governments through CMO support to civil administration (SCA) as well as providing security to governmental leaders and institutions of all branches of the government. Efforts to support transitional governance are shared between DOS and DOD, with leadership depending on the circumstances.

c. **Support local governance.** Even before national governance institutions and processes are established, the joint force should support the establishment of effective governance at the local level. Local governments are necessary to restore and protect the essential services that provide the basic foundations of security and economic stabilization. Additionally, finding political solutions at the local level tends to inform the search for a political settlement at higher levels. The military support to local governance may include restoring essential services as required, providing CMO SCA, or providing security to governmental leaders and institutions of all branches of the government. Local governance support is led by DCHA, with support from DRL.

d. **Support anticorruption initiatives.** Corruption undermines confidence in the state, impedes the flow of aid, concentrates wealth into the hands of a generally unelected, unaccountable, and illegitimate minority, and provides elites with illicit means of protecting their positions and interests. It provides insurgents, and sometimes legitimate opposition groups, information detrimental to long-term stability. At the same time, the political elites who benefit from corruption and oppose anticorruption initiatives may be the same elites with whom intervening forces must work toward political settlement; this requires a delicate balance in governance programs. Support to anticorruption initiatives is led by INL, with support from DCHA and DOJ.

(1) There is no absolute test of corruption; practices that are acceptable in some societies are considered corrupt in others. Some practices such, as bribery, embezzlement, fraud, and extortion, are considered corrupt in all societies. Nepotistic activities, such as patronage, or client-based systems, are accepted in varying degrees. Local customs and norms should guide the CDR in his assessment.

(2) It may be useful to distinguish between significant and petty corruption. "Grand corruption" refers to practices pervading the highest levels of government, leading to

an erosion of confidence in the rule of law. Petty corruption involves the exchange of small amounts of money or the granting of minor favors by those seeking preferential treatment. The critical difference between the two is that grand corruption involves the distortion of the central functions of the state, whereas petty corruption exists within the context of established social frameworks. Only where petty corruption exceeds what is acceptable within local norms, or impinges on the security and well-being of the population, will it need to be controlled as part of a stabilization mission. Otherwise, petty corruption is best dealt with by host government agencies.

(3) Providing legal guidance and assistance to the HN government can help mitigate the near-term effects of corruption. Long-term measures, assisted by civilian agencies, ensure lasting success. The strongest military contribution, other than the provision of legal expertise, is the example set by CDRs at all levels.

e. **Support elections.** The ability of the state and its local subdivisions to stage fair and secure elections is a significant milestone toward establishing legitimate, effective governance. While civilian agencies and organizations that maintain strict transparency guide the elections process, military forces provide the support that enables broad participation by the local populace. This certainly includes security, but may also include logistic support. Support to elections and other participation programs is led by DCHA with support from DRL.

25. Local Governance and Building on Local Capacities

a. Joint force governance efforts should build on the foundations of existing capacity—however insubstantial they are, be they formal or informal, be they national or local. By identifying existing capacities on which to build, governance capacity building is more likely to develop approaches that are both systemically desirable and culturally feasible.

b. While some capacities may be self-evident, many will need to be rendered explicit, often for the first time. Local knowledge will be critical to determining what is likely to work and what will not, while concurrently guarding against the dangers of misjudging the ability of local elites to gain the confidence of and subsequently mobilize the wider population. As such, intervening partners will need to assess the relationships between elites and the constituencies they claim to represent.

c. The reach of fragile states often does not extend to all parts of the country, and some localities may have weak or absent formal state institutions. Different forms of non-state authority, which derives its legitimacy from a mixture of force and local acceptance, often fills a vacuum in state governance. Though not always a panacea, strengthening these informal forms of governance may be a better choice than embarking on slow, costly, and potentially inappropriate state-building exercises. Poorly designed institution building may make matters worse by eroding what local capacity exists.

d. Establishing effective governance at the local level is necessary before developing governance institutions and processes throughout the state. Initially, effective local governance almost depends entirely on the ability to provide essential civil services to the people; restoring these services is also fundamental to humanitarian relief efforts. Essential tasks may include an initial response in which military forces establish mechanisms for local-level participation.

e. In an ongoing conflict or post-conflict environment, support to local governance tasks should normally be conducted by a PRT or some other interagency field-based team (e.g., FACT) with military support and participation. These interagency teams combine expertise with operational capacity to directly support HN local institutions in establishing legitimate and effective governance. Where these interagency teams are not established, local CDRs should attempt to work with USG and other civilian agencies to assess, plan, and conduct governance stability operations.

26. Essential Services

a. Whether following a US intervention or during PKO, COIN operation, or other intervention, or in response to a natural disaster, the restoration of essential services in a fragile area is a key action to achieve security. This basic function of local governance is often lost during conflict and other disasters; efforts to restore governance, particularly at the local level, should focus on essential services—generally referred to as SWEAT-MSO: sewage, water, electricity, academics (meaning schools), trash, medical, safety, and other considerations.

b. Decisions about what state functions intervening forces should restore, and how to prioritize these, should be made in consultation with USG agencies responsible for transition and development assistance, local authorities, and established local sensitivities. Local confidence in government is enhanced by the visible involvement of HN government authorities in the provision of core functions. As such, whenever possible, intervention forces should work through and with local authorities, and be prepared to execute tasks that local authorities lead. However, due to the humanitarian concerns in regard to essential service, in UGAs or areas in which military governance has been established, this preference should not override the need to restore services as quickly as possible.

c. As with all stability operations, the joint force follows the lead of other USG agencies, particularly USAID, in the restoration of essential services. In many circumstances, local or international development and humanitarian organizations may be operating in theater and able to fulfill this function. The military contribution will be focused on enabling them to expand their access to the population. However, only military forces may be able to operate in some areas.

d. Rudimentary service levels can often be restored by locating and working with key existing employees, though new managers may need to be brought in or outside consultants may be required to serve as mentors. As such, experts in public utilities, including CA personnel, should be part of the planning process and deploy with a joint force that will need to restore essential services, to include information and communications technology.

e. Securing the provision of essential services is an integral part to providing physical protection to the population. Because essential services are often a clear sign of effective governance, facilities and personnel that provide these services are often perceived as high-impact targets for insurgents and other adversaries.

27. Elections

a. In a post-conflict environment, elections are often one of the first and most visible steps toward nonviolent political transition, signaling the transfer of authority from the international community to HN leaders. Further, elections can significantly contribute to stability by providing for peaceful dispute resolution and, by giving a voice to members of opposition movements, providing the broad based support and contributing to the legitimacy of the government. In this context, the ability of US or multinational forces to conduct an election support mission successfully, in particular through achieving a secure environment, can be critical to the establishment of a legitimate government and attainment of overall mission objectives. Without the establishment of a secure environment, an election is prone to failure. Rather than promoting the government's credibility and the capabilities of indigenous security forces, extensive violence during an election can highlight the government and security force ineffectiveness.

b. While consideration must be given to the timing of the elections to ensure that they are not conducted before the government and HN security forces are prepared, it does not necessarily follow that all threats must be defeated prior to holding an election.

c. The HN government should implement the election process; however, where HN forces and agencies generate feelings of intimidation and insecurity within the population, international forces and monitoring agencies may be required to oversee and secure the election process. As such, understanding how the local population perceives local elites, HN government authorities, and international forces and agencies will influence the plan for delivering an election.

d. JFCs should anticipate that some military tasks will need to be executed continuously through the entire election process while others will only be required during one or more election stages. While it should be anticipated that joint forces will be mainly concerned with security and logistics tasks, in some cases they may be needed to perform tasks that support HN, USG, and other international civilian agencies election efforts if and when a hostile or uncertain environment precludes these bodies from operating.

(1) **Tasks in All Phases of the Election Process**

(a) **Security.** If HN security forces do not have the capacity, the joint force should conduct security operations to deter and defeat threats to the election process that may occur before, during, and after the election. Security should be closely coordinated with HN security forces and with election officials; these operations should be used, where possible, as opportunities for SFA. Security forces should pay careful attention to the security of key election facilities where ballots and other sensitive election materials are produced and stored.

(b) **Logistics.** Because of its presence and capacity, the joint force may need to provide logistic support for key election events.

(c) **Public Affairs.** PA officers should be prepared to provide public information and civic education in coordination with the US embassy and the HN election authority. Additionally, local media coverage of the election should be supported and monitored.

(d) **Unified Action.** The JFC, or LNOs, should participate in principals, donors, implementing agencies coordination to help coordinate and integrate security and election implementation strategies.

(2) **Tasks in the Pre-Election Phase**

(a) **Elections Security.** The joint force staff should develop a pre-election security assessment and mission analysis, preferably in cooperation with HN authorities. Based on this analysis and assessment, planners should develop plans for elections security, coordinating the plans with HN authorities and participating in (and, if necessary, helping to establish) election security planning groups at the national, subnational/provincial, and local/municipal levels. It may be appropriate to establish a joint election security operations group with appropriate liaison to US, HN, and IGO officials.

(b) **Legal Framework for Elections.** The JFC should be prepared to protect government officials and facilities involved in the development of a new legal framework for elections. Additionally, the joint force may provide election experts, generally SJA and CA personnel, to election legal working groups, if needed.

(c) **Voter Registration.** Plans for elections support should include plans for registration efforts. Voter registration will present the first major security and logistic challenges of the election, particularly during efforts to register nomads, armed forces, and DCs.

(d) **Electoral System.** Military support may be needed to support the establishment of election facilities (offices and polling centers) at the local, regional, and national levels. Additionally, considerations should be made for monitoring candidate security, noting any private security arrangements.

(e) **Host Nation Security Force Training and Mentoring.** If necessary, provide election-specific training for HN security forces (police and military), including principles or best practices in maintaining public order, PA, conduct at polling stations, counting centers, and other election sites.

(f) **Public Affairs and Civil-Military Operations.** PA and CMO efforts should assist in informing citizens and candidates about election deadlines, regulations, and requirements and encouraging participation. It may be necessary to secure critical media infrastructure for election communication.

(3) **Tasks During Campaign and Voting**

(a) **Protection of Election Materials.** Joint force support may be required to support and secure the distribution and transport of sensitive election materials (ballot papers, official voter registration lists, and protocol forms for reporting election results) by authorized election workers before during and after voting. This may include escorting authorized election officials who are transporting ballots and boxes, preferably in the presence of observers, to district election commission HQ.

(b) **Election Day Security.** The joint force should plan to conduct area security in key population centers and along lines of communications and to deploy quick reaction forces with coverage of key population centers. On election day, the progress of elections and reports of violence, interference with voters, or disruption of established voting and counting procedures at polling stations, counting centers, or at district or national election commission HQ should be monitored and responded to as required.

(c) **Election Observation, Monitoring, and Supervision.** Consideration should be given to the security of international agencies that are sending observers to the election. The joint force should coordinate with representatives of stakeholder and donor organizations regarding election security preparations and potential risks to international observers and other foreign civilians who are in the HN to support the elections.

(4) **Tasks Following Elections**

(a) **Collection and Storage of Ballots and Election Materials.** Joint force support may be required to secure subnational/district and national election commission HQ where vote counts are being tabulated and election results validated. During this period, voted ballots and other election materials should be secured during transport, storage, and validation.

(b) Additional security may be required during announcement of election results and government installation, including investiture events.

28. Media

a. A free, responsible, and robust media is an important component of participation. The media can be an important accountability mechanism for the government, helping to maintain the rule of law. Additionally, media can be useful in identifying gaps in government services through advocacy. By providing communications about public and government activities, the media encourage civic participation and empowerment. In short, the media play an important role in stable society, and the development of a free press in an important step in stabilization and reconstruction. Although the development of strong, independent local media is not a primary responsibility of the military, it merits support from the JFC and should be a continuous element of planning primarily assigned to CMO and PA elements of the joint force.

b. Joint forces may establish media outlets to meet the need to convey information to the public immediately, to dispel rumors, and to counteract the effects of hate speech and inflammatory propaganda. These efforts are often designed to preempt or compete with media outlets controlled by adversaries. The joint force may need to fill the vacuum in the provision of critical information to the population about stabilization activities, especially when free and independent media are lacking. Examples include information on the movement of peacekeeping forces, land mine and IED awareness, refugee returns, food and shelter programs, and voter registration and other election information. Outlets may take the form of radio stations, television stations, newspapers, magazines, the Internet, and mobile phones. The establishment of an international media outlet does not replace the need to nurture indigenous media, but it acknowledges that the latter task may take a substantial amount of time. The JFC's PA officer plays an important role in executing this capability of the joint force, and in working with other members of the staff to ensure that public communications, whether through joint force sponsored media or local and international press, help fulfill the SC requirements of the CDR.

c. International and local authorities make decisions about how to develop the media, including whether to focus on private or public media outlets. A key issue is funding, as even private media outlets may not be able to support themselves. Key tasks include the creation of a legal framework for media operations, such as a licensing structure, professional standards, and associations for publishers, editors, and journalists; construction and rehabilitation of publishing houses, presses, transmitters, and other media equipment; and training and education programs for publishers, broadcasters, and journalists.

d. Media supported or controlled by the joint force may be viewed as biased. In addition, media outlets run by the joint forces may attract local talent away from the local media, weakening these outlets and leaving a vacuum when the international intervention is over. At the same time, indigenous media outlets are likely to be associated with contending political factions. The challenge is to navigate between the short-term requirement for providing immediate, critical information to the public and the longer-term imperative of creating healthy, free, independent media.

e. The intervening authorities need to examine the current capacity of the media to print, distribute, and transmit news, as well as the capacity for media education and training. Before designing a media strategy, there are several questions to be answered. Who are the main participants in the crisis? Who are the opinion makers, as well as how? How does the population get information and weather? Do the citizens have radios, televisions, and access to print media and the Internet? The literacy rate among the population is also a critical factor.

f. One of the main challenges in building a free, independent media is establishing an impartial, transparent legal regime that upholds freedom of speech, establishes fair licensing practices, permits the independent media to operate without harassment, and minimizes the advantages that public media may have over private providers. Laws and regulatory regimes often take longer to develop and realize than other governance goals affecting the media. In some cases, postwar governments fail to enact legal measures to support and guide media.

29. Support to Civil Administration

a. SCA is assistance to stabilize a foreign government. SCA consists of planning, coordinating, advising, or assisting with those activities that reinforce or restore civil administration.

(1) SCA in friendly territory includes advising friendly authorities and performing specific functions within the limits of authority and liability established by international treaties and agreements.

(2) SCA in occupied territory encompasses the establishment of a transitional military authority, as directed by SecDef, to exercise executive, legislative, and judicial authority over the populace of a territory that US forces have taken from an enemy by force of arms until an indigenous civil government can be established.

b. The joint force may allow the existing government structure to continue under its control and supervision. This arrangement does not mean the US approves of the existing regime or condones its past actions. It represents the easiest basis for developing a functioning government on short notice, since it is already in place.

(1) The JFC may elect to retain all public officials or, for political or security reasons, may replace all or selected personnel with other qualified people. In some cases, the JFC may find it necessary to reorganize, replace, or abolish selected agencies or institutions of the existing government.

(2) SCA programs directed toward effecting political reform, strengthening government agencies and institutions, and developing self-government at the national and local level are carried out as necessary. This may include performing specific functions of governance, such as essential services restoration and security, as well as providing CA and legal expertise to support and assist HN political and governmental leaders.

c. Replacing the existing government and building a new structure is the most drastic option. The JFC should adopt this COA only if the old regime has completely collapsed or is so hostile or poses such a threat to peace and stability that its continued existence cannot be tolerated. The President must direct establishment of civil administration to exercise temporary executive, legislative, and judicial authority in a FN. The US forces will only assume control prescribed in directives to the US CDR. Within its capabilities, the military authorities must maintain an orderly government in the subject territory.

(1) Territory is considered occupied when it is actually placed under the authority of the hostile armed forces. The occupation extends only to territory where such authority has been established and can effectively be exercised. Occupation exists whenever an HN government is incapable of exercising its authority in an area and intervening forces are in a position to substitute. Occupation establishes a specific relationship between intervening forces and the civilian population, involving rights and responsibilities on both sides. In particular, where an intervening force is deemed to be in occupation, it becomes responsible for the protection of the population as well as the administration of the territory. Here military substitution for absent HN governance becomes both a legal obligation and an operational necessity.

(2) When required to establish military governance, the JFC should establish a transitional military authority to exercise functions of civil administration. These functions include providing for the safety, security, and well-being of the populace; reestablishing and

maintaining public order; and restoring essential services. Establishing a transitional military authority will require joint forces to execute tasks typically performed by the HN government. Transitional military authorities act on the behalf of the population and, in the case of occupation of enemy territory, to secure the occupying force. A UN Security Council resolution or similar authority may prescribe specific or additional roles of the transitional military authority.

For further details on military governance, refer to Appendix D, "Transitional Military Authority."

30. Other Considerations

a. During stability operations, JFCs influence events and circumstances normally outside the bounds of the military instrument of national power. By virtue of their responsibilities to the local populace, they become the executors of national and international policy. They are often required to reconcile long-standing disputes between opposing parties, entrusted with responsibilities more suited to civilian rather than military expertise. They are frequently called on to restore HN civil authority and institutions, to facilitate the transition toward a desired political end state that supports national and international order. The burdens of governance require culturally astute leaders and joint forces capable of adapting to nuances of religion, ethnicity, and a number of other considerations essential to success.

b. **Respect for Religious Customs and Organizations.** The depth to which religious and political factors interact in other societies drives the motivations and perceptions of the local populace. The religious conventions and beliefs of a society may significantly influence the political dimension of conflict. Depending upon how that influence is leveraged often determines whether conflict and instability give way to peaceful outcomes. International law mandates that the religious convictions and practices of members of the local populace be respected. The military force should, consistent with security requirements, respect the religious celebrations and the legitimate activities of religious leaders. Places of religious worship should remain open unless they pose a specific security or health risk to the military force or the local populace.

c. **Archives and Records.** Archives and records, current and historical, of all branches of the former government should be secured and preserved. These documents are of immediate and continuing use to the military force as a source of valuable intelligence and other information. They are of even greater importance to transitional governments by providing invaluable information in running the government. Therefore, the military force must seize, secure, and protect archives and records.

d. **Mail.** Large quantities of mail and other documents are often found in post offices or at other points of central communications. These may also represent an important source of intelligence and other information. The joint force should seize, secure, and protect such materials until the forces can process and deliver them.

e. **Shrines, Cultural Sites, Monuments, and Art.** In general, the joint force protects and preserves all historical and cultural sites, monuments, and works; religious shrines and objects of art; and any other national collections of artifacts or art. The destruction or vandalization of these institutions not only presents potential violations of international law, but also can provide significant propaganda victories to adversaries. The 1954 Hague Cultural Property Convention, ratified by the US in 2009, requires joint occupation forces to "as far as possible support the competent national authorities of the occupied country in safeguarding and preserving its cultural property."

f. **Vetting.** Successful capacity building relies on dependable vetting processes to screen potential civil servants from the HN. These processes help CDRs select qualified, competent officials while reducing the threat of security risks. Vetting processes should include the participation of local inhabitants to ensure transparency, cultural sensitivity, and legitimacy. CDRs should monitor these processes closely to prevent the exclusion of specific religious, ethnic, or tribal groups.

31. Transitions

a. Poorly timed and conceived transitions create opportunities for hostile groups to exploit. This is particularly the case if the HN government fails to adequately discharge a responsibility that was previously successfully discharged by intervening organizations. Such an outcome severely undermines population confidence in the government. However, an overly cautious and slow approach to transition can also lead to a loss of confidence in the government, or a dependant culture that institutionalizes the international presence and prolongs the intervention.

b. The transition of governance to HN authorities will not occur by default. Establishing sustainable governance must involve extensive international and interagency coordination from the very beginning to ensure a successful transition. Joint force support to governance should focus on restoring the capacity of the HN, as well as enabling the other USG agencies and IGOs. The goal is to transfer all efforts to HN, USG civilian agencies, IGO, or NGO ownership to permit an orderly reduction of the joint force involvement and presence. All MOE, end state, transition, and termination planning should reflect this goal.

Intentionally Blank

APPENDIX A
ASSESSMENT FRAMEWORKS

1. Introduction and Overview

a. Assessment is a process that measures progress of the joint force toward mission accomplishment. A constant challenge during stability operations is the difficulty to effectively analyze progress using systematic reliable indicators and data collection methods. Every operation will be unique, and a standard assessment cannot be provided in this appendix. This generic discussion of assessment must be tailored to the situation. Success can be measured by a wide variety of measures such as the reduction of ethnic-on-ethnic violence, reduction in crime, reduced IED attacks, or improvement in public utility performance. An assessment criteria utilized one week may not be valid the subsequent week. Assessment can be highly subjective due to the difficulty in developing a valid assessment framework. CDRs' intuition at all levels may be a useful measure.

b. **Measures of Effectiveness.** MOEs assess changes in system behavior, capability, or operational environment. They measure the attainment of an end state, achievement of an objective, or creation of an effect; they do not measure task performance. These measures typically are more subjective than MOPs, and can be crafted as either qualitative or quantitative. MOEs can be based on quantitative measures to reflect a trend and show progress toward a measurable threshold.

(1) Measurable results to a particular action may not appear for some time. This time lag complicates assessment enormously, because in the meantime the joint force may have executed other actions, which will make assessing cause and effect even more difficult.

(2) Assessment of ongoing operations can provide more than just progress of the joint force toward mission accomplishment. The assessment process and related measures should be relevant, measurable, responsive, and resourced so there is no false impression of accomplishment.

c. **Measures of Performance.** Tactical-level assessment typically uses MOPs to evaluate task accomplishment. The results of tactical tasks are often physical in nature, but also can reflect the impact on specific functions and systems. Tactical-level assessment may include assessing progress by phase lines; neutralization of enemy forces; control of key terrain or resources; and security, relief, or reconstruction tasks. Assessment of results at the tactical level helps CDRs determine operational and strategic progress, so JFCs must have a comprehensive, integrated assessment plan that links assessment activities and measures at all levels.

d. **Assessment Metrics.** The staff should develop metrics to determine if operations are properly linked to the JFC's overall strategy and the larger hierarchy of operational and national objectives. These metrics evaluate the results achieved during joint operations. Metrics can either be objective (using sensors or personnel to directly measure results) or subjective (using indirect means to ascertain results), depending on the metric applied to either the objective or task. Both qualitative and quantitative metrics should be used to avoid unsound or distorted results. Metrics can either be inductive (directly observing the operational environment and building situational awareness cumulatively) or deductive (extrapolated from what was previously known of the adversary and operational environment). Success is measured by indications that the effects created are influencing enemy, friendly, or neutral activity in desired ways among various target systems.

For further information on assessment, refer to JP 3-0, Joint Operations, *and JP 5-0,* Joint Operation Planning.

2. **Interagency Conflict Assessment Framework**

a. The ICAF is a framework that can be used to help people from different USG departments and agencies work together to reach a shared understanding of a country's conflict dynamics and consensus on potential entry points for additional USG efforts. This assessment will provide for a deeper understanding of the underlying conflict dynamics in your country or region.

b. ICAF teams are situation-specific and should include department/agency representatives with relevant technical or country expertise. ICAF teams are often co-led by the Conflict Prevention division of S/CRS and USAID's CMM because people in those offices have conflict assessment expertise, but anytime two or more departments/agencies want to conduct an ICAF, they may do so. Unless they have conflict assessment experience, however, they should request assistance from S/CRS Conflict Prevention or USAID CMM.

c. An ICAF allows an interagency team to identify potential entry points for future USG efforts in conflict prevention and conflict transformation, but it does not make direct recommendations for program design. That is the role of the sectoral assessment. Use of sectoral assessments is consonant with use of ICAF in the following ways:

(1) Results from sectoral assessments performed in the past provide data that is fed into the ICAF;

(2) During a situation assessment, the results of an ICAF identify sectors most critically in need of an in-depth sectoral assessment prior to planning; or

(3) After an ICAF is conducted and a plan has been created, sectoral assessments are conducted to assist in the design of programs.

d. When members of the interagency perform a conflict/instability assessment together, they reach a shared understanding of the conflict dynamics. The ICAF has been developed by the interagency community and has interagency acceptance. Using the ICAF, members of an interagency team are able to focus their discussion on the conflict they are analyzing and avoid being caught up in a disagreement on the process they are using to analyze the conflict.

e. The USG departments/agencies most likely to participate in the use of the ICAF are agencies with responsibilities for planning or programming foreign assistance funds or other international engagements. However, on occasion, USG agencies implementing domestic programs may have technical or country expertise to contribute to an ICAF even if they do not have international programs.

For more information, refer to JP 3-08, Interorganizational Coordination During Joint Operations, *and* Interagency Conflict Assessment Framework *at: http://www.crs.state.gov/shortcut.cfm/C6WW.*

3. Measuring Progress in Conflict Environments

a. To bring goals and resources into better balance and to provide feedback on the efficacy of strategies being implemented, policy makers require an objective system of metrics that will enable them to take stock of the magnitude of the challenges before intervening and to continuously track the progress of their efforts toward stabilization.

b. The USACE, United States Institute for Peace, Office of the Secretary of Defense, and US Army PKSOI developed *Measuring Progress in Conflict Environments (MPICE)* as a framework and a user's handbook—refer to http://www.usip.org/resources/measuring-progress-in-conflict-environments-mpice-0.

4. The District Stability Framework

a. The District Stability Framework (DSF) is a methodology designed for use by both military and civilian personnel to identify the underlying causes of instability and conflict in a region, devise programs to diminish the root causes of instability and conflict, and measure the effectiveness of programming. It is employed to gather information using the following lenses: operational environment, cultural environment, local perceptions, and stability/instability dynamics. This information then helps identify, prioritize, monitor, evaluate, and adjust programming targeted at diminishing the causes of instability or conflict.

b. The DSF has four major components: gaining situational awareness (from the four lenses of data mentioned above); analyzing that data; designing effective programming based on that analysis; and monitoring and evaluating programming.

c. USAID conducts training for deploying personnel on DSF. Wherever possible, USAID seeks to raise awareness of development and conflict mitigation and to help preempt these issues before military and civilian personnel are sent into hostile areas in reaction to them.

Refer to http://www.usaid.gov/our_work/global_partnerships/ma/dsf.html for more information.

5. The Criminal Justice Sector Assessment Rating Tool

a. A fundamental and vital component of rule of law development is instituting a vigorous and impartial criminal justice sector. Proficiency in how to effectively use and measure this foreign assistance, however, continues to develop accompanied by the requirement to organize complex efforts into transferable knowledge for all of USG policy makers and implementers.

b. CJSART is designed to assist policy makers and program managers prioritize and administer HN criminal justice sectors needing assistance. Once the assistance programs are under way, the CJSART is a systematic tool designed to measure progress and accomplishments against standardized benchmarks. Used in its entirety, the CJSART holistically examines a country's laws, judicial institutions, law enforcement organizations, border security, and corrections systems as well as a country's adherence to international rule of law standards such as bilateral and multilateral treaties.

For more information, refer to the Criminal Justice Sector Assessment Rating Tool.

6. Democracy and Governance Assessment

Conducting a DG Assessment: A Framework for Strategy Development provides a framework for constructing donor, in particular USAID, democracy and governance strategies. The framework guides a political analysis of the country, leads to program choices, and incorporates what researchers and practitioners have learned from comparative experience. While every country is unique in some manner, there are important commonalities. This is what makes anthropology or comparative political science possible. Most countries have political systems with elements and basic construction that resemble at least some other countries. Donors, such as USAID, have found that political issues are as important to a country's development as other issues such as health and economic growth and that many developmental plans have floundered on political shoals. In particular, donors believe that support for democracy should be part of their development assistance both because it is good in itself and because it best supports the developmental effort. Host countries also agree, at least officially, since most have signed the Universal Declaration of Human Rights and other international agreements that include elements of democracy. The strategic assessment framework is designed to help define a country-appropriate program to assist in the transition to and consolidation of democracy. As such, it is useful in developing strategies that address the core democracy and governance problem(s) in a country and that identify primary influences and rules of particular institutional arenas.

APPENDIX B
OPERATING WITH THE WHOLE OF GOVERNMENT

1. Introduction and Overview

a. A whole-of-government approach integrates the collaborative efforts of the departments and agencies of the USG to achieve unity of effort toward a shared goal. Under unified action, a whole-of-government approach is driven by the search for those combinations of USG resources and activities that reinforce progress made in one sector or enable success in another. To do this, interagency members must, to the greatest degree possible, resist seeing their resources (financial, diplomatic, military, development, intelligence, economic, SC, law enforcement, consular, commerce) as belonging to any one agency, Service, or entity. All are tools of USG power.

b. The IMS was developed to provide a structural framework for whole-of-government planning in reconstruction and stabilization.

c. Although certain IMS-like structures have been established, the IMS has never been activated. PRTs and other civil-military or multiagency structures may be established in situations where the IMS has not been activated.

2. Interagency Management System for Reconstruction and Stabilization

a. The IMS is guidance designed to provide policymakers in Washington, COMs, and military CDRs with flexible tools to achieve:

(1) Integrated planning processes for unified USG strategic and implementation plans, including funding requests;

(2) Joint interagency deployments at all levels of planning and execution of USG policy (e.g., national, subnational, GCC); and

(3) A joint civilian operations capability including shared communications and information management.

b. Although a full IMS crisis response has never been activated, IMS component structures have been deployed in crises outside of the formal IMS response mechanisms and without using IMS nomenclature. The IMS has also been tested in exercises and experiments to improve JFC coordination with civilian counterparts while conducting stability operations.

c. The IMS could be used to organize the USG civilian response for post-conflict situations, and to help stabilize and reconstruct societies in transition from conflict or civil strife. This whole-of-government planning framework utilizes the *Post-Conflict Reconstruction Essential Tasks,* among other analytical tools, to assist in reconstruction and stabilization planning.

d. A full IMS response would be composed of the country reconstruction and stabilization group (CRSG), the integration planning cell, the advance civilian team (ACT), and if needed, FACTs. These structures are designed to augment existing NSC, GCC, and country structures, respectively.

(1) **Country reconstruction and stabilization group.** Policy formulation is facilitated by, informed by, and organized by the CRSG, a Washington-based full-time interagency secretariat that performs planning and operations functions and mobilizes resources. The CRSG would serve a crisis-specific interagency decision-making body, ideally a crisis-specific Interagency Policy Committee (IPC). Such an IPC would be co-chaired by the regional assistant SECSTATE for the country in question, the S/CRS Coordinator, and the appropriate NSC senior director.

(2) **Integration planning cell.** The IPC consists of interagency planners and regional and sectoral experts who deploy to the relevant geographic combatant command or multinational HQ to assist in harmonizing ongoing planning and operations between civilian and military agencies or the USG and multinational HQ.

(3) **Advance civilian team.** The ACT supports the COM in country to develop, execute, and monitor plans. The ACT provides interagency management, deployment, and logistic capabilities. **When established, the ACT is the integrating civilian counterpart of the JTF at the country level.**

(4) **Field advance civilian team.** If an ACT has been established at the country level, a decision to deploy FACTs to sub national regions or provinces may follow. FACTs, which are an element of the ACT and report to the ACT (and through the ACT ultimately to the COM), are responsible for implementing plans pertaining to their particular geographic area of responsibility (AOR) and for informing revisions of the overall USG strategic plan and interagency implementation plan. They are also responsible for coordinating planning with any US military entities operating in their AOR. FACTs are primarily local, on-the-ground operational entities, but their role in assessments, plan revisions, and sub national field level planning is also important.

e. The IMS can be activated by a direct request from SECSTATE, ideally with recommendations from the Reconstruction and Stabilization IPC, crisis-specific IPC (if stood up), DOS regional assistant secretary, and COM, and in consultation with the Principals Committee, Deputies Committee, and NSC. The IMS is a flexible structure that may be deployed in whole or in part. The purpose of the IMS is to provide a whole-of-government structure to respond to an international crisis when the USG determines that a US response is in the national strategic interest.

For further details on IMS, refer to JP 3-08, Interorganizational Coordination During Joint Operations.

3. Interagency Coordination Mechanisms

a. Whether or not the IMS is activated, US military and civilian leaders should establish appropriate integration mechanisms to ensure unity of effort at each political level of the HN government. When appropriate, these mechanisms should include military and civilian representatives of the HN and other partner nation members. The joint interagency coordination group (JIACG), the US country team, an executive steering group (ESG), civil-military coordination boards (CMCBs), CMOCs, and joint interagency task forces (JIATFs) are key civil-military integration mechanisms that are normally located inside the designated operational area.

b. **Joint Interagency Coordination Group.** The primary role of the JIACG is to enhance interagency coordination at the combatant command HQ. JIACGs help GCCs support stabilization by facilitating unified action in support of plans, operations, contingencies, and initiatives. Whether operating as a full-time element of the GCC's staff or activated during contingencies or operations, the JIACG will assist with the reception of the IPC of the IMS into the staff. JIACGs include representatives from other federal agencies, partner DOD commands and agencies, and other IGO and NGO partners tailored to a GCC's particular AOR and missions.

For further details on JIACGs, see JP 3-08, Interorganizational Coordination during Joint Operations, *and the* Commander's Handbook for the Joint Interagency Coordination Group.

c. **US Country Team.** All stabilization efforts that are undertaken to support an HN government are managed through the elements of the US country team, led by the COM. The US country team is the primary interagency coordinating structure that is the focal point for unified action in stabilization. As permanently established interagency organizations with deep reservoirs of local knowledge based on long interaction with the HN government and population, country teams represent a priceless resource during stability operations.

For further details on country teams, see JP 3-08, Interorganizational Coordination during Joint Operations.

d. **Executive Steering Group.** The COM and a JTF CDR can jointly form an ESG. The ESG may be composed of the principals from the JTF, the US embassy, IGOs, or NGOs present in the operational area, and other organizations as appropriate. Lacking another similar forum, the ESG can provide high-level outlet for the exchange of information about operational policies as well as for resolution of difficulties arising among the various organizations. The ESG may be charged with formulating, coordinating, and promulgating local and theater policies required for the explanation, clarification, and implementation of US policies. The ESG should either be cochaired by the JFC and COM or assigned outright to either individual, depending on the nature of the US mission and possibly based on the security situation.

For further details on ESGs, see JP 3-08, Interorganizational Coordination During Joint Operations.

e. **Civil-Military Coordination Board.** A CMCB is a vehicle to coordinate CMO support. Military membership is typically restricted to key representatives from the JTF staff sections. A senior member of the JTF staff, such as the JTF deputy CDR or chief of staff, serves as chairperson of this board. If a CMOC has been established at the JTF level, the

CMOC director would be a key member of the board and also may serve as its chairperson. The type of C2 structure and the level of staff integration in the JTF should drive the decision to establish a CMCB and determine its membership.

For further details on CMCBs, refer to JP 3-08, Interorganizational Coordination During Joint Operations.

f. **Civil-Military Operations Centers.** The CMOC is a mechanism for bringing a wide variety of civil, HN, and military elements together for coordination, and it serves as a meeting place for these elements. CMOCs coordinate the interaction of US and multinational military forces with a wide variety of civilian agencies. A CMOC is not a C2 element; it is useful for exchanging information and facilitating complementary efforts. CDRs build a CMOC around a nucleus of organic assets that typically includes CA, logistic, legal, and communications personnel. CDRs invite representatives from nonmilitary organizations, preferably in a coordinated effort with civilian advisors or representatives, when they are present. The size, structure, location, and numbers of CMOCs are situation dependent.

For further details on CMOCs, see JP 3-08, Interorganizational Coordination during Joint Operations, *and JP 3-57,* Civil-Military Operations.

g. **Joint Interagency Task Force.** JIATFs are formal organizations usually chartered by the DOD and one or more civilian agencies and guided by a memorandum of agreement or other founding legal documents that define the roles, responsibilities, and relationships of the JIATF's members. The JIATF is staffed and led by personnel from multiple agencies under a single CDR or director. JIATFs may be separate elements under the JFC, or they may be subordinate to a functional component command, a joint special operations task force, or a staff section such as the J-3. JIATF members can coordinate with the country team, their home agencies, JIACGs in the area of interest, and other JIATFs to defeat complex networks. Because they use more than the military instrument of national power, JIATFs are generally not a lethal asset, but rather develop and drive creative nonlethal solutions and policy actions to accomplish their mission.

For further details on JIATFs, see JP 3-08, Interorganizational Coordination During Joint Operations.

4. **Provincial Reconstruction Teams**

a. A PRT is an interim interagency organization designed to improve stability in a given area by helping build the legitimacy and effectiveness of an HN local or provincial government in providing security to its citizens, delivering essential government services, and encouraging fair, transparent, and responsive governance. PRTs vary in structure, size, and mission. PRTs can temporarily augment the HN capability and capacity and facilitate reconstruction. While the PRTs are primarily concerned with addressing local conditions, they also work on building and improving communication and other linkages among the central, regional, and local government.

b. A PRT is a civil-military organization that assists with development and governance below the national level in an uncertain security environment. PRTs operate by combining military CA, security, and other functional specialties with civilian personnel to form a cohesive team. Common military specialties may include CA, IO, intelligence, medical, military police, and engineering. The military provides force protection for the base and convoy operations. In addition, the military normally provides support functions such as administration, logistics, life support, medical care, communications, and vehicle maintenance. The PRT leader can be from either DOS or DOD. Personnel serving in a PRT continue to work for their parent agency and are subject to operating guidelines of their original chain of command for performance, discipline, etc., but are expected to follow the PRT leader's guidance regarding security and internal military PRT rules, policies, and procedures. Although the agency providing the PRT leader may differ from one PRT to the next, the DOS, DOD, and USAID senior members generally form a command group. Deconfliction, consensus, and collaboration should be the PRT objective, but maintaining situational awareness of member activities and plans is essential to maximize USG efforts. PRTs facilitate the campaign plan in a collapsed state setting or the IDAD strategy in COIN or FID that supports an HN.

c. Direction and coordination of PRTs or other civil-military teams is conducted by a national-level interagency steering committee, under the supervision of the COM and JFC (for US-led PRTs) or a multinational executive committee (for coalition-led PRTs). This body will also conduct liaison with the HN national government to support PRT operations. Both embassy and JTF personnel staff the steering committee. Regional authorities may be established with regional CDRs overseeing a number of PRTs to ensure coordination between provinces and with national-level objectives. The regional authority coordinates the deployment and operations of all US PRTs in the operational area, including ensuring that PRTs have a long-term vision nested with either the campaign plan or the IDAD strategy, whichever is appropriate at the time, and the mission strategic plan or other relevant USG whole-of-government plans. The PRT should identify any inconsistencies in USG planning or guidance to their respective chains of command, preferable as a unified effort through the command group.

For further details on PRTs, refer to JP 3-24, Counterinsurgency Operations, *and JP 3-08,* Interorganizational Coordination during Joint Operations.

Intentionally Blank

APPENDIX C
SECURITY SECTOR REFORM

1. Introduction

a. Second only to providing security as required, the major joint force role in stabilization efforts is to help reform the HN security sector and build partner capacity to make it an enabler of long-term stability. The security sector comprises both military and civilian individuals and institutions responsible for the safety and security of the HN and the population at the international, regional, national, and subnational levels. As illustrated in Figure C-1, this includes state security providers, governmental security management and

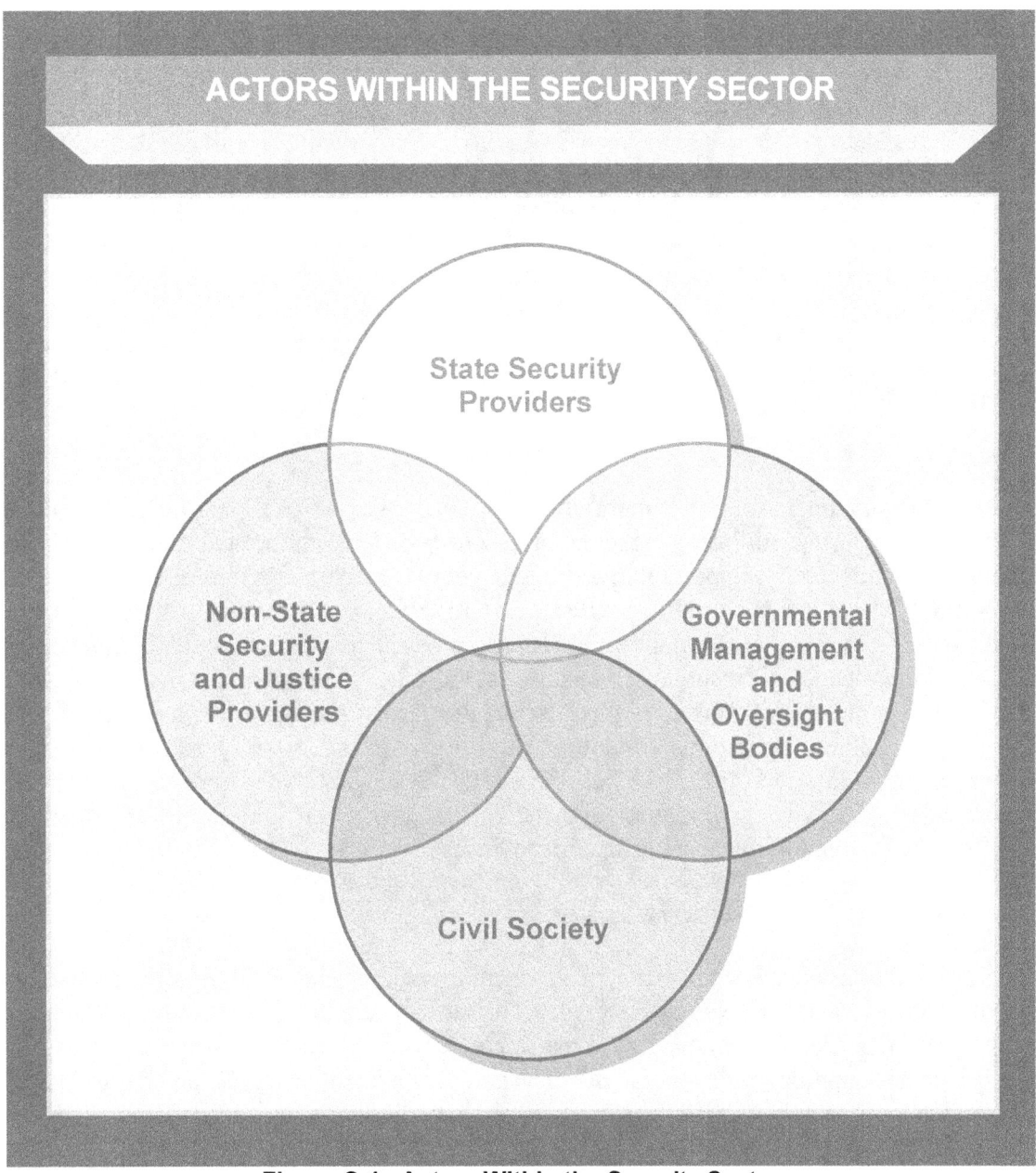

Figure C-1. Actors Within the Security Sector

oversight bodies, civil society, and non-state providers of justice and security. Helping to build HN capacity in the security sector includes stability operations from the security, rule of law, and governance functions; such operations fall under the rubric of SSR.

b. Development assistance benefits from being part of a comprehensive approach in which it is fully coordinated with security-related assistance, as development is at risk without basic security. With that understanding, the USG, along with like-minded bilateral and multilateral donors, has begun to develop a more comprehensive approach to SSR by better integrating defense and other security-related programs with development, and diplomatic tools and resources to assist partner governments to provide effective, legitimate, and accountable security for their citizens. SSR refers to a comprehensive set of programs and activities undertaken to improve the way an HN provides safety, security, and justice. Through SSR, the USG assists the HN to respond appropriately to threats within and outside its borders. SSR may include activities in support of security force and intelligence reform; justice sector reform; civilian oversight and management of military support and intelligence services; community security; and DDR.

c. SSR includes, but extends well beyond, the narrower focus of more traditional security assistance on defense, intelligence, and policing. Forces enhanced through traditional security assistance comprised of equipment and training can better carry out their responsibilities if the institutional and governance frameworks necessary to sustain them are equally well developed. SSR programs should be developed in light of the linkages among security, governance, development, and conflict. Integrating security sector, governance, and rule of law programs into a comprehensive package—in support of US and HN priorities—ultimately proves more successful and sustainable than a series of individual programs.

d. Stability operations in support of SSR take place across the range of military operations. During military engagement, security cooperation, and deterrence, NA operations conducted to support relatively stable yet vulnerable states normally include SSR as a primary component. During crisis response and limited contingency operations, such as COIN or PO, the JFC should emphasize SSR programs and activities to build the capacity of the HN to contend with insurgency, terrorism, and other threats to security, even while conducting combat operations against those threats. During major operations and campaigns, stability operations conducted during and in the wake of sustained combat operations should support SSR to help generate the capacity of the resulting political institutions in security, governance, and the rule of law as an important component of conflict transformation to ensure a sustained peace.

2. Unified Action in Security Sector Reform

a. SSR is a whole-of-government effort and requires the full support of all USG departments and agencies with an SSR role. The most successful outcomes will result only if the activities of all relevant USG departments and agencies are fully integrated in a comprehensive approach to support SSR. The complex and enduring characteristics of SSR demand an approach that capitalizes on the strengths of collective expertise in the USG.

(1) **Department of State.** DOS leads US interagency policy initiatives and oversees policy and programmatic support to SSR through its bureaus, offices, and overseas missions and leads integrated USG reconstruction and stabilization efforts. DOS's responsibilities also include oversight of other USG foreign policy and programming that may have an impact on the security sector.

(2) **Department of Defense.** DOD's primary role in SSR is supporting the reform, restructuring, or reestablishment of the armed forces and the defense sector across the range of military operations.

(3) **US Agency for International Development.** USAID's primary SSR role is to support governance, conflict mitigation and response, reintegration and reconciliation, and rule of law programs aimed at building civilian capacity to manage, oversee, and provide security and justice.

(4) **US Domestic Agencies.** Effective SSR should draw on capabilities across the USG, as appropriate. In addition to DOS, DOD, and USAID, other USG departments and agencies provide important capabilities in the conduct of SSR programs. In particular, DOJ, DHS, Department of Energy, Department of Agriculture, and Department of Treasury may play substantial or leading roles in the development and execution of SSR. These programs should be coordinated among the departments and agencies at the strategic level as well as through country teams consistent with COM authority.

b. The USG is not alone in its pursuit of comprehensive approaches to SSR. The UN is integrating SSR across different UN offices and agencies, including the UN Development Program and the UN Department of Peacekeeping Operations (DPKO). The North Atlantic Treaty Organization (NATO), the EU, OECD, and major bilateral donors have advanced a more holistic SSR concept through combined funding mechanisms and enhanced collaboration among defense and development agencies.

For further details, refer to OECD/Development Assistance Committee (DAC) publication, The OECD DAC Handbook on Security System Reform (SSR): Supporting Security and Justice.

c. Donors for SSR programs will normally operate through IGOs to deliver SSR as part of a broader development plan for the HN, and HN governments may have a preference for working with established IGOs and NGOs. However, some IGOs and NGOs may have a narrow focus and may not be sensitive to wider SSR priorities and the need to build a broad-based HN capability in a coherent manner, so they must be incorporated into a comprehensive reform plan. Partner nations may also bring valuable capabilities that the USG cannot provide, such as paramilitary forces. The UN can take a leading role in DDR, which itself is a multi-agency activity. NGOs may also contribute niche capabilities and consultancy advice, such as in the justice and rule of law sector, and provide local knowledge and established community links.

d. As with other areas of stabilization, the Armed Forces may be required to conduct significant portions of SSR that are normally the provenance of civilian agencies, particularly when the security situation prevents significant civilian participation.

3. Military Contribution to Security Sector Reform

a. SSR planning should seek to ensure balanced development of the entire security sector, as imbalanced development can undermine the long-term success of SSR efforts. The activities of military forces are generally focused on reforming the HN military forces, but those actions may need to be only part of a broader, comprehensive effort to reform various elements of the security sector, as described throughout this section. Figure C-2 portrays the various elements within the security sector and their relationships. Military forces gradually transfer the responsibilities they may have accumulated during combat operations to other participants in the SSR effort, whether from one military force to another, or to civilian groups or agencies. Transitions allow the military force to focus their efforts on their primary tasks of securing the HN and building up HN security forces.

b. The relationship of the HN military and law enforcement is critical in providing internal security to the state. In many post-conflict societies appropriate distinctions between military and law enforcement roles and missions have eroded or disappeared entirely. That erosion could lead to inappropriate military involvement in local community and political affairs, including corruption of criminal justice and law enforcement functions by military forces. A fundamental task of SSR may be to restore the distinction between military and law enforcement functions and to provide robust mechanisms to sustain their separation.

c. **Defense Reform.** Military forces are developed primarily to counter external threats to the HN. The design of these forces develops from the analysis of those threats and the specific capabilities required to counter them. Providing HA and countering certain types of internal military threats can also be a necessary capability. In addition to the capability to conduct operations, military capacity building must include the administrative support and development of a functioning HN defense ministry and chain of command. A coherent SSR program directed at defense forces should focus on the provision of training and advisor teams, simultaneous delivery of equipment and infrastructure, operational support through provision of fires and logistic support and delivering financial and managerial support for the security forces. This must also include oversight and control mechanisms and processes that ensure the various elements of the defense sector are accountable to elected and politically appointed civilian leadership, both in the executive and legislative branches. Accountability is essential to establishing a sound foundation for defense budget planning and program implementation.

(1) Advisors, trainers, mentors, and liaison staff should be carefully selected, with maturity, experience, and patience being desirable traits, as dealing with foreign and possibly immaturely developed military forces will contribute to setbacks and frustrations. They will require more extensive predeployment training than more conventional forces. Continuity of personnel and a consistent approach enables SSR to progress coherently. Tour lengths for advisors should be long enough for relationships to be forged and a deep understanding of how best to develop the indigenous force to emerge. The nuances of language must be

addressed, either through formal language training, or through dedicated interpreters, who are able to conduct all activities required of embedded mentors.

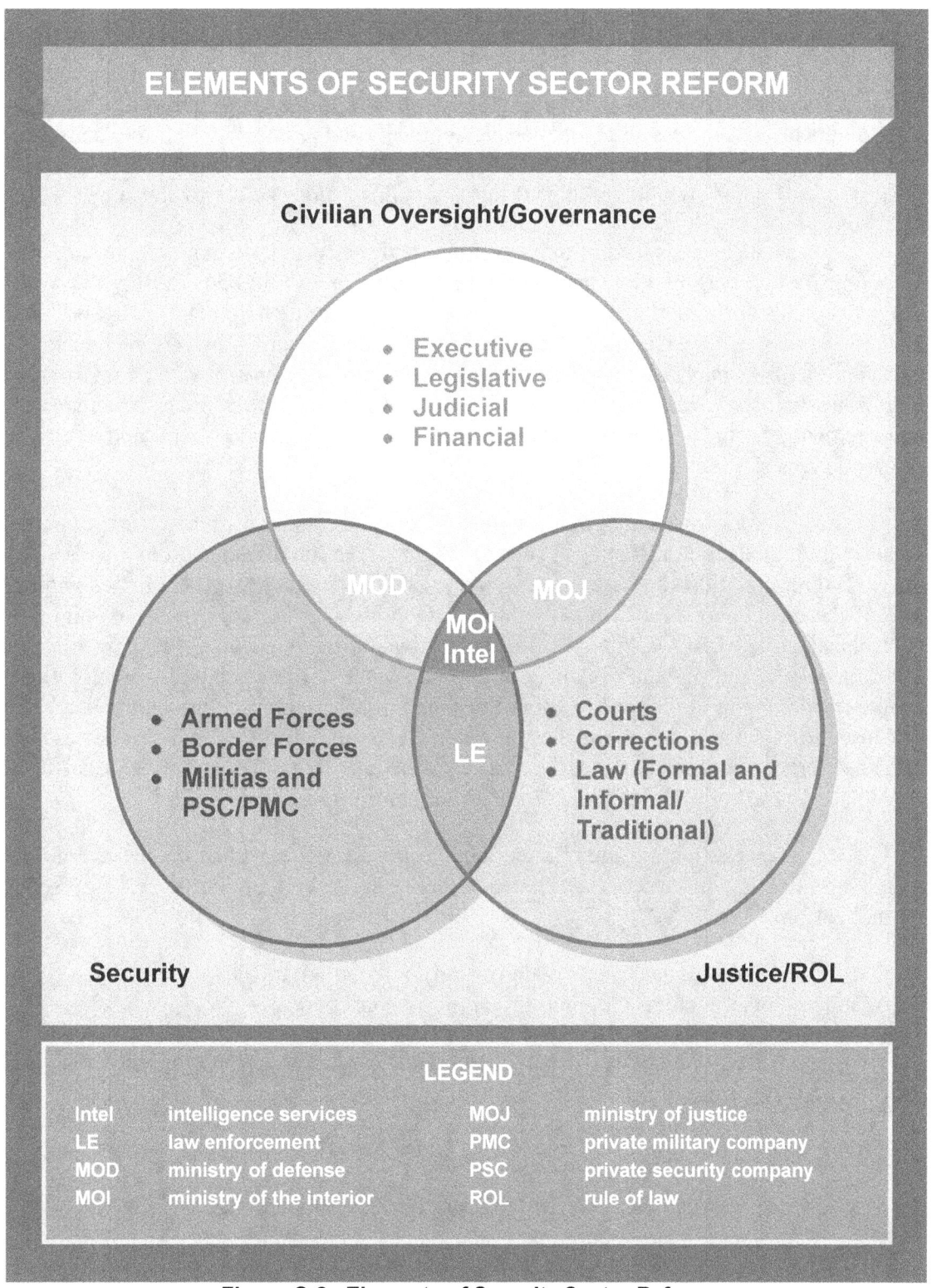

Figure C-2. Elements of Security Sector Reform

(2) The mentor organization and equipment should reflect the role and structure of the HN unit and the unit's activity in ongoing operations. Mentors embedded at various levels from government ministries to tactical units need to have ready access to each other to monitor and influence issues and decisions made by HN forces to inform both the overall SSR program and the higher military chains of command.

(3) A clear understanding of the command relationship and responsibilities between partner nation and HN forces is critical to the successful transition of authority. Advisors and trainers provide the essential link between both HN and partner nation forces and have a significant role within the transition process. HQ elements on the ground should have a dedicated staff branch dealing with SSR that maintains a close link with any superior HQ.

(4) A state needs to control its territory, and access to it, to maintain its authority. The control of border areas by state-sanctioned border forces will be necessary to prevent any movement of irregular activists into a failed state under development, or a weak state that requests assistance to strengthen its capability. While HN capability is being developed, intervention forces may need to provide the necessary border control, as well as advisors and trainers to help build capacity and provide coordination. Border control includes the management of land borders, airspace, coastal waters, territorial waters, and exclusive economic zones.

(5) Border forces are often involved in detecting and preventing crime in border areas, including illegal trafficking and entry. These forces can include border guards, coast guard, and immigration and customs personnel. Their activities are closely linked with the role of the customs service in facilitating and securing legal trade, as well as migration control and antiterrorism. In many states, ineffective border management systems frustrate efforts to detect and prevent organized crime and other irregular activity. Such failures enable trafficking in illicit arms, commodities, and people, which in turn can fuel conflict and insecurity. Border forces can also be associated with corruption, which reduces state revenues, erodes confidence, and discourages trade and economic activity. Issues to be considered in the initial development of a border control force are:

(a) Facilitating the efficient and regulated movement of people and goods, thereby achieving an appropriate balance between security, commerce, and social normalization.

(b) Building capacity to detect and combat illicit trafficking, organized crime, terrorism, and other factors leading to insecurity in border areas.

(c) Strengthening revenue generating capacity, promoting integrity, and tackling corruption.

(d) Establishing a border guard under central government control.

(e) Harmonizing border control and customs regulations regionally and enhancing cross-border cooperation.

(f) Establishing cross-border protocols with adjoining states.

(6) A key element of defense reform is SFA, which is defined as DOD activities that contribute to unified action by the USG to support the development of the capacity and capability of foreign security forces and their supporting institutions. SFA developmental activities provide enabling capabilities, which can support broader SSR programs as well as other security capacity building activities. It is conducted across the range of military operations and may begin or terminate in any of the joint phases. While SFA is normally part of the larger SSR effort, it may be tied to simply building partner capacity to achieve other strategic purposes. See Figure C-3.

(a) SFA improves the capability and capacity of HN or regional security organization's security forces. These forces are composed of all the state-sanctioned security

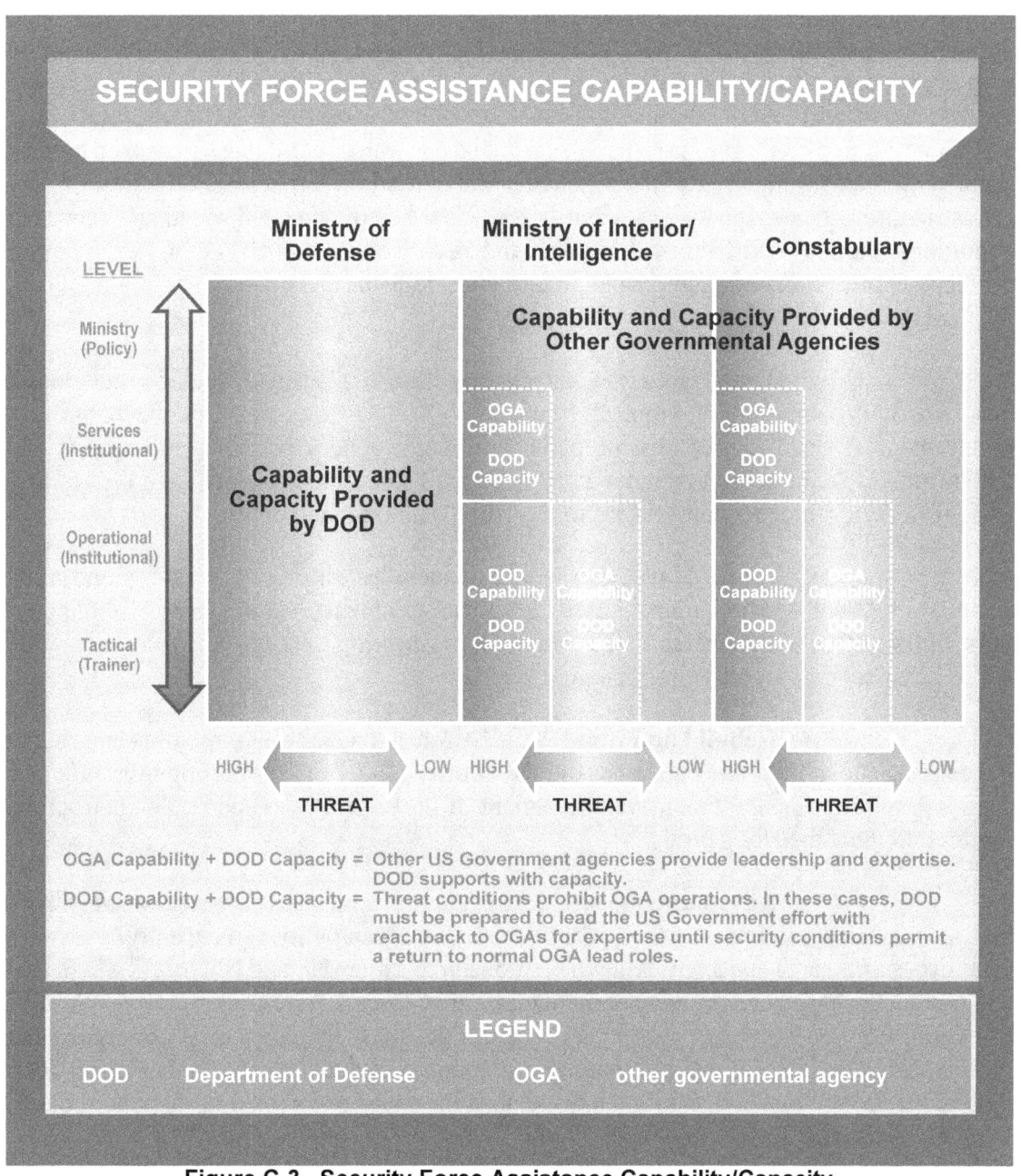

Figure C-3. Security Force Assistance Capability/Capacity

forces that provide security for an HN and its relevant population or support a regional security organization's mission, including but not limited to, military, paramilitary, police, and intelligence forces; border police, coast guard, and customs officials; and prison guards and correctional personnel. Conducting SFA and other capacity-building activities are the primary way that military forces support a comprehensive SSR program.

(b) SFA can be designed to support SSR by establishing conditions that support the HN's development of legitimate, credible, competent, capable, committed, and confident security forces. This requires HN forces capable of securing their borders, protecting their population, regulating the behavior of those that pose a security risk, and holding individuals accountable for criminal activities. There are five SFA tasks—organize, train, equip, rebuild and build, and advise and assist. When supporting the development of the HN security forces, the JFC must understand the command's role with the HN or the regional security organization they are supporting. These tasks facilitate the JFC and the staff to assess and allocate resources.

<u>1.</u> **Organize** is the SFA task that encompasses all measures taken to assist security forces in improving its organizational structure, processes, institutions, and infrastructure. Organizing the HN security force is based on the local social and economic conditions, cultural and historical factors, and security threats. SFA aims to create an efficient organization with a command, intelligence, logistic, and operations structure viable for the HN.

<u>2.</u> **Train** is the SFA task that assists security forces by developing programs and institutions to train and educate. These efforts must fit the nature and requirements of their security environment. Training is conducted in institutions, in units, and by individual trainers. It includes a broad range of subject matter, including the key SSR issue of security force responsiveness to a civilian oversight and control.

<u>3.</u> **Equip** is the SFA task that includes all efforts to assess and assist security forces with the procurement, fielding, and sustainment of equipment. All equipment must fit the nature of the operational environment. Ensuring long-term sustainment by the HN is a critical consideration for this task.

<u>4.</u> **Rebuild and build** is the SFA task that assesses, rebuilds, and builds the existing capabilities and capacities of HN security forces and supporting infrastructure. This task requires a comprehensive assessment of the capability, capacity, and structures required to meet the HN's needs.

<u>5.</u> **Advise and assist** is the SFA task in which US personnel work with the HN security forces to improve their individual and unit capability and capacity. Advising establishes a personal and a professional relationship between US and HN forces where trust and confidence influence the development of security forces. Assisting involves US forces providing required support or sustainment capabilities for the security forces to accomplish their objectives. The level and intensity of advice and assistance is based on local operational conditions and should continue until the security forces establish the required systems to provide for themselves.

(c) End states for SFA are described as follows:

<u>1.</u> Competent from the ministerial level to the individual soldier and police officer, across all related fields of interest and functional specialties.

<u>2.</u> Capable in size and effective enough to accomplish missions, remain sustainable over time, and maintain resources within state capabilities.

<u>3.</u> Committed to the security and survival of the state, the preservation of the liberties and human rights of the citizens, and the peaceful transition of authority.

<u>4.</u> Confident in the ability to secure the country; earning the confidence of the citizenry, the government, and the international community.

For further details on SFA, refer to JP 3-22, Foreign Internal Defense.

d. **Justice Reform.** The HN justice system encompasses an array of formal and informal institutions, groups, and individuals. These institutions can include the ministry of justice, law enforcement, law schools and bar associations, and legal advocacy organizations. The groups and individuals can include members of the judiciary, legislature, corrections, and prosecutor's office; public defenders; ombudsmen; regulatory bodies; and human rights and public interest groups. The legal framework includes the constitution, laws, rules, and regulations. Peace agreements may also constitute part of the legal framework in post-conflict countries. Justice systems differ significantly across national boundaries; there may also be multiple justice systems functioning in a country. To enhance HN legitimacy, justice reform should build upon the existing legal frameworks. This may include common law, civil law, criminal codes, traditional or religious law, and international law. SSR planners must avoid imposing their concepts of law, justice, and security on the HN, except, perhaps, where characteristics are in dire need of reform such that they do not meet HN treaty obligations or customary international law with regard to human rights. Implementing such reform, even where warranted, will doubtless entail a sophisticated political analysis on whether to undertake the change. The HN's systems and values are central to its development of justice system reform.

(1) **Legal System.** An effective legal and judicial system is vital to the rule of law. The lack of clear, widely accepted, and enforceable laws, and ready access to justice, are significant barriers to sustainable national and economic development. Consequently, legal and judicial reform has traditionally formed an important part of SSR, with the focus on national laws, the court system, and judges. A formal justice system may be complemented by the informal customary or traditional justice systems that are unique to particular areas, cultures, or regions. Sometimes referred to as "non-state justice systems," traditional justice systems frequently provide important alternatives to formal, codified systems and provide greater access to justice to remote or underserved populations. Traditional justice systems may enjoy high levels of legitimacy with HN populations and may possess unique advantages as a means of promoting SSR programs in a broader context. Conversely, non-state systems may not adhere to international human rights law. At the very least, SSR

planners should gain a thorough knowledge of any alternative systems that may be operating in a particular HN and how they will fit into the overall SSR program.

(2) Any transitional justice scheme is likely to be part of a wider reconciliation process and handling of unresolved justice concerns from past or ongoing conflicts, including war crimes. In such cases, special venues and processes for conflict-related justice and reconciliation may be necessary. Such processes sometimes are incorporated in the comprehensive peace agreements that form the foundation of conflict transformation. Issues to be addressed in the initial development of a legal and judicial system are:

(a) Fair and impartial laws and effective enforcement mechanisms.

(b) Independent, impartial, and competent courts and judges.

(c) Accountability and transparency in the judicial system.

(d) Timely access to justice.

(e) Transparent cooperation between state and traditional institutions.

(f) An integrated approach with other components of the criminal justice system including police and prison/penal reform bodies.

(3) Again, these considerations are politically sensitive and require evaluation at the highest levels to determine the level of reforms to be pursued toward these ideals. The Western notions of "fair and impartial laws" and "timely access to justice" may not comport with the cultural norms of the HN, where those cultural norms do not otherwise violate or are not otherwise inconsistent with international legal obligations.

(4) **Law Enforcement.** Law enforcement (especially police) forces supporting an effective and accountable justice system are central to a legitimate security sector. Although military forces may be involved initially in developing the justice and law enforcement forces, this task should be assumed by other agencies as soon as possible. Qualified, professional justice sector and police trainers, normally from non-DOD sources, support an improved advising process and ensure sustainable development with appropriate civilian oversight. Reform of the security sector may need to include the demilitarization of police forces and a re-focusing on providing greater security for citizens, rather than the security of the state. This may involve the creation of a community-based police service, with a clear separation between the roles of the police and military forces.

(5) Trainers and advisors who are tasked with the initial development of HN police services should:

(a) Assess police roles, responsibilities, structures, management, and practices.

(b) Understand the traditional role of police within the HN's society. From that starting point, they develop a force that conforms to internationally accepted law.

Changing the institutional mentality of the police force to one that secures and protects the population requires extensive effort, time, and resources.

(c) Support links across the justice system to ensure system wide functionality.

(d) Improve police training, including the police education system. In the aftermath of conflict, it is important to focus training on investigative processes, including the gathering, handling, and preserving of evidence to support ongoing prosecutions.

(e) Enhance the ability of police services to plan and develop criminal intelligence analysis skills.

(f) Strengthen police accountability.

(g) Develop an integrated approach that complements the broader SSR program.

(6) Law enforcement reform is nested within the larger justice system reform. The justice system consists of a number of interrelated steps—arrest, detention, prosecution, adjudication, corrections, and parole or rehabilitation. Functionality requires that all work together as a system. Law enforcement reform that outpaces the rest of the justice sector may result in more arrests with inadequate detention facilities and no means of adjudication.

(7) **Corrections System.** The justice system as a whole contributes to a secure, just, peaceful, and safe society through the use of appropriate and reasonable sanctions. As part of the justice system, corrections contributes to the protection of society by actively encouraging offenders to take advantage of opportunities that will assist them in becoming law-abiding citizens, while exercising only the degree of control necessary to provide for the safety of society. In the context of failing and failed states, overcrowded and poorly managed prisons are often characterized by abuse and torture and often present major health risks to the whole community. In some states, prisoners are often detained without charge or trial. In these cases, specific SSR action is needed to reform and develop corrections systems quickly, placing immediate demands on military participation. Corrections reform is necessary to support developments in police and justice systems and needs to be reformed simultaneously. Issues that should be considered in the initial development of a corrections system are:

(a) Ensuring respect for the human rights of detainees.

(b) Reducing pretrial detention.

(c) Improving health and social services in prisons.

(d) Increasing HN civilian and multinational oversight of prisons.

(e) Promoting rehabilitation and reintegration.

(f) Developing an integrated approach with the judicial system.

(8) Priorities for technical assistance to the corrections system include staff development and training, management training, policy development, conditions of youth in detention, and the promotion of activities to address prison overcrowding. A sound policy framework is essential for the effective and efficient governance of any correctional system. However, policies must be based on the rule of law and be respective of other international, regional, and national standards for corrections and the protection of human rights. Overall goals of corrections reform should include systemic improvements in corrections and criminal justice policies and legislation through a consistent approach to offenders based upon shared values and principles; effective programs to safely reintegrate offenders into society; and increased staff professionalism.

e. **Non-State Security Forces.** Local militias, hunting societies, neighborhood crime watches, citizen security patrols, and tribal forces are a frequent response when the state is unable to provide effective security to local communities and may be significant employers within local communities. SSR programs must acknowledge the presence of these non-state groups and determine how best to deal with them. Indeed, intervening forces may quickly achieve a measure of local legitimacy by partnering with local non-state security groups in such situations. Because non-state security forces lack accountability mechanisms and oversight systems, over time they tend to become major abusers of human rights and predators in their own and other communities. This tendency is exacerbated by lack of training as law enforcement officers and the use of force in a community policing role. As violence increases in frequency and becomes more intense, lack of effective control over militia activities incurs proportionally greater costs. Uncontrolled violence, once accepted, tacitly or otherwise, by state authorities or intervening forces, is very difficult to restrain. To the extent that a partnership has developed between local forces and the intervening force, the declining legitimacy and problematic functionality of local militias will accrue to their sponsors as well. As discussed earlier, the DDR of non-state security forces is essential to reforming an HN's security sector. DDR is particularly challenging for local forces. Where bearing weapons is a socially accepted feature of adulthood, disarmament will be problematic at best. Disarmament processes may require a nuanced approach that differentiates between personal weapons and heavy or crew-served weapons. Without an effective demobilization process supported by segregation and encampment of former fighters, however, conflict-era associations, militia chains of command, and the pathologies of violent behavior are likely to endure. The perception that former combatants are receiving benefits that are not broadly available to civilians may generate resentment, if not open hostility, among those civilians.

(1) **Private Military and Security Forces.** The private security industry comprises those individuals and institutions that provide security for people and property under contract and for profit. The activities of an uncontrolled or poorly regulated private security industry can present unique governance problems and act as an obstacle to SSR programs of both military and law enforcement forces. Increased security provision by non-state organizations is prevalent in all regions of the world. SSR planners therefore must consider the potentially serious implications of the private security industry in the HN, as well as the effects of limited regulation and accountability of a market, which continues to grow in both size and importance. While SSR programs now recognize the value of properly scoping and reforming public security agencies such as the military and police as key to

transition and democratization, the need to introduce similar levels of professionalism and accountability in the private sector has typically been neglected by SSR programs. This is despite the fact that the sector often represents one of the largest armed groups within a country. There are many types of organizations that compose the private security industry, including:

(a) Service providers that conduct mine clearance, logistics and supply, and risk consulting.

(b) Private security companies (PSCs) that protect industrial and commercial sites, humanitarian aid missions, embassies, very important persons, and conduct surveillance and investigation, and risk assessment and analysis.

(c) Private military companies (PMCs) that support military training, military intelligence, and offensive combat.

(2) There are significant challenges to incorporating elements of the private security industry into a comprehensive SSR program. SSR planners need to develop a comprehensive system providing for effective regulation and oversight of this industry. In the absence of adequate legislation and regulation there may be no control over the type or quality of services providing these elements. Untrained staff with questionable backgrounds may use weaponry force in an illegitimate way. More important to an effective SSR program, the introduction of armed PSCs/PMCs weakens the state's monopoly over the use of force and, where unregulated, hinders rather than helps law enforcement. In states with a history of ethnic or other sectarian conflict there is the potential for PSCs/PMCs to be misused against ethnic as well as political rivals. Specific objectives of SSR programs will be dependent upon the context of the security environment. They should be formulated with the overall aims of increasing democratic oversight and accountability of the entire sector. This can be achieved by formulating a comprehensive system of legislation and regulation for the private security industry, developing effective mechanisms for oversight, and encouraging a culture of professionalism. An example of this would be comprehensive licensing systems clearly defining the type of services that PSCs/PMCs may be allowed to provide and providing for the revocation of licenses in certain cases.

f. **Intelligence and Security Service Reform.** Intelligence and security service reform is a key element of SSR because intelligence both supports SSR and is the target of reform activities. Intelligence and security services are normally located within central government, typically reporting directly to senior decision makers. They should provide warnings and insights about threats and trends which impact on the security and economic well-being of a state and allow decision makers to shape policy. The most crucial task facing countries embarking on SSR processes is to build a nationally owned and led vision of security. This can be achieved through a national security review to elaborate on overarching threats to the country's security and to support the development of a policy on national security. Such a review allows the HN government to distinguish between legitimate and illegitimate security activities, and delineates between the competing claims for resources. Intelligence services can make a significant contribution to this process through the provision of accurate intelligence on the range of threats faced by the state.

(1) In addition to assisting the overall SSR process intelligence services themselves frequently require reform. Intelligence services of the state may have been involved in human rights abuses or participated in the rule of a corrupt or tyrannical regime. Thus, there may be a requirement to reform the intelligence services and structures of a state as a part of the comprehensive SSR program. Indicators of where services may require reform include:

(a) Balance between the necessary secrecy of the intelligence services and transparency regarding their mandates and their powers.

(b) Existence of oversight structures to minimize maladministration.

(c) Extent of control over and public accountability for the financing of intelligence services.

(d) Controls in place to govern the use of intrusive methods of intelligence collections.

(e) Professionalism and ethics of intelligence officers.

(2) There are three types of intelligence services that may be present in an HN:

(a) Intelligence on foreign or external threats.

(b) Intelligence on threats to internal security.

(c) Intelligence-led advice on policy and decision making.

(3) Two of the main drivers behind a foreign intelligence capability today are to learn and understand as much as possible about other states' capabilities and to prevent a foreign power achieving strategic surprise. This requires access to both secret and open-source information, primarily focused on national security, military and defense, political, economic, and foreign policy issues. Primary examples of the capability centered on this type of activity are the Central Intelligence Agency and the UK Secret Intelligence Service.

(4) Security intelligence focuses on those threats that operate internally to the HN. Security intelligence is generally distinctive to the law enforcement sector. However, these distinctions are often blurred as domestic and foreign intelligence activities increasingly overlap, particularly in the realm of activities such as counterterrorism, which can encompass threats to domestic targets, overseas embassies, armed forces, or commercial interests in foreign countries.

(5) Intelligence can also be used to support policy-formulation and decision-making processes of an HN government. This can occur through the provision of tactical or strategic intelligence assessments that provide a long-term view of a particular issue. It allows governments to reduce uncertainty and manage risk through scoping the possible set of future threats with which the government may be faced.

(6) In reforming and training intelligence organizations, as with the rule of law, the military is not the ideal lead, though military intelligence personnel may need to be factored into the development of the HN military capacity. Traditionally, US civilian intelligence agencies have taken the lead in building intelligence capacity in countries where reconstruction efforts are ongoing.

4. Guidance for Security Sector Reform

a. **Support Host Nation Ownership.** The HN's history, culture, legal framework, and institutions must inform the principles, policies, laws, and structures that form an SSR program. As a result, the needs, priorities, and circumstances driving SSR will differ substantially from one country to another. Accounting for the basic security concerns of the HN population is essential for attaining buy-in and is essential to the success of SSR. To ensure the sustainability of reforms, assistance should be designed to meet the needs of the HN population and to support HN agencies, processes, and priorities. To accomplish this, SSR generally should be developed to serve longer-term goals.

b. **Incorporate Principles of Good Governance and Respect for Human Rights.** Accountability, transparency, public participation, respect for human rights, and legitimacy must be mainstreamed in security force development. Military and civilian security forces must carry out their core functions in accordance with these principles. This is particularly important in rebuilding countries where the legacy of abuse by security personnel may have eroded public confidence in the sector overall. SSR programs should include accountability and oversight mechanisms, including thorough direct collaboration with civil society, to prevent abuses of power and corruption, and to build public confidence. Vetting is routinely done prior to giving provisional assistance or training to security forces. Likewise, SSR programs must incorporate an explicit focus on security sector governance. Strengthening the overall legal, policy, and budgetary frameworks should be an important component of SSR into any country.

c. **Balance Operational Support with Institutional Reform.** Incentives, processes, resources, and structures must be put in place so that externally supported reforms, resources, and capacities are sustained after assistance ends. Equal emphasis should be placed on how the forces and organizations that US and international assistance strengthen through capability building programs will be financed, managed, monitored, deployed, and supported by partner nation governments. Training platforms and materiel assistance must be coordinated with efforts to develop HN infrastructure, personnel and administrative support systems, logistic and planning procedures, and an adequate and sustainable resource base. Success and sustainability depend on developing the institutions and processes that support security forces as well as the human capacity to lead and manage them.

d. **Link Security and Justice.** A country's security policies and practices must be founded upon the rule of law and linked to the broader justice sector. SSR should aim to ensure that all security forces operate within the bounds of domestic and international law, and that they support wide-ranging efforts to enforce and promote the rule of law. The police in particular should operate as an integral part of the justice system and directly support other parts of the justice sector, including the courts and corrections institutions.

Assistance to the police and other state security providers may need to be complemented with other efforts to strengthen these institutions, to avoid unintended consequences, and to ensure that the security forces operate according to the law. Experience demonstrates, for example, that police assistance undertaken absent efforts to strengthen other parts of the justice system can lead to increased arrests without the necessary means to adjudicate cases, or defend, incarcerate, or rehabilitate suspected offenders. In addition, although the tendency may be to focus on criminal justice systems, civil justice reform may have important implications for law and order, particularly with respect to the resolution of potential conflict drivers, such as land disputes.

e. **Foster Transparency.** Effective SSR programs should be conducted transparently and openly whenever possible. Program design should include a robust SCC to foster awareness of reform efforts among HN officials and the population, neighboring countries, the donor community, and others with a potential stake in program outcomes. Likewise, DOS, DOD, and USAID practitioners should engage in broad consultation with other USG agencies, NGOs, IGOs, international donors, and the media, to enhance program development and program execution.

f. **Do No Harm.** In complex environments, donor assistance can become a part of the conflict dynamic serving either to increase or reduce tension. As with any activity that involves changes to the status quo, SSR planners and implementers must pay close attention to minimize adverse effects on the local population and community structures, the security sector, or the wider political, social, and economic climate in unanticipated or unintended ways. Developing a thorough understanding of the system for which change is sought, and the actual needs that exist, is a prerequisite for the success of any SSR-related activity. Practitioners should conduct a risk assessment prior to implementation and be prepared to adjust activities over the lifetime of the SSR program.

5. **Planning for Security Sector Reform**

a. **Comprehensive Plan.** The military contribution to an SSR program should be incorporated within a comprehensive reform plan, which should be developed by all the stakeholders, including the intervention force where applicable, IGOs, NGOs, and HN leadership. During a FID or COIN operation, the IDAD strategy is the overarching strategy for SSR. In any case, the overarching strategy should set out a realistic timeline for reform that recognizes the context of the issues, as well as the resources available, the HN leadership capacity to deliver change, and existing institutional capabilities. The strategic reform plan should take into account certain factors:

(1) A comprehensive vision for the security sector. It should articulate all threats and responses to those elements that seek to destabilize state institutions. This may take the form of a national security strategy that coordinates security, political, and economic policies.

(2) Priorities among the various SSR tasks, the lead element for each, and their funding sources.

(3) The structure of the security sector. This should also designate roles and responsibilities for the various aspects of the sector defined and measures to strengthen the relationships developed within the sector.

(4) Transfer of responsibility. All elements of the strategic reform plan must have an end state of turning over responsibility to institutions of the HN.

b. **Objectives.** There are four primary objectives when conducting SSR:

(1) Increase effective governance, oversight, and accountability in the security sector.

(2) Improve delivery of security and justice.

(3) Assist local leadership in developing an ownership of the reform process.

(4) Support the development of sustainable security and justice delivery.

c. **Lines of Effort.** In SSR the needs of each situation and each country vary greatly. As such, reform efforts must be context-driven. The USG should formulate SSR in a holistic way that encompasses institutional structures, resource management, operational capacity, and civilian oversight and governance.

(1) **Institutional Structures.** From the outset, SSR should support the HN's national structures that will manage the implementation of SSR, since national ownership and leadership are essential for effective security sector development. The design of SSR should focus on the organizational structures and management processes within security sector organizations. Merely training and equipping judges, prosecutors, corrections officers, soldiers, or law enforcement officers would be ineffective and unsustainable. Managerial systems and planning capacities need to be developed and supported in coordination with training and equipping programs at the various levels of government—national, provincial, and local—and need to correspond closely to local capabilities. They must also be integrated with governance reform programs.

(2) **Resource Management.** Sustainable SSR programs must take into account basic resource issues such as the number of qualified personnel, their skill levels, and existing materiel support in the HN. Capacity development is an essential component of SSR programs that must take into account the existing resource management structures and resources on hand to enhance basic security and other service delivery, while also working to increase the governance and regulatory capacities of the state.

(3) **Operational Capacity.** Capacity development refers to the ability of US and partner nation forces to train and advise HN individuals and institutions to develop security strategies, set priorities, solve problems, and achieve results with the resources available. It is a broader concept than the training and technical assistance approaches that are usually employed to address capacity shortfalls. Capacity development requires a comprehensive approach from all USG agencies in coordination with partner nations, IGOs like the UN, and NGOs, and that addresses capacity gaps while tailoring them to the operational environment.

Strengthening capacity in HN governments to develop, manage, and implement SSR should be a central aspect of all reform programs. Capacity needs are present throughout the security sector, and not just within state institutions. In the past, capacity development programs have failed because wider governance issues (e.g., systematic corruption) have not been understood. For this reason a thorough assessment must inform the SSR planning process.

(4) **Civilian Oversight and Governance.** Civilian oversight bodies are those institutions authorized by the state to manage and oversee the activities and governance of security forces and agencies. They can be formal or informal. They may include (but are not limited to) the executive branch and ministries of defense, interior, justice, and foreign affairs; judicial branch, national security coordination and advisory bodies; the legislative branch and its committees; traditional and customary authorities; the ministry of finance and other financial management bodies; civilian review boards and compliance commissions; and local government structures. Local government structures in security include governors, municipal councils, auditing bodies, civilian review boards, and public complaints commissions.

d. **Design and Planning Considerations.** SSR planning must account for several interrelated factors that influence reform, including cultural awareness, leadership capacity building, public trust and confidence, HN dependency, perseverance, and end state. Interactions among the security sector and these factors complicate reform efforts. Actions taken to reform one aspect of the security sector affect reform activities in another. Effective assessment of these factors, together with the sector in its entirety, will drive the process and help define success.

(1) **Cultural Awareness.** Regardless of the need to develop an HN's security forces quickly, SSR requires considerable tolerance, cultural awareness, and an environment of mutual respect. Organizations and individuals working closely with HN security forces must respect the security culture of the HN. This culture is shaped by history, language, religion, and customs and must be understood. Cultural awareness and sensitivity are necessary to dispel the natural tensions that arise when external authorities dictate the terms and conditions of SSR for the HN. Responsiveness, flexibility, and adaptability to local culture help limit resentment and resistance to reform while generating local solutions to local problems. Local help fosters acceptance and strengthens the confidence of the citizens in reform.

(2) **Leadership Capacity Building.** Challenges associated with developing capable, legitimate, and accountable security forces require capable leadership in the HN security sector at all levels. To establish the conditions for long-term success, SSR may help the HN identify and begin training and advising security force leaders as early as possible. Such efforts must avoid undermining HN legitimacy while recognizing that assistance, advice, and education may be needed. Programs focused on developing senior leaders, such as those conducted by the DOD regional centers for security studies, may prove helpful. Often the HN can augment programs for officer training and staff college courses of participating forces and may even develop similar institutions. This participation ensures

that future leaders gain the knowledge and skills to manage security forces effectively while meeting the broader responsibilities normally associated with leaders in the security sector.

(3) **Public Trust and Confidence.** In rebuilding the institutions of a failed state, CDRs must engender trust and confidence between the local populace and the security forces. As SSR proceeds, these security forces carry a progressively greater burden in ensuring public safety. Frequently, they do so in an environment characterized by crime and violence. This proves true in areas recovering from violent, predatory forces. Recovery requires a community-based response that uses the unique capabilities of the security forces and police. Operating in accordance with the laws of the HN, the success of these forces will help gain the trust and confidence of the local populace. Furthermore, increased public confidence engenders greater desire among the people to support the efforts of the security forces. External participants in SSR must focus on enhancing the functionality of HN security forces while sustaining and strengthening the perception of legitimacy for civilians. Public confidence is further strengthened as HN forces support activities that foster civil participation. These activities, such as providing security for elections, associate the security forces with positive processes; this improves the credibility of HN security forces while providing visible signs of accountability and responsibility.

(4) **HN Dependency.** During reform, the risk of building a culture of dependency is mitigated by adopting a training process. This process sequentially provides training and equipment to security forces, a dedicated advising capability, and an advisory presence. After initial training efforts, this reform helps HN security forces progress toward the transition of security responsibility. A robust transition plan supports the gradual and coherent easing of HN dependency, typically in the form of increased responsibility and accountability. Depending on the security environment, external forces in SSR may need to protect new HN security forces from many direct and immediate threats during their development. While this requirement usually applies only during initial training, security forces remain at risk throughout their development during SSR; these threats may contribute to problems with discipline, dependability, and desertion. In extreme circumstances, protecting HN security forces may necessitate training outside the physical boundaries of the state.

(5) **Perseverance.** SSR is a complex activity, and participants must demonstrate persistence and resilience in managing the dynamic interactions among the various factors affecting the reform program. Within the SSR processes, some failures are likely. Early identification of potential points of failure, such as corruption within the police force, allows for mitigating action.

e. SSR and the international assistance that supports it are inherently political processes. The processes that are initiated by reforms inevitably create winners and losers as they challenge traditional interests and existing power relationships. SSR therefore has an explicitly political objective to ensure that security is provided in a manner consistent with US and internationally accepted democratic norms, human rights principles, and the rule of law. Security can be provided and governed by state and non-state institutions in many ways and ultimately is driven by a country's balance of power. Therefore, SSR is best approached as a comprehensive governance issue and not simply as a technical and military activity.

6. Security Sector Reform During Nation Assistance

a. SSR during NA is often initiated following a diplomatic request for assistance from another country and may be managed through the UN. The focus for this activity is likely to be the reform of existing security institutions and specific capability strengthening initiatives, such as improving indigenous counterterrorism capabilities or providing intelligence training and police investigative skills. The scope for this activity is wide and each act of assistance should be carefully matched to local conditions. Initial delivery of assistance to a country may lead to further engagement across the full range of security sector activity.

b. **Ministry.** USG personnel may provide advice to HN officials to enable reform in these areas:

(1) High-level reform aims to assist senior officials in the HN security sector to link threats with capabilities, leading to affordable plans for developing the sector.

(2) Reform should encourage governments to include security expenditure within standard public resource management in a transparent way and to ensure that affordability is a driving consideration.

(3) Advice on change and project management may strengthen HN capacity to deliver reform.

c. **Training.** Professional military training is the most prominent activity for routine contribution by US military forces. Routine military assistance often takes the form of a military training team that provides military advice and training for HN military forces.

d. **Education.** The US military and other countries have long exchanged instructors and students in professional military command and staff courses. With its strong reputation in staff and officer training, the US is well-placed to advise other nations on the restructuring or development of their military education systems. Education should include the role of military forces in a democratic society.

7. Disarmament, Demobilization, and Reintegration

a. DDR usually forms part of a peace agreement and is conducted within a wider post-conflict recovery process. DDR seeks to increase the stability of the post-conflict security environment by ensuring that combatants, and their weapons, are taken out of the conflict and provided with at least a minimal transition package so that they can return to their civilian life and forgo returning to arms again. The complex DDR process has dimensions that include culture, politics, security, humanity, and socioeconomics. DDR can potentially provide incentives for CDRs and combatants to enter negotiations to facilitate political reconciliation, dissolve belligerent force structures, and present opportunities for former combatants and other DDR beneficiaries to return to their communities.

b. While the process is focused on the ex-combatants, the wider community will also feel the benefits of a successful DDR program that enhances security and is a clear sign of progress to peace. However, communities will require assistance to successfully absorb such ex-combatants. DDR is complex and fraught with potential unforeseen consequences. If combatants are disarmed too quickly, this may create a security vacuum, if they are detained for too long in encampments this may create unrest. Without a fully funded reintegration program, militia leaders may simply reform their groups for criminal purposes, creating a different security problem. Gender, ethnic, and minority issues must also be considered in the design of DDR programs. The immediate goal of DDR is to appropriately scope the armed forces to the security requirements of the HN. Typically, a DDR program transitions from disarmament and demobilization to reintegration. Disarmament and demobilization refers to the act of releasing or disbanding an armed unit and the collection and control of weapons and weapons systems. Reintegration helps former combatants return to civilian life through benefit packages and strategies that help them become socially and economically embedded in their communities.

c. **Importance of DDR to Stability.** The DDR program is a critical component of peace and security and should be accounted for in initial planning. Often, the terms of this program are negotiated in cease-fire or peace accords. DDR focuses on the immediate management of people previously associated with armed forces and belligerent groups. DDR sets the foundation of a secure environment and for sustaining the communities in which these individuals live as contributing, law-abiding citizens. The DDR program is a central contributor to long-term peace, security, and development. DDR dictates, and are dictated by, a variety of priority areas in planning for full spectrum operations and SSR. The promise of DDR to formerly competing fighting forces often plays a crucial role in achieving a peace agreement. DDR planning directly ties to SSR, determining the potential size and scope of military, police, and other security structures. In addition, reintegration of former combatants back into their communities sets the foundation for—and determines the success of—long-term PB and development programs. The success of DDR depends on integrating strategies and planning across all the sectors. The employment opportunities extended to disarmed and demobilized former combatants result from an effectively governed, viable economy. If the DDR program expires without providing alternative economic opportunities to the former combatants, the likelihood of a return to violence substantially increases. DDR closely coordinates with security reform efforts in all sectors to ensure an integrated approach that synchronizes activities toward a common end state.

d. Generally, the military does not lead the planning and execution of the DDR program. However, military forces must be integrated in the planning of DDR from its inception and may be involved more directly in the disarmament and demobilization stages. Military forces and police, whether from external sources or the HN, are fundamental to the broad success of the program, providing security for DDR processes.

e. Successful DDR programs use many approaches designed for specific security environments. Each program reflects the unique aspects of the situation, culture, and character of the state. The best interests of children and their protection from violence and abuse are overarching principles during DDR.

f. In operations involving the welfare of children, the entire process emphasizes integration and inherently is a community process. To the greatest extent possible, children associated with armed groups (child soldiers) should be immediately released and reintegrated into civil society. Cash payments to demobilized minors are harmful and should therefore be avoided. Juvenile justice considerations, which may involve restorative as well as retributive actions, are central to any DDR program involving child soldiers. International DDR approaches must comply with *The Principles and Guidelines on Children Associated with Armed Forces or Armed Groups*, also known as the *Paris Principles*. The SJA is the staff principal responsible for providing command guidance on any situations pertaining to child combatants.

For more information on DDR, refer to JP 3-24, Counterinsurgency Operations, *and JP 3-07.3,* Peace Operations.

8. Transitions

a. SSR programs should be monitored throughout implementation to ensure they deliver sustainable results while minimizing unintended negative consequences. Program evaluation at key decision points and at the close of specific projects will provide important measures of effectiveness to adjust ongoing programs and to provide lessons for future SSR programs. Program evaluation should identify expected outcomes.

b. Military forces gradually transfer the responsibilities they have accumulated during combat operations to other participants in the SSR effort, whether from one military force to another or to civilian groups or agencies. Transferring security responsibility from intervening to HN security forces should be done according to the tactical, operational, and strategic conditions identified during SSR planning. As forces establish suitable conditions, responsibility for security gradually transitions to the local, provincial, and national government. During the transition of authority, progress through transition should be gauged by a process that confirms the performance and capabilities of each respective HN security force. These capabilities can be gauged through exercises similar to those used to validate the readiness of US and multinational forces for contingency operations. This prevents a premature transition of authority which can lead to a loss of confidence and cause the populace to seek alternative means of security, damaging the overall SSR program.

APPENDIX D
TRANSITIONAL MILITARY AUTHORITY

1. General

a. A transitional military authority is a temporary military government exercising the functions of civil administration in the absence of a legitimate civil authority. It exercises temporary executive, legislative, and judicial authority in a foreign territory. A transitional military authority may be required in UGAs, occupied territory, or an allied or neutral territory liberated from enemy forces, including insurgent or rebelling forces. The authority to establish military governance resides with the President. US forces will only assume control prescribed in directives to the JFC.

b. Occupying forces establish military governance pursuant to international law, including the Hague Convention and Geneva Convention relative to the Protection of Civilian Persons in Time of War. The authority of such an interim government is limited in scope by international law; UN Security Council resolutions or similar authority may provide authority additional to that provided by traditional sources of international law. In other circumstances, a transitional military authority may be established pursuant to a UN Security Council resolution or a similar international legal authority, which will also describe the limits of that authority.

c. The objective for a transitional military authority is to establish a government that supports US objectives, restores and maintains public order, ensures the safety and security of the local populace, and provides humanitarian assistance and essential civil services. The time during which a transitional military authority exercises authority varies based on the requirements of both the military operation and international law.

d. The goal of US civil administration of an occupied territory is to create an effective civil government. This government should not pose a threat to future peace and stability. The CDR of a transitional military authority has the right, within the limits set by international law and US laws and treaties, to demand and enforce law and order in an occupied area to accomplish the mission and properly manage the area. In return for such obedience, the inhabitants have a right to freedom from unnecessary interference with their individual liberty and property rights. Subject to the requirements of the military situation, CDRs must observe the principle of governing for the benefit of the governed.

2. Organization

a. The JFC is responsible for the detailed planning and operations of the transitional military authority under the general guidelines received from the President and SecDef. The JFC may execute the authorities of civil administration directly, invest the authority in subordinate operational CDRs, or establish a separate JCMOTF.

(1) Concentrating authority and responsibility in the CDR or in subordinate operational commands helps ensure that activities related to civil administration, including relations between the military and HN civilians, are integrated consistently with ongoing

operations. However, the higher the tempo within the operational area, the less the CDR is able to address the requirements of civil administration. This is partly because areas of high operational tempo will normally require frequently changing civil administration policies. Finally, operational HQ are not always assigned operational areas corresponding to existing political subdivisions.

(2) The establishment of a separate JCMOTF to conduct civil administration may institute a concentration of expertise and focus on stability operations. However, a command dedicated to stability operations, including civil administration, represents a separate chain of command from combat forces, particularly if the JCMOTF does not report to the JFC executing combat operations in the operational area. In this case, activities of the transitional military authority must be carefully coordinated with those of combat forces.

b. The head of an established civil administration system is the civil administrator, often called the military governor. The administrator is a military CDR or other designated person who exercises authority over the occupied territory. The military governor may command subordinate military governors assigned to political subdivisions throughout the territory.

c. A transitional military authority may draw assistance from experienced civilians from the HN, the USG, or other agencies and organizations. These agencies and organizations have the expertise to establish a system of government that fosters the gradual transition to a legitimate HN authority. This cooperation facilitates the transition while ensuring that all activities complement and reinforce efforts to establish conditions necessary to achieve success.

d. Where practical, the transitional military authority should retain subordinate officials and employees of the HN government. These officials can continue to properly discharge their duties under the direction and supervision of appropriately trained military personnel. Even with the use of local civilians, the occupying forces still retain the power to exercise supreme authority. HN officials working for the transitional military authority should be appropriately compensated.

(1) The transitional military authority should thoroughly assess the capability of the remaining HN government officials to determine if those officials can support and contribute to the transitional military authority. If permitted by international law, offices that are unnecessary or detrimental to the transitional military authority may close temporarily.

(2) The authority should also vet officials, and those who refuse to serve the best interests of the transitional military authority may be suspended. Generally, if a transitional military authority needs to be established, high-ranking political officials of the former government, such as cabinet ministers and other political elites, will not continue to hold office. Typically, mere membership in unfriendly organizations or political groups should not typically be considered sufficient grounds for removal from office; however, officials who have served as active leaders of such organizations or political groups may need to leave office. Similarly, officials who prove unreliable, involved in potential war crimes, or corrupt must leave office through legal action or through an open, transparent administrative process.

The willful failure of retained officials to perform their duties satisfactorily is sufficient reason for dismissal.

(3) Military officials of the transitional military authority should refrain from developing or maintaining unofficial relationships with local officials and HN personnel. Military personnel must refuse personal favors or gifts offered by local government officials or the local populace unless authorized by higher authority. DOD ethics rules provide appropriate guidelines for the relationships among military supervisory officials and HN subordinates.

e. Any member of the joint force may contribute relevant information on the local populace and other aspects of the operational environment. Foreign area officers, CA personnel, and others normally concentrate their efforts on specific aspects of local culture, and general customs and behaviors. Intelligence analysts will use all this information to produce timely and relevant intelligence and distribute appropriate products throughout the joint force and interorganizational partners, as appropriate.

3. Existing Laws, Customs, and Boundaries

a. The laws of the territory subject to military authority/control may not be changed, except to the extent permitted by the Geneva Convention relative to the Protection of Civilian Persons in Time of War. CDRs must consult closely and carefully with their legal advisors before attempting to change any local laws.

b. In general, the military authority should not impose the customs of another nation on the governed territory. Implementing changes or reforms inconsistent with local customs may foster active or passive resistance, adding friction to an already complex effort. CDRs and their legal advisors must recognize that laws and customs often vary between political divisions of a country, such as between provinces or municipalities. CDRs need to identify issues related to ethnic and minority groups so policies of the transitional military authority do not inadvertently oppress such groups.

c. Local boundaries and political divisions may not be redrawn except to the extent permitted by international law. Where possible, boundaries of operational areas covered by separate or subordinate military governments should normally reflect these boundaries as closely as possible.

4. Guidelines for Transitional Military Authority

a. **Treatment of the Population.** Fair treatment of the local populace can help reduce the chance that it will be hostile to US forces and increase the chance for obtaining its cooperation. The proper and just treatment of civilians helps military forces establish and maintain security; prevent lawlessness; promote order; and secure local labor, services, and supplies. Such treatment promotes a positive impression of the military force, the United States, and multinational and IGO partners. It strengthens the legitimacy of the operation and the transitional military authority in the eyes of the populace, bordering nations, and other members of the international community.

(1) A policy of proper and just treatment does not prevent the imposition of restrictive or punitive measures necessary to secure the objectives of the transitional military authority. In particular, such measures may be needed in an area where the population is actively and aggressively hostile.

(2) The military's policies for treating any population vary depending on several factors. These factors include characteristics of the population, such as their attitude toward the governing forces, the degree of technical-industrial development, socioeconomic conditions, the political system, and local history and culture. Another determining factor is the policies of the US with respect to the HN government. The CDR must become familiar with HN customs, institutions, and attitudes and establish policies accordingly.

(3) When determining policies for treating the local populace, CDRs should consider the following:

(a) Generally, less restrictive measures are appropriate for civilians of friendly or neutral states. More restrictive measures generally are needed with civilians of hostile states.

(b) Depending on the culture, the local populace may perceive certain actions as characteristic of an illegitimate or weak military government. On the other hand, certain actions, though permissible under international law, may aggravate an already complex civil situation or reduce the effectiveness of the force in imposing civil control.

(c) Force may be used to subdue those who resist the transitional military authority or to prevent the escape of prisoners or detainees suspected of crimes. Force is limited to what is necessary and must be consistent with international law. Legal advisors should be consulted when formulating policies for the use of force and the treatment of prisoners, detainees, and other persons.

(4) Military CDRs are inherently empowered to take all prudent and proportional measures necessary to protect their forces. However, during stability operations, the nature of the threat can often inhibit the ability of friendly forces to differentiate between hostile acts, hostile intent, and normal daily activity among civilians. For this reason, military CDRs and forces must retain the authority to detain civilians and an acceptable framework under which to confine, intern, and eventually release them. This authority has the most legitimacy when sanctioned by international mandate or when bestowed or conveyed from the local or regional government power. The initial or baseline authority granted to military forces to use force and detain civilians will ultimately determine the status of the persons they detain. The status of detained persons will further determine the manner in which they are processed, the degree of due process they are afforded, and whether their offense is military or criminal in nature.

b. **Economic Stabilization and Recovery.** In certain circumstances, military forces may need to act with regard to economic conditions to promote security and law and order. When international law and the governing mandate permits a transitional military authority to engage in economic stabilization and recovery activities, two immediate goals generally exist for the economic sector. The first goal aims to use all available goods and services as efficiently as possible to meet the essential needs of the local populace. The second aims to revive the economy at the local level to reduce dependence on external support.

(1) Issues such as stabilizing monetary policy, controlling inflation, and reestablishing a national currency generally exceed expertise resident in the transitional military authority. This lack of expertise underscores the necessity of introducing appropriate civilian expertise as soon as practical or puts the success of broader economic recovery programs at risk from the outset of operations.

(2) When resources are scarce, an equitable distribution of necessities—such as food, water, shelter, and medicine—supports economic stability. To this end, it may be necessary to establish and enforce temporary controls over certain aspects of the local economy. These controls may be designed to affect the prices of goods and services, wage rates and labor practices, black market activity, hoarding of goods, banking practices, imports or exports, and production rates within industry. However, these controls may also have adverse effects that can lead to renewed violence. These adverse effects may consist of causing potential shortages of goods and services, impeding economic progress, and causing corruption, conflict over limited resources, and social tension. CDRs must weigh the decision to implement economic controls very carefully. In doing so, they should seek guidance from higher echelons and from personnel and organizations with appropriate expertise.

For further details on resources control, refer to JP 3-57, Civil-Military Operations.

c. **Public Health.** Establishing the public health policy is a primary concern of the transitional military authority for security, public safety, economic, and humanitarian reasons.

(1) Generally, the joint force lacks the HSS capacity to provide sustained medical care for civilians; however, with appropriate resources and security, the transitional military authority may open and secure humanitarian access to the local populace. It may also take steps such as establishing temporary clinics, training local health professionals, and augmenting existing medical facilities.

(2) The transitional military authority should take steps to secure the public health infrastructure. Such steps can enable functioning hospitals and clinics to remain open so local medical personnel can continue to serve civilians. The transitional military authority can also repair critical transportation infrastructure to ensure continued delivery of medical supplies and accessibility for emergency patient transport. The transitional military authority should ensure the continued functioning of essential services infrastructure so that adequate power, water, and sanitation are available to support health care facilities. Public health policy should also focus on burying or cremating remains; disposing of sewage, garbage, and refuse properly; purifying local water supplies; inspecting food supplies; and controlling insects and disease.

d. **Justice Systems.** The ordinary courts in areas under control of the transitional military authority generally continue to function during a military occupation. They may only be suspended if judges abstain from fulfilling their duties, the courts are corrupt or unfairly constituted, or the administration of the local jurisdiction has collapsed. In such cases, the transitional military authority may establish its own justice system.

(1) The penal laws of the occupied territory remain in force during the occupation. However, the transitional military authority may suspend them during an occupation if they constitute a threat to security or an obstacle to the application of the Geneva Conventions.

(2) During an occupation, the transitional military authority may enact special decrees and penal provisions essential for it to fulfill its obligations under the Geneva Convention relative to the Protection of Civilian Persons in Time of War, maintain orderly civil administration, and ensure the security of the occupying forces. It may not declare that the rights and actions of enemy nationals are extinguished, suspended, or unenforceable in a court of law. Penal provisions enacted by the transitional military authority during an occupation may not be enforced until they are made public to the population of the subject territory in the national language of that territory. Such penal provisions may not be retroactive and the penalty must be proportionate to the offense. Courts may only apply those provisions of law that were applicable prior to the alleged offense and are in accordance with the general principles of law.

(3) The transitional military authority may establish courts to hear cases on alleged violations of the special decrees and penal provisions enacted by the transitional military authority. It may also establish courts and administrative boards for other certain purposes. These might include considering the cases of detainees and reconsidering the refusals of requests by aliens to leave the occupied territory.

5. Transitions

a. The JFC should transfer control to a duly recognized government as quickly as possible. Authority and control can transfer either to the legitimate sovereign or to another civil authority. As conditions in the territory subject to transitional military authority stabilize, the degree of control exercised by the military can decrease; however, granting authority to civilian government officials does not of itself terminate the transitional military authority's responsibility in the occupied territory. A formal transfer to an authority capable of fulfilling the responsibilities of government and fully recognized by the USG must occur.

b. The transitional military authority should identify, screen, and train reliable civilians to ease this transfer. As the situation permits, the responsibility for civil administration transfers to HN or other civil authority to help it return to full self-governance. The joint force may continue to advise and train HN officials to build capacity, particularly in the security sector, after transferring governance authorities.

APPENDIX E
LEGAL AND FISCAL CONSIDERATIONS

This appendix summarizes some of the laws and policies that bear upon US military operations in support of stability operations. No summary provided in this document can replace a consultation with the unit's supporting SJA.

1. The Law of War and the Department of Defense Policy on Stability Operations

a. As stability operations are a core military function, there is no change regarding the obligation to comply with all applicable law and regulations. US forces conducting such missions remain bound to adhere to the principles of the law of war, to US laws and treaties, and to customary international law regarding human rights.

b. The nature of stability operations anticipates that they will be conducted in countries, regions, or areas that lack governmental structures capable of completing basic functions and providing services to the local population. Where the environment is not sufficiently permissive to allow civilian governments, agencies, or NGOs to provide adequate assistance to local populations, US military forces may be required to conduct operations in those areas. The operation of US forces in these circumstances generates several legal issues that will be of concern to CDRs at all echelons.

2. Authority to Assist a Foreign Government

a. DOS has the primary responsibility, authority, and funding to conduct foreign assistance on behalf of the USG. Foreign assistance encompasses any and all assistance to a FN, including security assistance (assistance to the internal police forces and military forces of the FN), development assistance (assistance to the foreign government in projects that will assist the development of the foreign economy or their political institutions), and humanitarian assistance (direct assistance to the population of an FN). The legal authority for DOS to conduct foreign assistance is found in the Foreign Assistance Act.

b. The Armed Forces of the United States have limited authority to provide assistance to foreign governments. For FID, US forces may be authorized to make limited contributions. Assistance to police by US forces is permitted, but not with DOD as the lead governmental department.

3. Non-International Armed Conflict

a. Although stability operations can be carried out while the HN is involved in armed conflict with another state, they are generally focused on the need to preserve the HN's internal security. Most often, stability operations are conducted in a country with existing conflict between government forces and armed non-state actors. As such, the main body of the law of war dealing with international (inter-state) armed conflict does not strictly apply to these conflicts—a legal position that can be a source of confusion to CDRs and US Service

GENEVA CONVENTIONS—COMMON ARTICLE 3

In the case of armed conflict not of an international character occurring in the territory of one of the High Contracting Parties, each Party to the conflict shall be bound to apply, as a minimum, the following provisions:

(1) Persons taking no active part in the hostilities, including members of armed forces who have laid down their arms and those placed "hors de combat" by sickness, wounds, detention, or any other cause, shall in all circumstances be treated humanely, without any adverse distinction founded on race, colour, religion or faith, sex, birth or wealth, or any other similar criteria.

To this end, the following acts are and shall remain prohibited at any time and in any place whatsoever with respect to the above-mentioned persons:

    (a) Violence to life and person, in particular murder of all kinds, mutilation, cruel treatment and torture;

    (b) Taking of hostages;

    (c) Outrages upon personal dignity, in particular humiliating and degrading treatment;

    (d) The passing of sentences and the carrying out of executions without previous judgment pronounced by a regularly constituted court, affording all the judicial guarantees which are recognized as indispensable by civilized peoples.

(2) The wounded and sick shall be collected and cared for.

An impartial humanitarian body, such as the International Committee of the Red Cross, may offer its services to the Parties to the conflict.

The Parties to the conflict should further endeavor to bring into force, by means of special agreements, all or part of the other provisions of the present Convention.

The application of the preceding provisions shall not affect the legal status of the Parties to the conflict.

members. It bears emphasis, however, that Article 3 common to all four of the 1949 Geneva Conventions is specifically intended to apply to non-international (including intra-state or "internal") armed conflicts.

b. By specifying that its application does not affect the legal status of the parties to a conflict, Common Article 3 makes clear that those taking an active part in the hostilities have no special status under international law. They are not, when captured, prisoners of war, but may be held for the duration of hostilities for analogous reasons. They may also be prosecuted as criminals for bearing arms against the government and for other offenses, so long as they are accorded the minimum protections described in Common Article 3. US forces should remember that they are criminal suspects within the legal system of the HN. US forces must carefully preserve weapons, witness statements, photographs, and other evidence collected at the scene. This evidence will be used by the HN legal system and thus promote the rule of law by holding persons accountable for their crimes.

c. During all such military operations, CDRs must be aware of Common Article 3 and the status of civilians under the laws of the HN. The importance of having awareness is heightened in stability operations because the crux of the overall campaign plan is to provide training and support to HN governments and security forces. The most effective means of maintaining legitimacy in stability operations is to conduct the mission in a professional manner consistent with international legal standards.

d. Status-of-forces agreement (SOFAs) establish the legal status of foreign military personnel in an HN. Criminal and civil jurisdiction, taxation, and claims for damages and injuries are some of the topics usually covered in SOFAs. Other documents which may reflect the legal status of military personnel include diplomatic letters, memorandums of agreement, and memorandums of understanding. In the absence of an agreement or some other arrangement with the HN, DOD personnel may be subject to HN laws.

e. The role of the International Committee of the Red Cross (ICRC) in Common Article 3 situations as an impartial humanitarian organization is formally recognized in the Geneva Conventions. In non-international armed conflicts, the ICRC formally declares itself available for carrying out its Common Article 3 designated tasks. The ICRC's efforts in non-international armed conflicts include protecting the lives and dignity of victims of armed conflict and endeavouring to prevent suffering.

4. Detainee Operations

a. Detainee operations of civilians, in general, should not be undertaken unless they are well planned, coordinated with the HN, and directed by the highest authority. The detention of civilians in a stability operations environment is a complex task. Detention is a highly politically sensitive issue, and the manner in which detainee operations are carried out can have a large negative impact on the civilian populace and could affect the success or failure of a stability operations campaign.

b. There are two primary issues that must be considered at the base level prior to taking detainees into custody. One issue is the legal basis for detention. This will define all other actions and processes used to handle detainees. The legal basis should address the circumstances where it is appropriate to detain civilians, how long they may be held, and possibly even a standard for continued detention or release from custody. The other issue that CDRs must consider is the standard for humane treatment of detainees, both from a legal perspective for US-held prisoners and from a training perspective when working with HN security forces. CDRs will specifically detail the parameters of detainee operations in an operations order which is incorporated into all subordinate units' missions.

c. **Standards for Detention and Internment.** Regardless of the precise legal status of those persons captured, detained, or otherwise held in custody by US forces, they must receive humane treatment until properly released. They also must be provided the minimum protections articulated in Common Article 3 of the Geneva Conventions. Specially trained, organized, and equipped military police units in adequately designed and resourced facilities should accomplish prolonged detention. Such detention must follow the detailed standards contained in Department of Defense Directive (DODD) 2310.01E, *The Department of Defense Detainee Program,* and CJCSI 3290.01C, *Program for Detainee Operations.* The interrogation of detainees may only be conducted by qualified and certified personnel and must be in accordance with DODD 3115.09, *DOD Intelligence Interrogations, Detainee Briefings, and Tactical Questioning,* and JP 2-01.2, *Counterintelligence and Human Intelligence Support to Joint Operations.* The military police personnel operating detention facilities shall not be used to assist in or "set the conditions for" interrogation.

d. **Transfer of Detainees to the Host Nation.** There are certain conditions under which US forces may not transfer the custody of detainees to the HN or any other foreign government. US forces retain custody if they have substantial grounds to believe that the detainees would be in danger in the custody of others. Such danger could include being subjected to torture or inhumane treatment.

e. **The Role and Contributions of the ICRC**

(1) Subject to essential security needs, mission requirements, and other legitimate, practical limitations, the ICRC must be permitted to visit prisoners of war and provide them certain types of relief. Typically, the USG will invite the ICRC to observe prisoners of war, civilian internee or detainee conditions as soon as circumstances permit. The invitation to the ICRC for its assistance is made by the USG (DOS, in coordination with DOD), and not by the CCDR. Reporting of all ICRC contacts, inspections, or meetings through operational channels is accomplished in accordance with DOD guidance.

(2) The SJA should serve as the escort and LNO with the ICRC. The SJA can quickly identify and resolve many law of war issues before they become a problem for the JFC. The SJA can best serve as the JFC's skilled advocate in discussions with the ICRC concerning the law of war.

(3) Both the JFC and the SJA should recognize that the ICRC, as an impartial humanitarian organization, is not a political adversary, eagerly watching for and reporting law of war violations. Rather, it is capable of providing assistance in a variety of ways. In recent conflicts, the ICRC assisted in making arrangements for the transportation of the

remains of dead enemy combatants and for repatriating prisoners of war and civilian detainees.

(4) Involving the ICRC is a central issue when considering detainee issues. Because detention facilities, even during multinational operations, are usually administered by individual nations, the confidential reports provided by the ICRC tend to be directed to national governments.

For more information, refer to JP 3-63, Detainee Operations, *and the* Operational Law Handbook.

5. Investigations

a. Investigations are an essential tool to allow CDRs to understand events that take place within the operational area. They are tools that allow for the enforcement of discipline when misconduct has been demonstrated. However, investigations are more than that. They allow CDRs to have a record of actions taken in battle that may be disputed in the future, whether by outside organizations like the media, or by enemy IO efforts. Properly conducted investigations can be used to demonstrate a commitment to professionalism by US forces and assist in gaining or maintaining legitimacy with a local population.

b. In the event an investigation is required in a joint environment, judge advocates should determine which Service's regulation is most applicable and then an investigation under that regulation should be conducted. When determining which Service's regulation is most applicable consider the possible uses of the investigation, whether a particular Service requires a certain investigation, which Service has the most at stake in the outcome of the investigation, any local or command guidance regarding joint investigations, and other matters that would contribute to an informed decision.

c. Since investigations in all Services follow similar basic concepts and will result in a thorough investigation if conducted properly, the regulation ultimately used is not as important as is choosing and following a particular authorized regulation. Under no circumstances should regulations be combined and a "hybrid" investigation be created. The Services are shown great deference in regards to administrative matters as long as regulations are followed correctly.

6. Criminal Jurisdiction over Civilian Personnel and Contractors

Modern operations involve many DOD civilians as well as contractors authorized to accompany the force (CAAF). Article 2(a)(10) of the Uniform Code of Military Justice now allows for the prosecution of people accompanying US forces in times of declared war or contingency operations. The Military Extraterritorial Jurisdiction Act further allows for the prosecution in federal courts of DOD civilians and CAAF. Typically, DOD civilians and CAAF implicated in criminal activities will be referred to the DOJ for action. However, military courts may be used to prosecute those serving with or accompanying US forces in the field during declared war or contingency operations. So, DOD civilians and CAAF may be made subject to general orders. They are also subject to US laws and to the laws of the HN; they may be prosecuted or receive adverse administrative action by the United States or contract employers. DOD directives contain further policy and guidance pertaining to allegations of criminal activity against US civilians and CAAF.

7. Funding Issues

a. A basic tenet of fiscal law is that expenditure of public funds may be made only when expressly authorized by Congress. The fiscal rules surrounding stability operations are a web of statutes, annual appropriations, policies, regulations, and directives that may be confusing. The financial impacts of stability operations are a major concern of the JFC. Planning must take into account the legal authority, authority limits, funding sources, and mechanisms that allow US forces to dispense supplies and services. The SJA and the comptroller should be involved in planning for stability operations as early as possible. It is important that the JFC coordinate expenditures with the appropriate agency prior to funds being expended.

b. Congress specifically appropriates funds for foreign assistance. The USAID expends such funds under the legal authorities in Title 22, USC. Provisions of Title 10, USC, authorize small amounts of money. These funds are appropriated annually for CDRs to provide humanitarian relief, disaster relief, or civic assistance in conjunction with military operations. These standing authorities are narrowly defined and generally require significant advance coordination within DOD and DOS. As such, they can be of limited value in a rapidly evolving operational environment.

c. As was stated previously, federal law generally prohibits DOD from expending funds to provide training or materiel support to foreign security forces. Generally, such expenditures must be made through DOS foreign assistance funds under Title 22, USC. While DOS has supervision and control of Title 22, USC, foreign assistance programs, DOD frequently ends up as the implementer of these programs. DOD 5105.38-M, *Security Assistance Management Manual,* should be thoroughly reviewed for an understanding of the major security assistance programs as well as the relationship between DOD and DOS in implementing those programs. The major types of security assistance programs authorized under Title 22, USC (from the Foreign Assistance Act and the Arms Export Control Act), as well the administrator of each program and the funding request and approval timeline for these programs should be understood.

d. There are two exceptions to the general rule requiring the use of Title 22, USC, funds for foreign assistance:

(1) Interoperability, Safety, and Familiarization Training: DOD may fund the training (as opposed to goods and services) of foreign militaries with operations and maintenance (O&M) dollars only when the purpose of the training is to enhance interoperability, familiarization, and safety training. O&M funds may not be used for security assistance training. This exception applies only to interoperability training.

(2) Congressional appropriation or authorization to conduct foreign assistance: DOD may fund foreign assistance operations if Congress has provided a specific appropriation or authorization to execute the mission.

e. Effective foreign forces need training and equipment. US laws require Congress to authorize such expenditures. US laws also require the DOS to verify that the HN receiving the assistance is not in violation of human rights.

f. All training and equipping of foreign security forces must be specifically authorized. Usually, DOD involvement is limited to a precise level of man hours and materiel requested from DOS under the Foreign Assistance Act. The President may authorize deployed US forces to train or advise HN security forces as part of the operational mission. In this case, DOD personnel, operations, and maintenance appropriations provide an incidental benefit to those security forces. All other weapons, training, equipment, logistic support, supplies, and services provided to foreign forces must be paid for with funds appropriated by Congress for that purpose. Examples of additional appropriations to allow DOD to provide training and assistance to foreign forces include the Iraq Security Forces Fund and the Afghan Security Forces Fund. Moreover, the President must give specific authority to the DOD for its role in such "train and equip" efforts. In May of 2004, the President signed a decision directive that made the CDR, US Central Command, under policy guidance from the COM, responsible for coordinating all USG efforts to organize, train, and equip Iraqi Security Forces, including police. Absent such a directive, DOD lacks authority to take the lead in assisting an HN to train and equip its security forces.

g. In addition to the aforementioned authorities, Congress has recently (since 2005) passed a number of special foreign assistance authorities that are not made permanent law within the USC, but rather are stand-alone authorities contained in annual authorization and appropriations acts. These special authorities often contain "dual key" or co-approval provisions that grant a certain foreign assistance authority to SecDef, with the concurrence of SECSTATE (or in other cases, with the concurrence of the relevant COM). Keeping track of the currency of these authorities can be very challenging, as they frequently expire at the end of each fiscal year (FY), making their continued availability entirely dependent upon annual renewals by Congress. Some of the major special authority programs passed by Congress since 2005 follow (Note: These references are current at the time of publication, however they may expire before this publication is updated. Consult the local SJA and comptroller for current fiscal authority. The authorities listed below are provided for historical purposes to inform the reader that temporary authorities may exist outside the traditional Title 22, USC, planning cycle.)

(1) **Authority to Build the Capacity of Foreign Military Forces.** Section 1206 of the FY 06 National Defense Authorization Act (NDAA), as amended through FY 11, authorized (through FY 12) SecDef, with the concurrence of SECSTATE, to:

(a) Conduct or support a program to build the capacity of a foreign country's national military forces in order for that country to conduct counterterrorist operations; or participate in or support military and stability operations in which the Armed Forces of the United States are participating; and

(b) Build the capacity of a foreign country's maritime security forces to conduct counterterrorism operations.

(c) Additionally, Title 10, USC, Section 168, provides statutory authority for SecDef and CCDRs to conduct military-to-military contacts and comparable activities that are designed to encourage a democratic orientation of defense establishments and military forces of other countries.

(2) **Support of Special Operations to Combat Terrorism.** The FY 05 NDAA (as amended through FY 11), authorized SecDef, with the concurrence of the relevant COM, to expend up to $45,000,000 during any FY (through FY 13) to provide support to foreign forces, irregular forces, groups, or individuals engaged in supporting or facilitating ongoing military operations by US SOF to combat terrorism.

(3) **Pakistan COIN Fund.** In addition to these authorities, Congress has granted temporary "dual key" authorities to region-specific areas, such as the previously mentioned Iraqi Security Forces Fund and Afghanistan Security Forces Fund. The Pakistan COIN fund is an example of an authority that is not an "out of O&M hide" fund, meaning that it has its own appropriated fund to draw from, compared to 1206 and 1208 funds, which simply come out of the DOD O&M fund. Most recently (June of 2009), Congress established in the Treasury of the United States the "Pakistan Counterinsurgency Fund," which provided $400,000,000 (available until 30 September, 2011, as amended in NDAA for FY 2011 assistance required to be provided in a manner that promotes the observance of, and respect for, human rights, as well as the respect for legitimate civilian authority within Pakistan) to SecDef, with the concurrence of SECSTATE, to provide assistance to Pakistan's security forces, to include:

(a) Program management and the provision of equipment, supplies, services, training, and funds;

(b) Facility and infrastructure repair, renovation, and construction to build the COIN capability of Pakistan's military and Frontier Corps;

(c) $2,000,000 for urgent humanitarian assistance to the people of Pakistan only as part of civil-military training exercises for Pakistani security forces receiving assistance under the "Pakistan Counterinsurgency Fund" and to assist the Government of Pakistan in creating such a program beginning in FY 10.

(4) **Regional Defense Combating Terrorism Fellowship Program (CTFP)**

(a) In addition to the above temporary authorities, in 2003 Congress enacted a permanent DOD authority known as CTFP (codified at Title 10, USC, Section 2249c), which authorizes DOD appropriated funds to be used to pay any costs associated with the education and training of foreign military officers, ministry of defense officials, or security officials at military or civilian educational institutions, regional centers, conferences, seminars, or other training programs conducted under the Regional Defense CTFP, including the costs of transportation and travel and subsistence costs.

(b) According to the FY 07 DOD Report to Congress on the CTFP, the CTFP's goals are to: build and strengthen a global network of combating terrorism (CbT) experts and practitioners at the operational and strategic levels; build and reinforce the CbT capabilities of partner nations through operational and strategic-level education; contribute to efforts to counter ideological support to terrorism; and provide the US military with a flexible and proactive program that can respond to emerging CbT requirements. The Assistant Secretary of Defense for Global Security Affairs provides policy oversight. The DSCA provides financial management. CTFP requires approval from the COMs prior to any event or engagement.

(5) **Combatant Commander Initiative Fund.** Title 10, USC, Section 166a, authorizes the Chairman of the Joint Chiefs of Staff (CJCS) to provide to a CCDR DOD funds for the following activities:

(a) Force training

(b) Contingencies

(c) Selected operations

(d) C2

(e) Joint exercises (including activities of participating foreign countries)

(f) HCA, to include urgent and unanticipated humanitarian relief and reconstruction assistance

(g) Military education and training to military and related civilian personnel of foreign countries (including transportation, translation, and administrative expenses)

(h) Personnel expenses of defense personnel for bilateral or regional cooperation programs

(i) Force protection

(j) Joint warfighting capabilities. This statute further states that the CJCS, "in considering requests for funds in the Combatant Commander Initiative Fund, should give priority consideration to:

1. Requests for funds to be used for activities that would enhance the war fighting capability, readiness, and sustainability of the forces assigned to the CDR requesting the funds;

2. The provision of funds to be used for activities with respect to an area or areas not within the AOR of a GCC that would reduce the threat to, or otherwise increase, the national security of the United States; and

3. The provision of funds to be used for urgent and unanticipated humanitarian relief and reconstruction assistance, particularly in a foreign country where the armed forces are engaged in a contingency operation."

(6) The DSCA provides FHA program assistance and support for geographic combatant commands via OHDACA funding.

h. The **"Leahy Amendment"** contains additional constraints on government funding of SFA/FID missions. The law, first enacted in the 1997 Foreign Operations Appropriation Act (i.e., the annual DOS Appropriations Act), prohibits the USG from providing funds to the security forces of a foreign country if DOS has credible evidence that the foreign country or its agents have committed gross violations of human rights, unless SECSTATE determines and reports that the government of such country is taking effective measures to bring the responsible members of the security forces unit to justice.

i. **Humanitarian Relief and Reconstruction.** In military operations, commands require specific authority to expend funds. That authority is normally found in the DOD Appropriations Act, specifically, O&M. In recent contingency operations, Congress appropriated additional funds to CDRs for the specific purpose of dealing with stability operations and related mission types like COIN. Recent examples include the CERP, the Iraq Relief and Reconstruction Fund, Iraq Freedom Fund, and Commander's Humanitarian Relief and Reconstruction Program funds.

j. **Commanders Emergency Response Program**

(1) Beginning in November of 2003, Congress authorized use of a specific amount of O&M funds for a CERP in Iraq and Afghanistan. The legislation was renewed in successive appropriations and authorization acts. It specified that CDRs could spend the funds for urgent humanitarian relief and reconstruction projects. These projects had to immediately assist the Iraqi and Afghan peoples within a CDR's operational area. Congress did not intend the funds to be used as security assistance such as weapons, ammunition, and supplies for security forces; salaries for Iraqi or Afghan forces or employees; rewards for information; payments in satisfaction of claims made by Iraqis or Afghanis against the United States (specific legislation must authorize such payments).

(2) The CERP is not a standing program. Any similar future program should be governed by whatever specific legislative provision Congress chooses to enact. In any program similar to CERP, CDRs and staffs must make sound, well-coordinated decisions on how to spend the funds. They must ensure that maximum goodwill is created. CDRs must verify that the extra cash does not create harmful effects in the local economy. One such side effect would be creating unsustainable wages that divert skilled labor from an HN program essential to its legitimacy. CDRs must also ensure that projects can be responsibly administered to achieve the desired objective and that they avoid inadvertently financing insurgents.

k. **Foreign Claims**

(1) Under the Foreign Claims Act (FCA), meritorious claims for property losses, injury or death caused by Service members or the civilian component of the US forces may be settled "[t]o promote and maintain friendly relations" with the HN. Claims that result from "noncombat activities" or negligent or wrongful acts or omissions are also

compensable. Categories of claims that may not be allowed include: losses from combat; contractual matters; domestic obligations; and claims that are either not in the best interest of the US to pay, or are contrary to public policy.

(2) In adjudicating claims under the FCA, the Foreign Claims Commission applies the law of the country in which the claim arose to determine both liability and damages. This includes the local law or custom pertaining to contributory or comparative negligence and joint tortfeasors. Payments for punitive damages, court costs, filing costs, attorneys' fees, and bailment are not allowed under the FCA.

(3) As a general rule, the FCA will not apply in foreign countries where the US has an agreement that "provides for the settlement or adjudication and cost sharing of claims against the United States arising out of the acts or omissions of a member or civilian employee of an armed force of the United States." For example, if a unit deploys to Korea, Japan, or any NATO or Partnership for Peace country, claims matters will be managed by a command claims service under provisions outlined in the applicable status SOFA.

l. **Condolence or Solatia-Like Payments**

(1) Condolence or solatia payments are monetary or in-kind payments provided to an individual or their family as an expression of sympathy or condolence for an injury or a death. Condolence and solatia payments are not claims payments. These payments are only made in certain cultural groups where payments in sympathy or in recognition of loss are common.

(2) These payments are meant to be made immediately, and are generally nominal. The individual or unit involved in the damage has no legal obligation to pay; compensation is simply offered as an expression of sympathy in accordance with local custom. Condolence and solatia payments are not paid from claims funds. Instead, solatia payments are made from a unit's O&M funds while condolence payments may also derive from other sources (e.g., CERP Funds in Iraq were authorized to cover condolence payments in 2005).

(3) Prompt payment of condolence/solatia ensures the goodwill of local national populations, thus allowing the US to maintain positive relations with the HN. Condolence or solatia payments should not be made without prior coordination with the GCC.

Intentionally Blank

APPENDIX F
KEY STABILITY OPERATIONS DOCUMENTS

1. Overview

This appendix provides general summaries of stability operations documents from key government and nongovernment agencies.

2. United States Department of State

Various offices within DOS have authored key documents of import in a stability operation. As tools to assist accomplishing these reconstruction tasks, S/CRS in particular has developed a number of key documents that have been vetted with other USG departments and agencies. These include:

a. *Interagency Management System for Reconstruction and Stabilization*: Describes a framework and processes for whole-of-government actions in reconstruction and stabilization efforts in complex operational environments. The IMS is discussed throughout this JP.

b. *Principles of the USG Planning Framework for Reconstruction, Stabilization, and Conflict Transformation*: Lays out key principles and processes to be used in planning for stabilization efforts; it establishes a four-stage process including situation analysis, policy formulation, strategy development, and interagency implementation planning.

c. *Triggering Mechanisms for Whole-of-Government Planning for Reconstruction, Stabilization, and Conflict Transformation*: Describes the conditions under which whole-of-government planning is necessary (both in crisis and contingency scenarios) in a certain country, including political or economic collapse, increased ethnic tension, and other situations with conflict implications; outlines the authorities that can trigger and oversee the establishment and prioritization of those country engagements.

d. *Civilian Response Corps Active Concept of Operations*: The Civilian Response Corps active component is made up of civilians from various agencies within the USG who are deployed approximately 50 percent of the year, have sectoral expertise, training, and experience in stabilization efforts. They may assist with whole-of-government planning, assessments, HN engagement, and a variety of other tasks.

e. *Civilian Response Corps Standby Concept of Operations*: The Civilian Response Corps standby component is made up of civilians from various agencies within the USG who are full-time employees of their home agency but who have received additional training in stabilization and are deployable with 30 days' notice to a specific effort with permission from their supervisor. Their qualifications and potential duties are the same as the Civilian Response Corps active component.

f. *Demobilization, Disarmament, and Reintegration (DDR) in Stabilization and Reconstruction Operations*: This document provides USG personnel with guidance in strategic-level planning to disarm armed elements and facilitate the return of ex-combatants to civilian life.

g. *Transition Elections and Political Processes in Reconstruction and Stabilization Operations*: Best practices for one of the most visible and important steps toward democratic political transition, including information for policymakers, strategic planners, implementers, and monitors.

h. *Post-Conflict Reconstruction Essential Tasks*: Outlines key stabilization tasks within five broad areas: security, governance and participation, humanitarian assistance and social well-being, economic stabilization and infrastructure, and justice and reconciliation. They are organized into short-, medium-, and long-term phases. Many tasks are cross-cutting and require consideration of other tasks, especially when prioritizing efforts. The ETM is designed to evolve as it is used and as best practices emerge.

3. United States Agency for International Development

a. USAID is an independent federal government agency that receives overall foreign policy guidance from SECSTATE.

b. In its efforts to be successful as an instrument of US foreign policy and national security, the agency has developed nine principles of development and reconstruction assistance. These principles are a summary of characteristics for successful assistance, and include the following:

(1) **Ownership.** Build on the leadership, participation, and commitment of a country and its people.

(2) **Capacity Building.** Strengthen local institutions, transfer technical skills, and promote appropriate policies.

(3) **Sustainability.** Design programs to ensure their impact endures.

(4) **Selectivity.** Allocate resources based on need, local commitment, and foreign policy interests.

(5) **Assessment.** Conduct careful research, adapt best practices, and design for local conditions.

(6) **Results.** Focus resources to achieve clearly defined, measurable, and strategically focused objectives.

(7) **Partnership.** Collaborate closely with governments, communities, donors, IGOs, NGOs, the private sector, and universities.

(8) **Flexibility.** Adjust to changing conditions, take advantage of opportunities, and maximize efficiency.

(9) **Accountability.** Design accountability and transparency into systems and build effective checks and balances to guard against corruption.

4. United States Institute of Peace

a. The United States Institute of Peace is an independent, nonpartisan, national institution established and funded by Congress to prevent and resolve violent international conflicts, promote post-conflict stability and development, and increase conflict management capacity, tools, and intellectual capital worldwide.

b. In 2005, the Working Group on Civil-Military Relations in Nonpermissive Environments, facilitated by the US Institute for Peace, was created, which ultimately produced the *Guidelines for Relations Between US Armed Forces and Non-Governmental Humanitarian Organizations in Hostile or Potentially Hostile Environments* (http://www.usip.org/resources/guidelines-relations-between-us-armed-forces-and-nghos-hostile-or-potentially-hostile-envi). These guidelines seek to mitigate frictions and facilitate interaction between the Armed Forces of the United States and NGOs engaged in humanitarian relief efforts in hostile or potentially hostile environments.

c. *Guide to IGOs, NGOs, and the Military in Peace and Relief Operations* (http://bookstore.usip.org/books/BookDetail.aspx?productID=51290) provides short scenarios of typical international involvement in peace missions, natural disasters, and stability operations, as well as an introduction to the organizations that will be present when the international community responds to a crisis. Included are descriptions of the roles of the UN and other international institutions, NGOs, the US military, and USG civilian agencies.

d. The *Guiding Principles for Stabilization and Reconstruction* presents the first strategic "doctrine" ever produced for civilians engaged in PB missions. It is a practical roadmap for helping countries transition from violent conflict to peace.

5. United Nations

a. The Inter-Agency Standing Committee (IASC) is the UN's policy-making body in humanitarian affairs. It is the primary mechanism for inter-agency coordination of humanitarian assistance, and is a unique forum involving the key UN and non-UN humanitarian partners. It was created to strengthen coordination and effectiveness of humanitarian assistance. *Civil-Military Guidelines & Reference for Complex Emergencies* is the first collection of core humanitarian instruments developed by the UN and IASC on civil-military relationship in complex emergencies. Its aim is to assist humanitarian and military professionals to deal with civil-military issues in a manner that respects and appropriately reflects humanitarian concerns at the strategic, operational, and tactical levels in accordance with international law, standards, and principles.

b. The DPKO plans, prepares, manages, and directs UN PKO. It provides policy guidance and strategic direction to UN PKO, and works to integrate the efforts of UN, governmental, and nongovernmental entities in the context of PKO. It also provides guidance and support on military, police, mine action, and other relevant issues to other UN political and PB missions.

(1) The DPKO, along with the Department of Field Support, has evolved a major reform effort, *Peace Operations 2010,* aimed at strengthening and professionalizing the planning, management, and conduct of UN PKO.

(2) The UN peacekeeping doctrine framework is currently divided into six major guidance "series" (1000–6000). It includes the capstone publication, *United Nations Peacekeeping Operations: Principles and Guidelines*, and the *Handbook on United Nations Multi-Dimensional Peacekeeping Operations*.

6. United States Army Peacekeeping and Stability Operations Institute

a. PKSOI serves as the US military's center of excellence for mastering stability and PO at the strategic and operational levels to improve military, civilian agency, international, and multinational capabilities and execution.

b. PKSOI writes and contributes to concept and doctrine development through its interactions with organizations and authors responsible for stability operations concept and doctrine development. PKSOI provides subject matter expertise, technical review, and writing expertise to doctrine and concept preparing agencies. The institute facilitates integration of doctrinal changes with other PKSOI sections to ensure second and third order effects are considered with respect to policy, training, education, research, and the after action review process. Its publications can be accessed through: https://pksoi.army.mil/Index.cfm.

APPENDIX G
REFERENCES

The development of JP 3-07 is based upon the following primary references.

1. National Policy and Strategy

a. Presidential Policy Directive-1, *Organization of the National Security Council System.*

b. *National Military Strategy of the United States of America.*

2. Department of Defense

a. Department of Defense Instruction (DODI) 3000.05, *Stability Operations.*

b. DODI 6000.16, *Military Health Support for Stability Operations.*

c. DODI 8220.02, *Information and Communications Technology (ICT) Capabilities for Support of Stabilization and Reconstruction, Disaster Relief, and Humanitarian and Civic Assistance Operations.*

d. DODD 2310.01E, *The Department of Defense Detainee Program.*

e. DODD 3115.09, *DOD Intelligence Interrogations, Detainee Briefings, and Tactical Questioning.*

3. Chairman of the Joint Chiefs of Staff

a. CJCSI 3121.01B, *Standing Rules of Engagement/Standing Rules for the Use of Force for US Forces (U).*

b. CJCSI 5130.01D, *Relationships Between Commanders of Combatant Commands and International Commands and Organizations (U).*

4. Joint Publications

a. JP 1, *Doctrine for the Armed Forces of the United States.*

b. JP 2-0, *Joint Intelligence.*

c. JP 2-01.3, *Joint Intelligence Preparation of the Operational Environment.*

d. JP 3-0, *Joint Operations.*

e. JP 3-05, *Joint Special Operations.*

f. JP 3-07.3, *Peace Operations.*

g. JP 3-07.4, *Joint Counterdrug Operations.*

h. JP 3-08, *Interorganizational Coordination During Joint Operations.*

i. JP 3-13, *Information Operations.*

j. JP 3-13.1, *Electronic Warfare.*

k. JP 3-16, *Multinational Operations.*

l. JP 3-22, *Foreign Internal Defense.*

m. JP 3-24, *Counterinsurgency Operations.*

n. JP 3-29, *Foreign Humanitarian Assistance.*

o. JP 3-31, *Command and Control for Joint Land Operations.*

p. JP 3-57, *Civil-Military Operations.*

q. JP 3-61, *Public Affairs.*

r. JP 4-0, *Joint Logistics.*

s. JP 4-10, *Operational Contract Support.*

t. JP 5-0, *Joint Operation Planning.*

5. Other Documents

a. *Achieving Unity of Effort: A Case Study of US Government Operations in the Horn of Africa*, Institute for Defense Analyses.

b. *Allied Joint Doctrine for Peace Support,* AJP-3.4.1(A), NATO.

c. *Assessing Counterinsurgency and Stabilization Missions*, Jason Campbell, Michael O'Hanlon, Jeremy Shapiro, The Brookings Institution.

d. *Campaigning to Protect: Using Military Force to Stop Genocide and Mass Atrocities,* Lt Col Clint "Q" Hinote, USAF.

e. *Changing Tires on the Fly: The Marines and Postconflict Stability Ops*, Frank G. Hoffman, Foreign Policy Research Institute.

f. *Civilian Surge, Key to Complex Operations*, National Defense University.

g. *Civil-Military Coordination Officer Field Handbook,* UN Office for the Coordination of Humanitarian Affairs.

h. *Civil-Military Guidelines and Reference for Complex Emergencies,* UN Office for the Coordination of Humanitarian Affairs.

i. *Combating Serious Crimes in Postconflict Societies,* US Institute of Peace.

j. *Commander's Handbook for Strategic Communication,* Joint Warfighting Center.

k. *Commanding Heights, Strategic Lessons from Complex Operations,* Center for Complex Operations, National Defense University.

l. *Comprehensive Framework for Action, High-Level Task Force on the Global Food Security Crisis,* United Nations.

m. *Concept for Unified Action through Civil-Military Integration,* USMC.

n. *Conducting a DG Assessment: A Framework for Strategy Development,* USAID.

o. *Criminal Justice Sector Assessment Rating Tool,* Bureau for International Narcotics and Law Enforcement Affairs, US DOS, Version 2.0.

p. *Cultural Generic Information Requirements Handbook (C-GIRH)* DOD-GIRH-2634-001-08, US Marine Corps Intelligence Activity.

q. *Disarmament, Demobilisation, and Reintegration: A Practical Field and Classroom Guide,* German Technical Co-operation Corporation, The Norwegian Defence International Centre, Pearson Peacekeeping Centre, and Swedish National Defence College.

r. *Disarmament, Demobilization, and Reintegration in Reconstruction and Stabilization Operations,* S/CRS, US DOS.

s. *Evaluation of USAID's Community Stabilization Program (CSP) in Iraq: Effectiveness of the CSP Model as a Non-Lethal Tool for Counterinsurgency,* USID.

t. *General Guidance for Interaction between United Nations Personnel and Military and Other Representatives of the Belligerent Parties in the Context of the Crisis in Iraq,* UN Office for the Coordination of Humanitarian Affairs.

u. *Guidance for the Conduct of Tactical Stability Activities and Tasks,* ATP-3.2.1.1, NATO.

v. *Guide to IGOs, NGOs, and the Military in Peace and Relief Operations.*

w. *Guide to Rebuilding Governance in Stability Operations: A Role for the Military,* USA PKSOI.

x. *Guide to Rebuilding Public Sector Services in Stability Operations: A Role for the Military,* Strategic Studies Institute, US Army War College.

y. *Guide to Rule of Law Country Analysis: The Rule of Law Strategic Framework*, US AID.

z. *Guidebook for Supporting Economic Development in Stability Operations*, RAND.

aa. *Guiding Principles for Stabilization and Reconstruction*, US Institute of Peace, US PKSOI.

bb. *Guidelines for Humanitarian Organisations on Interacting with Military and Other Security Actors in Iraq*, UN Assistance Mission for Iraq.

cc. *Guidelines for the Interaction and Coordination of Humanitarian Actors and Military Actors in Afghanistan*, UN Assistance Mission for Afghanistan.

dd. *Guidelines for Relations Between US Armed Forces and Non-Governmental Humanitarian Organizations*, US Institute of Peace.

ee. *Improving Capacity for Stabilization and Reconstruction Operations*, RAND.

ff. *Integrating Civilian Agencies in Stability Operations*, RAND.

gg. *Interagency Conflict Assessment Framework*, S/CRS, US DOS.

hh. *International Security Assistance Force Provincial Reconstruction Team Handbook*, Edition 4.

ii. *MAGTF Command Element in Transition and Reconstruction Operations*, Marine Corps Center for Lessons Learned.

jj. *Managing Assistance in Support of Political and Electoral Processes*, US AID.

kk. *MARO—Mass Atrocity Response Operations: A Military Planning Handbook*, Carr Center for Human Rights Policy, John F. Kennedy School of Government, Harvard University, and the US PKSOI.

ll. *Measuring Progress in Stabilization and Reconstruction (MPICE)*, US Institute of Peace.

mm. *Military Participation in the Interagency Management System for Reconstruction and Stabilization*, United States Joint Forces Command Source (USJFCOM).

nn. *Military Support to Economic Normalization Handbook*, USJFCOM.

oo. *Military Support to Essential Services and Critical Infrastructure*, USJFCOM.

pp. *Military Support to Post-Conflict Governance, Elections, and Media Development*, USJFCOM.

qq. *Military Support to Rule of Law and Security Sector Reform*, USJFCOM.

rr. *Military-Humanitarian Integration, The Promise and the Peril*, Denis Kennedy, The Finnish Institute of International Affairs.

ss. *Post-Conflict Health Reconstruction: New Foundations for US Policy*, Leonard S. Rubenstein, US Institute of Peace.

tt. *Post-Conflict Reconstruction Essential Tasks*, S/CRS, US DOS.

uu. *Preventing Genocide, A Blueprint for US Policymakers,* United States Holocaust Memorial Museum, The American Academy of Diplomacy, and the Endowment of the US Institute of Peace.

vv. *Securing the Future, A Primer on Security Sector Reform in Conflict Countries*, US Institute of Peace.

ww. *Security and Stabilisation: The Military Contribution*, Joint Doctrine Publication 3-40, United Kingdom.

xx. *Security Sector Reform*, US AID, DOD, US DOS.

yy. *Stability Operations*, Field Manual 3-07, US Army.

zz. *The New Balance: Limited Armed Stabilization and the Future of US Landpower*, Strategic Studies Institute, US Army War College.

aaa. *The Rule of Law Handbook: A Practitioner's Guide for Judge Advocates*, The Judge Advocate General's Legal Center and School.

bbb. *The US Military's Experience in Stability Operations, 1789-2005*, Lawrence A. Yates, Combat Studies Institute Press.

ccc. *Topic Guide on Fragile States*, Claire McLoughlin, Governance and Social Development Resource Centre.

ddd. *US Department of State Foreign Affairs Manual.*

eee. *USAID Primer: What We Do and How We Do It.*

Intentionally Blank

APPENDIX H
ADMINISTRATIVE INSTRUCTIONS

1. User Comments

Users in the field are highly encouraged to submit comments on this publication to: Joint Staff J-7, Deputy Director, Joint and Coalition Warfighting, Joint and Coalition Warfighting Center, ATTN: Joint Doctrine Support Division, 116 Lake View Parkway, Suffolk, VA 23435-2697. These comments should address content (accuracy, usefulness, consistency, and organization), writing, and appearance.

2. Authorship

The lead agent for this publication is USJFCOM. The Joint Staff doctrine sponsor for this publication is the Director for Strategic Plans and Policy (J-5).

3. Change Recommendations

a. Recommendations for urgent changes to this publication should be submitted:

TO: JOINT STAFF WASHINGTON DC//J7-JEDD//

b. Routine changes should be submitted electronically to the Deputy Director, Joint and Coalition Warfighting, Joint and Coalition Warfighting Center, Joint Doctrine Support Division and info the lead agent and the Director for Joint Force Development, J-7/JEDD.

c. When a Joint Staff directorate submits a proposal to the CJCS that would change source document information reflected in this publication, that directorate will include a proposed change to this publication as an enclosure to its proposal. The Services and other organizations are requested to notify the Joint Staff J-7 when changes to source documents reflected in this publication are initiated.

4. Distribution of Publications

Local reproduction is authorized and access to unclassified publications is unrestricted. However, access to and reproduction authorization for classified joint publications must be in accordance with DOD 5200.1-R, *Information Security Program.*

5. Distribution of Electronic Publications

a. Joint Staff J-7 will not print copies of JPs for distribution. Electronic versions are available on JDEIS at https://jdeis.js.mil (NIPRNET), and http://jdeis.js.smil.mil (SIPRNET), and on the JEL at http://www.dtic.mil/doctrine (NIPRNET).

b. Only approved JPs and joint test publications are releasable outside the CCMDs, Services, and Joint Staff. Release of any classified JP to foreign governments or foreign nationals must be requested through the local embassy (Defense Attaché Office) to DIA,

Defense Foreign Liaison/IE-3, 200 MacDill Blvd., Joint Base Anacostia-Bolling, Washington, DC 20340-5100.

c. JEL CD-ROM. Upon request of a joint doctrine development community member, the Joint Staff J-7 will produce and deliver one CD-ROM with current JPs. This JEL CD-ROM will be updated not less than semi-annually and when received can be locally reproduced for use within the combatant commands and Services.

GLOSSARY
PART I—ABBREVIATIONS AND ACRONYMS

ACT	advance civilian team
AOR	area of responsibility
AXO	abandoned explosive ordnance
C2	command and control
CA	civil affairs
CAAF	contractors authorized to accompany the force
CBRN	chemical, biological, radiological, and nuclear
CbT	combating terrorism
CCDR	combatant commander
CDR	commander
CERP	Commanders' Emergency Response Program
CJCS	Chairman of the Joint Chiefs of Staff
CJCSI	Chairman of the Joint Chiefs of Staff instruction
CJSART	Criminal Justice Sector Assessment Rating Tool
CMCB	civil-military coordination board
CMM	Office of Conflict Management and Mitigation (USAID)
CMO	civil-military operations
CMOC	civil-military operations center
COA	course of action
COG	center of gravity
COIN	counterinsurgency
COM	chief of mission
CONOPS	concept of operations
CRSG	country reconstruction and stabilization group
CTFP	Combating Terrorism Fellowship Program
DAC	Development Assistance Committee (OECD)
DC	dislocated civilian
DCHA	Bureau for Democracy, Conflict, and Humanitarian Assistance (USAID)
DDR	disarmament, demobilization, and reintegration
DHS	Department of Homeland Security
DOD	Department of Defense
DODD	Department of Defense directive
DODI	Department of Defense instruction
DOJ	Department of Justice
DOS	Department of State
DPKO	Department of Peacekeeping Operations (UN)
DRL	Bureau of Democracy, Human Rights, and Labor (DOS)
DSCA	Defense Security Cooperation Agency
DSF	District Stability Framework (USAID)

EGAT	Bureau of Economic Growth, Agriculture, and Trade (USAID)
ERW	explosive remnants of war
ESG	executive steering group
ETM	essential tasks matrix
EU	European Union
FACT	field advance civilian team
FAS	Foreign Agricultural Service (USDA)
FCA	Foreign Claims Act
FHA	foreign humanitarian assistance
FHP	force health protection
FID	foreign internal defense
FN	foreign nation
FY	fiscal year
GCC	geographic combatant commander
GEOINT	geospatial intelligence
HAST	humanitarian assistance survey team
HCA	humanitarian and civic assistance
HN	host nation
HNS	host-nation support
HQ	headquarters
HSS	health service support
HUMINT	human intelligence
IASC	Inter-Agency Standing Committee (UN)
ICAF	Interagency Conflict Assessment Framework
ICITAP	International Criminal Investigative Training Assistance Program (DOJ)
ICRC	International Committee of the Red Cross
IDAD	internal defense and development
IDP	internally displaced person
IED	improvised explosive device
IGO	intergovernmental organization
IMS	Interagency Management System for Reconstruction and Stabilization
INL	Bureau of International Narcotics and Law Enforcement Affairs (DOS)
IO	information operations
IPC	interagency policy committee
IPI	indigenous populations and institutions
ISR	intelligence, surveillance, and reconnaissance
IW	irregular warfare

J-2	intelligence directorate of a joint staff
J-3	operations directorate of a joint staff
J-5	plans directorate of a joint staff
JCMOTF	joint civil-military operations task force
JFC	joint force commander
JIACG	joint interagency coordination group
JIATF	joint interagency task force
JIPOE	joint intelligence preparation of the operational environment
JP	joint publication
JTF	joint task force
LNO	liaison officer
MCA	military civic action
MOE	measure of effectiveness
MOP	measure of performance
MPICE	measuring progress in conflict environments
NA	nation assistance
NATO	North Atlantic Treaty Organization
NDAA	National Defense Authorization Act
NGO	nongovernmental organization
NSC	National Security Council
O&M	operation and maintenance
OECD	Organisation for Economic Co-operation and Development
OFDA	Office of United States Foreign Disaster Assistance (USAID)
OHDACA	Overseas Humanitarian, Disaster, and Civic Aid (DSCA)
OHDM	Office of Humanitarian Assistance, Disaster Relief, and Mine Action
OIA	Office of International Affairs (TREAS)
OPDAT	Office of Overseas Prosecutorial Development, Assistance, and Training (DOJ)
OPLAN	operation plan
OTA	Office of Technical Assistance (TREAS)
PA	public affairs
PB	peace building
PEO	peace enforcement operations
PKO	peacekeeping operations
PKSOI	Peacekeeping and Stability Operations Institute
PM	peacemaking
PMC	private military company

PO	peace operations
PRM	Bureau of Population, Refugees, and Migration (DOS)
PRT	provincial reconstruction team
PSC	private security contractor
QIP	quick impact project
ROE	rules of engagement
SC	strategic communication
SCA	support to civil administration
S/CRS	Office of the Coordinator for Reconstruction and Stabilization (DOS)
SecDef	Secretary of Defense
SECSTATE	Secretary of State
SFA	security force assistance
SJA	staff judge advocate
SOF	special operations forces
SOFA	status-of-forces agreement
SSR	security sector reform
TAG	technical assistance group
TIP	trafficking in persons
UGA	ungoverned area
UK	United Kingdom
UN	United Nations
USACE	United States Army Corps of Engineers
USAID	United States Agency for International Development
USC	United States Code
USG	United States Government
UXO	unexploded explosive ordnance

security sector reform. A comprehensive set of programs and activities undertaken to improve the way a host nation provides safety, security, and justice. Also called **SSR.** (Approved for incorporation into JP 1-02.)

Intentionally Blank

JOINT DOCTRINE PUBLICATIONS HIERARCHY

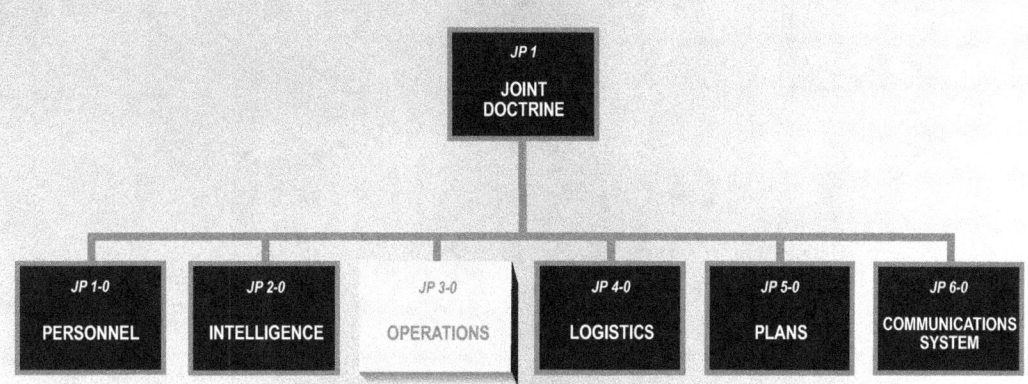

```
                          ┌──────────────┐
                          │     JP 1     │
                          │    JOINT     │
                          │   DOCTRINE   │
                          └──────┬───────┘
   ┌──────────┬──────────┬───────┼──────────┬──────────┬──────────┐
┌──────┐  ┌──────┐  ┌──────┐  ┌──────┐  ┌──────┐  ┌──────────┐
│JP 1-0│  │JP 2-0│  │JP 3-0│  │JP 4-0│  │JP 5-0│  │  JP 6-0  │
│PERSON│  │INTELL│  │OPERA │  │LOGIS │  │PLANS │  │COMMUNICA │
│ NEL  │  │IGENCE│  │TIONS │  │TICS  │  │      │  │  TIONS   │
│      │  │      │  │      │  │      │  │      │  │  SYSTEM  │
└──────┘  └──────┘  └──────┘  └──────┘  └──────┘  └──────────┘
```

All joint publications are organized into a comprehensive hierarchy as shown in the chart above. **Joint Publication (JP) 3-07** is in the **Operations** series of joint doctrine publications. The diagram below illustrates an overview of the development process:

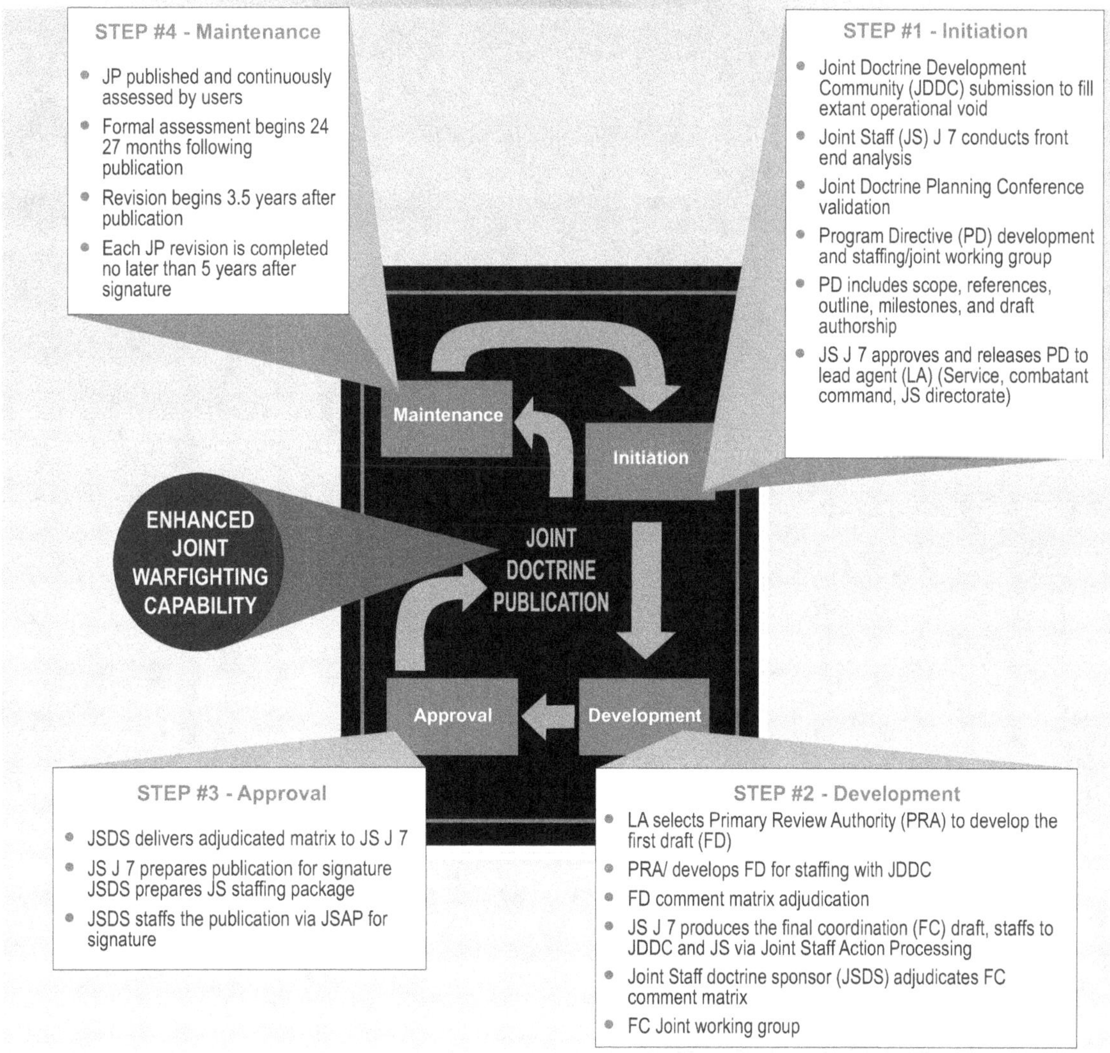

STEP #4 - Maintenance

- JP published and continuously assessed by users
- Formal assessment begins 24 27 months following publication
- Revision begins 3.5 years after publication
- Each JP revision is completed no later than 5 years after signature

STEP #1 - Initiation

- Joint Doctrine Development Community (JDDC) submission to fill extant operational void
- Joint Staff (JS) J 7 conducts front end analysis
- Joint Doctrine Planning Conference validation
- Program Directive (PD) development and staffing/joint working group
- PD includes scope, references, outline, milestones, and draft authorship
- JS J 7 approves and releases PD to lead agent (LA) (Service, combatant command, JS directorate)

ENHANCED JOINT WARFIGHTING CAPABILITY

JOINT DOCTRINE PUBLICATION

Maintenance — Initiation

Approval — Development

STEP #3 - Approval

- JSDS delivers adjudicated matrix to JS J 7
- JS J 7 prepares publication for signature JSDS prepares JS staffing package
- JSDS staffs the publication via JSAP for signature

STEP #2 - Development

- LA selects Primary Review Authority (PRA) to develop the first draft (FD)
- PRA/ develops FD for staffing with JDDC
- FD comment matrix adjudication
- JS J 7 produces the final coordination (FC) draft, staffs to JDDC and JS via Joint Staff Action Processing
- Joint Staff doctrine sponsor (JSDS) adjudicates FC comment matrix
- FC Joint working group

www.ingramcontent.com/pod-product-compliance
Lightning Source LLC
Chambersburg PA
CBHW081324310526
45789CB00018B/2317